WITHDRAWN

Rails Solutions
Ruby on Rails Made Easy

Justin Williams

friendsof

DESIGNER TO DESIGNER™

an Apress® company

Rails Solutions: Ruby on Rails Made Easy

ISBN-13 (pbk): 978-1-59059-752-1

ISBN-10 (pbk): 1-59059-752-4

Printed and bound in the United States of America 9 8 7 6 5 4 3 2 1

Trademarked names may appear in this book. Rather than use a trademark symbol with every occurrence of a trademarked name, we use the names only in an editorial fashion and to the benefit of the trademark owner, with no intention of infringement of the trademark.

Distributed to the book trade worldwide by Springer-Verlag New York, Inc., 233 Spring Street, 6th Floor, New York, NY 10013. Phone 1-800-SPRINGER, fax 201-348-4505, e-mail orders-ny@springer-sbm.com, or visit www.springeronline.com.

For information on translations, please contact Apress directly at 2560 Ninth Street, Suite 219, Berkeley, CA 94710. Phone 510-549-5930, fax 510-549-5939, e-mail info@apress.com, or visit www.apress.com.

The information in this book is distributed on an "as is" basis, without warranty. Although every precaution has been taken in the preparation of this work, neither the author(s) nor Apress shall have any liability to any person or entity with respect to any loss or damage caused or alleged to be caused directly or indirectly by the information contained in this work.

The source code for this book is freely available to readers at www.friendsofed.com in the Downloads section.

Credits

Lead Editor	**Copy Editor**
Chris Mills	Nancy Sixsmith
Technical Reviewers	**Assistant Production Director**
Ashish Bansal	Kari Brooks-Copony
Ryan J. Bonnell	
	Production Editor
Editorial Board	Katie Stence
Steve Anglin	
Ewan Buckingham	**Compositor**
Gary Cornell	Molly Sharp
Jason Gilmore	
Jonathan Gennick	**Artist**
Jonathan Hassell	April Milne
James Huddleston	
Chris Mills	**Proofreader**
Matthew Moodie	Linda Seifert
Dominic Shakeshaft	
Jim Sumser	**Indexer**
Keir Thomas	Michael Brinkman
Matt Wade	
	Interior and Cover Designer
Project Manager	Kurt Krames
Beth Christmas	
	Manufacturing Director
Copy Edit Manager	Tom Debolski
Nicole Flores	

CONTENTS AT A GLANCE

CONTENTS AT A GLANCE

CONTENTS

CONTENTS

CONTENTS

ABOUT THE AUTHOR

Justin Williams is a software developer in Evansville, IN. He is the owner of Second Gear (www.secondgearllc.com), a web and desktop application development firm, and was lead developer of the Porchlight issue-tracking system for small development teams. He graduated from Purdue University in West Lafayette, IN with a degree in Computer & Information Technology. His personal blog is located at www.carpeaqua.com.

When not building software, Justin spends countless hours playing video games, listening to talk radio, and visiting friends and family.

ABOUT THE TECHNICAL REVIEWERS

Ashish Bansal, a Senior Manager of Technology at Sapient (www.sapient.com), has more than eight years of experience in the IT world. He has been coding for more than 15 years (counting the games he wrote for his ZX Spectrum 128K). He has extensive experience in web application development and EAI.

Ashish is an avid open source follower and contributor. He is always looking to learn new things, including Google WebToolkit and Ruby on Rails, when he is not playing with his daughter. He is currently working on an Apress book on the Google WebToolkit and has published various articles on IBM developerWorks. Ashish has been a member of IEEE for more than 10 years. He can be reached at abansal@ieee.org.

Ashish lives in Mississauga, a suburb of Toronto, with his wife and daughter. He dreams of being a karate black belt who can also play the piano.

From the first two lines of code he wrote in 1984 on a 64K Apple computer, **Ryan J. Bonnell** discovered his one true love—and it's been a passionate affair ever since.

A self-starter and problem solver, Ryan's been working with the Web since the early 1990s and currently enjoys his position as lead web developer for Creative Arc (http://creativearc.com), a Minneapolis web design firm.

When he's not working, Ryan can be found refining his photography skills or sipping on a latté at the nearby Starbucks. A fine cigar or premium single-malt scotch is his celebration after a hard day's work.

INTRODUCTION

This book covers the Ruby on Rails programming framework, but don't let that frighten you. Unlike many other programming books out there, this one isn't written for programmers. This is a book for web designers and developers who are not at home when trawling through reams of code. More generally, this book is intended for anyone who is comfortable with Cascading Style Sheets (CSS) and XHTML, but might not have dabbled with any other languages.

Learning to program for the first time might seem to be a scary process because many people associate the process with memorizing strange keywords and syntax. I assure you that it's not. Ruby on Rails takes the pain and suffering out of web application programming, and what little bits it leaves in I hope to alleviate by putting things in plain English that anyone can understand.

The purpose of this book is to not only introduce you to programming and Ruby on Rails but also to make you comfortable enough that you can begin working on Rails applications on your own or as part of a team. This book covers the most important aspects of Ruby on Rails in depth, looking at the functionality you'll want to implement in your web applications from a task-based perspective instead of obsessing over all the code syntax. You'll be shown the code you need when you need it (and not before), and everything is explained thoroughly.

What lies ahead?

Chapter 1 introduces you to Rails, gives you a little bit of history, and explains the basics of how Rails works in terms of its overall architecture—just enough to give you what you need without going too deep.

Chapter 2 takes you step by step through installing Rails on Mac or Windows. The install process is not an easy one, but I'll take you very carefully through it.

The basics of programming are discussed in Chapter 3, in the context of the Ruby language on which Rails is built. Again, there is just enough to give you a basic grounding—giving you what you need.

Chapter 4 shows you how to build a bare-bones Rails application, including setting up a database to store the application data.

Chapters 5–11 build on this application, adding useful functionality, including forms for adding and editing data, user login, user interface enhancements, viewing user profiles, form validation, and more. Throughout this section of the book, you'll be looking at best practices and usability, and you'll learn about cutting-edge techniques such as Ajax, DOM scripting, and microformats—all made easier by Rails.

Chapters 12–13 introduce peripheral topics that although not essential to building up the application, are still useful to know about when developing Rails applications. These topics include plugins, engines, and scaffolding to further speed up your development, and efficient deployment of applications to a web server via Capistrano.

The book is rounded off with two appendices that cover caching and testing, which you will find useful after you master the basics.

Everything included in this book is something I have used in a real-world application. A lot of books focus on theory more than practice. Not here. I want to give you real-world knowledge (and code) that you can plug into your applications after you finish the book.

Code download and support

Speaking of the code, if you aren't a fan of typing, you can grab all the code used in this book from `www.friendsofed.com`. Just find this book's page on the site; you'll find a handy link to download all the code. If you do find any problems with the book, feel free to e-mail `feedback@friendsofed.com`. Folks there will be happy to help you.

Beyond that, there is also a companion website at `www.railssolutions.com` that will continue the discussion of Rails. My goal is to make the site a central location for all readers of this book to discuss their new knowledge and learn more than what is written on the forthcoming pages.

Let's get started—enjoy the book!

Layout conventions

To keep this book as clear and easy to follow as possible, the following text conventions are used throughout:

Code is presented in `fixed-width font`.

New or changed code is normally presented in **`bold fixed-width font`**.

Menu commands are written in the form Menu ➤ Submenu ➤ Submenu.

When I want to draw your attention to something, I highlight it like this:

> *Ahem, don't say I didn't warn you.*

Sometimes code doesn't fit on a single line in a book. When this happens, I use an arrow like this: ➡.

```
This is a very, very long section of code that should be written all on ➡
the same line without a break.
```

1 INTRODUCTION TO RUBY
   ON RAILS

Let's take a trip down memory lane back to 1991. Bryan Adams had the number one song, Terminator 2 was the number one movie, and Tim Berners-Lee became the first web developer by posting the first website online in August. Berners-Lee is credited as being the father of the World Wide Web because he developed the project as a method of writing hypertext on the Internet. That hypertext language was HTML.

As the Web matured, users and developers wanted more from the platform—mainly shopping and discussion areas. Obviously, this development couldn't be done with only HTML, so the Common Gateway Interface (CGI) was created in 1993. CGI enables client machines to pass data back to the web server. Instead of users just receiving static data on websites, they can now send data back to the site, be it messages to be posted or feedback to tell the site's creator that something is wrong with it. This is the basis of dynamic websites. The creation of CGI to send data back and forth between servers and client machines was a major breakthrough from the passive days of the first web pages. The first popular means of creating dynamic websites using CGI was the Perl programming language.

From the mid-90s to the beginning of the 21st century, languages such as PHP and Microsoft Active Server Pages (ASP) began to take the place of Perl as the de facto standards in terms of web application programming. While Perl still was used by many developers (and still is to this day), PHP and ASP enabled developers to easily create dynamic websites by adding dynamic code into regular HTML documents.

Another language that was giving developers the ability to embed dynamic behavior into the Web was JavaScript. Unlike PHP and ASP, whose code was executed on a web server, JavaScript was run on the client side in the user's browser. The beginning uses of JavaScript were basic form validation, rollover effects, and scrolling a banner across the browser status bar. It wasn't until recently that the full power of JavaScript began to be harnessed by web developers with the growth of Ajax (more on that later).

In 2006, PHP, ASP, and Perl are still on the scene, but the current trend is toward developing a site based off of a framework instead of writing everything from scratch in a programming language. Frameworks are semicomplete applications that provide specific functionality for common or repetitive tasks. In layperson's terms, frameworks provide a lot of prewritten functionality so that you don't have to reinvent the wheel. Frameworks are nothing new to the desktop development scene: Microsoft has been touting its .Net framework for many years as the preferred way to write new Windows applications, and Apple has given developers the Cocoa framework with the release of Mac OS X.

Both Apple and Microsoft realized that by giving third-party developers so much functionality from the start, they could release applications faster and more easily than ever before. By making the developer's life easier, both companies are helping to ensure that developers keep writing software for their respective platforms in the future.

Now the Web is beginning to catch up with the desktop in terms of both usability and development. The ability to easily collaborate with other users via web applications can be credited with the growth. Before eBay, there wasn't an easy way to put things up for auction with your computer. Now anyone can get online and easily set up an auction. Wikipedia has taken the creation of an encyclopedia out of the hands of a few authors at a single company and given that ability to the entire world. Anyone who is an expert on a subject can contribute to that subject's page on the wikipedia. This growth in collaborative web applications has been dubbed Web 2.0.

Because of the gain in popularity, in the past year more web application frameworks have come on the scene for every developer's language of choice. For instance, PHP developers have Cake, and Python has Django. The framework with the most buzz at the moment however is Rails, a framework built on the Ruby programming language.

This section takes a quick look at the history of Ruby and Rails before discussing the components that make up the Rails framework, the anatomy of a rail application, and how the application works with databases. Later on, I'll also say a few words about how secure Rails is. As you probably already know—or if not, you will know very soon—security is a very important issue in developing web applications.

A history of Ruby

Ruby is an object-oriented, interpreted programming language. Interpreted programming languages are read line by line instead of by compiling the code into an executable that is unreadable to a human being (but is much quicker to process by a computer.) Other interpreted languages include JavaScript and BASIC. If you open up your web browser on a page that uses JavaScript, you can read the source code by using your browser's window. Try opening up an application like your system's Calculator in a text editor. All you see is some garbled text because the Calculator application was written in a compiled language.

As Figure 1-1 shows, Ruby was developed in 1993 by Yukihiro Matsumoto, but first released to the public in 1995. Matsumoto designed Ruby primarily to reduce the workload of developers by following the principle of least surprise, meaning that the language typically behaves as the programmer expects: methods are named using common English terms that appropriately define the action being performed. For example, Ruby has actions called strip, split, delete, and upcase to perform actions on strings of text. Each of those names intuitively explains the action they perform.

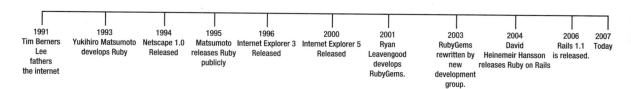

Figure 1-1. The Ruby timeline

Ruby started to gain popularity in 2001 with the commencement of Ryan Leavengood's work on RubyGems, which is an easy way to package and distribute applications and libraries. RubyGems' development stalled for several years because Leavengood left the project at version 0.4.0. In 2003, a group of developers reincarnated the RubyGems project and released a totally rewritten version under the same name. While they didn't share any of the same code, they shared the same principle: simple software distribution for Ruby.

Object-oriented programming

As mentioned previously, Ruby is an object-oriented programming language. The object-oriented programming paradigm is built on the premise that a computer application can be built using a collection of individual units called *objects*. These objects perform actions on one another. Object-oriented programming is different from its predecessor, known as *procedural programming*, in which applications are written simply as a list of instructions to the computer.

Object-oriented programming is built on three basic principles: inheritance, encapsulation, and polymorphism. *Inheritance* is the process of starting with a base object, taking the structure and actions of that base object, and then adding them to a dependent object. For example, you could create a base object called Person that defines height, weight, and a few other attributes. You could then inherit those characteristics as you create both a Student and Teacher object that each has its own unique characteristics, but also inherits the characteristics of Person as well. You can see an example of this in Figure 1-2.

Images courtesy of Wikimedia Project

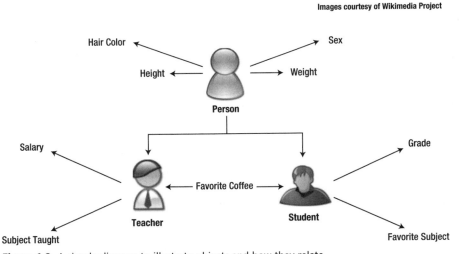

Figure 1-2. A simple diagram to illustrate objects and how they relate.

In Figure 1-2, you see a Person object that has the attributes of height, weight, hair color and sex. Where does the Person object get that data? It comes from a *class*, which is a blueprint for an object to be built from containing information about the attributes (called *properties*) and actions (called *methods*) that any object based on the class can have. In the case of a Person, its properties are the attributes that define the class; the methods it can perform might include eat, sleep, or walk. The creator of the class determines what properties it has to manipulate and what methods it has to perform actions with.

Encapsulation prevents outside objects from being able to see the implementation details of a specific object. The objects see only what they need to see to send data between the objects, which helps enforce the modularity of objects. Having little to no dependency on other objects is an essential concept for object-oriented programming. For the most part, objects need to be independent units of functionality, not reliant on each other for necessary information.

Finally, polymorphism describes the behavior of an object that varies depending on the input. The literal interpretation of the word polymorphism is *many shapes*, which is a great way to explain the concept. Let's assume that your Person object has a method called enroll. A Student and a Teacher can both enroll in a subject, but in different ways. If a Student enrolls in a subject, it is to take the course; if a Teacher enrolls, it is to teach the course.

Riding the Rails

In late 2003, David Heinemeier Hansson and 37Signals began working on a web-based project management solution for small teams. Initially, Hansson looked to create the application using PHP, but became frustrated with some of the shortcomings of the language. Many PHP programmers find themselves in the same shoes, repeating the same code in multiple places while building a system, for example. This process can be monotonous, redundant, and time-consuming, so why do it if you don't have to? Again, object oriented programming helps to clear up redundancy.

Instead of succumbing to the same development process again by using PHP, Hansson looked for a savior. He found Ruby. Using Ruby, Hansson developed 37Signals' popular web-based project management application called Basecamp on his own in two man-months. While developing Basecamp, Hansson realized that a lot of the code he was writing could be extracted into a framework that could be used as part of other future applications. In July 2004, he released his framework, Ruby on Rails, to the public.

Similar to the way the Ruby language itself follows the principle of least surprise, Rails was designed with the principle of don't repeat yourself (DRY) in mind. DRY basically means that no piece of a system should ever be duplicated. Changes to any one part of an application should have to be made in only a single place, similar in concept to the way you can use Cascading Style Sheets (CSS) to ensure that a change made to an h1 header has to be made in only one place.

Another principle followed by Rails is Convention Over Configuration. Rails does not have many configurable options, as other frameworks such as Cocoa and .Net do. Instead, it is opinionated and accomplishes tasks in a way that the Hansson and the Rails core team think is best. Because of this rationale, Rails is often referred to as selfish or opinionated software, which has been a point of contention for many of Rails' dissenters. Despite what they say, however, Rails' Convention Over Configuration mantra makes rapid application development a reality because developers can dive right into building applications.

> *Convention Over Configuration does not necessarily mean that you can't modify the framework's defaults to work the way you desire and that you are locked into a single way of thinking. That isn't the case. Advanced developers can modify the way the framework interacts with their applications with a bit of work. Most of the time, however, there is not a need to alter the way Rails behaves by default.*

Components of Rails

A Ruby on Rails application consists of several components, as you can see in Figure 1-3.

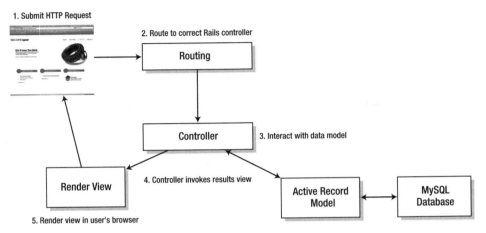

Figure 1-3. A generic Rails application

A simple web request can take quite a journey in Ruby on Rails. When a user first requests a page via the browser, the Rails controller (Action Controller) receives the request and redirects to the correct method based on the routing URL. After the correct method is called, the method is executed and grabs any data it needs from the SQL database using the Active Record model. After it has all the data it needs, it renders the final view (HTML, CSS, and images) in the user's browser.

At the base of any application are the data models that describe the business rules of your application. Models are based on real-world items such as a person, bank account, or vehicle. Each piece of data is represented by using a database table and is managed using Active Record, which is a Rails-provided object to simplify access to databases.

Active Record connects the data models and database tables by turning rows from the database into objects that can be manipulated. It also enables you to describe business rules via the use of an English-like syntax called Associations, which describes relationships between the different data models in your application. A person's family relationships can be described as follows:

```
class Person < ActiveRecord::Base
  has_many :brothers
  has_many :sister
  belongs_to :mother
  belongs_to :father
end
```

To manipulate these data models, there are controllers that perform all the actions your application performs. An application can have many controllers for each portion of the application. For example, if you have a model that describes a vehicle, you might also have a controller that describes how to add a new car, change its color, or remove it from the inventory. The controller logic is handled with the Rails component called Action Controller.

The previous two items are visible only from your perspective as the developer. The users of your application see only the views, which are built using a mix of HTML and basic Ruby embedded inside. The main method of creating the view is using Rails' Action View. Action View consists of embedded Ruby templates (RHTML), which have a syntax similar to a PHP page. A basic line to output a user's first name using RHTML templates could be described this way:

```
<p>Good morning, <strong><%= @user.first_name %></strong></p>
```

After the user submits a request, and Action Controller retrieves the results of the request, Action Controller then renders the result using RHTML templates in standard HTML. It replaces all instances of escaped Ruby code (the code between <%= %>) with standard HTML elements so the browser can fully understand the resulting page.

Being able to interpret a variety of results using the same standard RHTML view is an advantage of designing your applications using dynamic templates like this: even if the information you are working with changes over time, you can still continue using the same page to serve the information to your users.

Here's a quick example of a basic Rails application that manages a car dealership's inventory. Don't bother trying to run this code yet—you'll get to that point in the next few chapters. Right now, just observe the syntax and let's walk through how it functions.

First, I created three models: Salesman, Customer, and Vehicle. Salesmen sell many vehicles, and each customer can own many vehicles. Each vehicle is owned by a single customer and sold by a single employee. You can define these business rules using a Rails model:

```
class Vehicle < ActiveRecord::Base
  belongs_to :customer
  belongs_to :salesman
end

class Salesman < ActiveRecord::Base
  has_many :vehicles
end

class Customer < ActiveRecord::Base
  has_many :vehicles
end
```

With the models defined, you can then create a controller to work with vehicle data. This example controller is very basic: it adds new cars, lists all the cars in the system, and enables a car to be sold to a customer. This isn't exactly production-ready code (it doesn't take into account security issues or error correction, for example), but it gives you a taste of what Ruby code looks like.

```ruby
class VehicleController < ApplicationController
  def new
    @car = Car.new(params[:car])
    if @car.save
      redirect_to :controller => "vehicle", :action => "view_all"
    end
  end

  def delete
    @vehicle = Vehicle.find(params[:id])
    @vehicle.destroy
  end

  def sell
    @car = Car.find(params[:id])
    @salesman = Salesman.find(params[:salesman][:id])
    @customer = Customer.find(params[:customer][:id])
    @car.customer = @customer
    @car.salesman = @salesman
    if @car.update_attributes(params['car'])
      redirect_to :controller => "vehicle", :action => "view_all"
    end
  end

  def view_all
    @cars = Vehicle.find(:all)
  end
end
```

Finally, here's a very basic view for only one of the methods: view_all. The view_all method gives the user a listing of all the cars in the database. Rather than write out the entire HTML, you can focus on the Ruby portion of the template. This portion of the template iterates through the @cars variable defined in the controller to output the name of each of the cars.

```erb
<ul>
<% @cars.each do |c| %>
  <li><%= c.name %></li>
<% end %>
</ul>
```

> *Don't worry if all this code seems scary to you right now. This is only the beginning of your journey, and you'll be going through every part of the Rails architecture and code syntax in detail and with multiple examples. It'll seem like child's play by the end of the book.*

Model, View, Controller

Separating the basic anatomy of a Rails application into three separate model, controller and view components means that Rails is built using the Model-View-Controller (MVC) architecture. MVC separates an application's data model, user interface, and controller logic into separate components, as you can see in Figure 1-4.

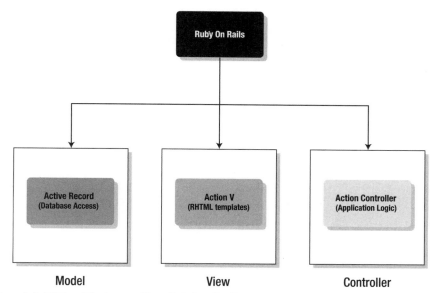

Figure 1-4. MVC architecture and how Rails handles it

The MVC architecture is great from a programmer's perspective because it separates each component of a Rails application into an isolated code base that is easily managed without having to worry about breaking other parts of your application. For instance, you can normally modify the layout of your views without having to worry about it having any impact on the controller or model code. If all this code were interspersed through a single HTML file that contained the template HTML as well as all the model and controller data, it would not be nearly as manageable and capable of being debugged. Design patterns such as MVC are created to make a developer's life easier. This is where Rails scores over PHP and even ASP, which don't follow any sort of paradigm.

You might be a bit confused right now, but don't worry. After you start working with Rails, you won't even realize that you are working in a design pattern. It all becomes natural to you after awhile.

Rails' database support

Active Record takes your model class and connects it with a table in your database using an object-relational mapping pattern. The most frequently used database for Rails development is MySQL, which is widely available on multiple platforms, easy to install, and freely available for development.

Aside from MySQL, there are database adapters for several other production databases, including PostreSQL, SQLite, Microsoft SQL Server, Oracle, and most other major database vendors.

Luckily, Rails makes the choice of a database vendor almost an afterthought because Active Record does not expose you directly to the database itself. Instead, you perform all your actions by calling Active Record and let it do the heavy lifting.

Who uses Rails?

While still in its infancy, many major developers have gotten aboard the Ruby on Rails bandwagon. 37Signals is one of the main developers, having released five applications powered by the framework. One of its most recent offerings, Campfire, is pushing the limits of the framework. Campfire is a web-based chat client that functions almost exactly like a normal Internet chat client, but uses Ajax technologies in your browser.

> *Ajax is the common method by which websites can load new data without having to reload the entire web page, enabling some impressive dynamic functionality and interaction not previously available on websites. A prime example of Ajax is Google's Gmail service. When Gmail checks for new e-mail messages, it doesn't refresh the web page. Instead, it pings the Google servers and pushes out the new messages almost instantly.*

Many modern web companies have adopted Rails because it enables them to release their applications to the public faster than ever before. Joyent released its online file storage system, Strongspace, as a Rails application. Second Gear's Porchlight bug-tracking system (see Figure 1-5) was built using Rails. Odeo (see Figure 1-6) released its podcast sharing and recording center early in the life of Rails. Even Google is on board with Rails because it recently purchased Measure Map, the Rails' blog statistics package.

1

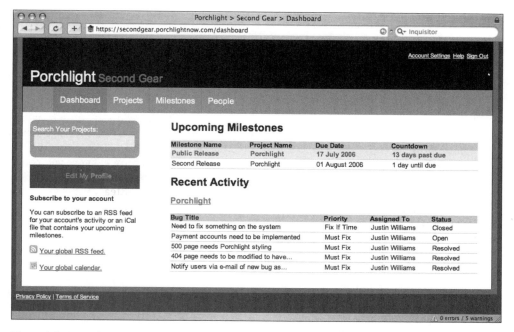

Figure 1-5. Second Gear's Porchlight bug-tracking system was built using Ruby on Rails in three months.

Figure 1-6. Odeo is a podcasting creation-and-sharing tool built on Rails.

Is Rails safe?

One of the questions developers ask as they consider a new framework or programming language in general is how safe it is. As with many other frameworks, Rails is as safe and secure as your knowledge of the topic. As long as you follow some general security precautions that I will outline in future chapters, your applications should be safe and secure.

For example, one of the most common security vulnerabilities you can run into when developing web applications is *SQL injection*, which allows hackers to execute SQL statements via your website. For example, a remote attacker could craft an SQL query to delete all the items in your database. The query could be passed into a form element and could be executed and cause havoc inside your application if not properly handled. Rails' Active Record functionality prevents SQL injection if you are not working directly with SQL statements by automatically quoting any dangerous characters in the data that is passed through.

Another type of attack is a *cross-site scripting (XSS)* attack, which allows hackers to steal the cookies from another user of the site, thereby stealing their private details—such as login name and password. Rails can prevent these attacks by wrapping your data with the h( ) helper method that prevents HTML from being executed by users.

> *Cookies, which are small files stored on your local computer, persist data when you are using a website and want to store details for later use, such as personal site preferences or the contents of your shopping cart.*

An example of the safety built into Rails is its transaction-based database manipulation. Using transactions, if there is any sort of problem with your database commit, the entire set of actions will be undone without affecting your existing data. By using transactions, data anomalies can be a thing of the past.

Summary

This chapter looked at the history of web programming from its very beginnings to today as well as the components of a Rails application. It covered the basics of Active Record, Action Controller, and Action View. It also discussed the database support afforded to Rails applications and who is using Rails. Finally, it wrapped everything up with a discussion of the security provided by the Rails framework. This introduction gives you a foundation from which to build your Rails knowledge.

Sound interesting? Let's get started!

2 INSTALLING RAILS

Before you can begin to learn how to create a Ruby on Rails application, you have to take the time to set up a proper development environment. Since all development tasks are best done on your local machine, you will be installing a few applications and utilities. For a very basic Ruby on Rails development environment, your toolbox needs to include the following:

- Ruby 1.8.4
- RubyGems 0.8.11
- Ruby on Rails framework itself
- Lighttpd 1.4.11
- MySQL 5.0.21
- MySQL bindings for Ruby

You don't need to download these tools yet because you will be doing it all in the next few pages as you work through the installation.

While this bare-bones system will get you up and running, your life will be easier with the installation of a few more utilities:

- FastCGI 2.4.0
- Readline 5.1
- PCRE 6.6
- FastCGI bindings for Ruby

The FastCGI libraries speed up the execution of your Rails application, and the FastCGI bindings enable the libraries to interface with Rails. Readline is needed so that the Rails' console mode will work. The console is an essential tool for debugging, and it's hard to imagine developing without it. Finally, the PCRE libraries enable regular expressions to be executed via Lighttpd.

I'll cover building a development environment for Rails on both Mac OS X 10.4 "Tiger" and Windows XP from the ground up. Building the system from scratch is the best way to ensure that it's easily upgradeable and capable of running the application independent of any required operating system. First, I'll cover installing Rails on Mac OS X. Grab a beverage of choice because this might take awhile.

Installing Rails on Mac OS X

Depending on your desires and proficiency with Mac OS X, you have two options for installing Rails on your system. The first is to do a manual installation, in which you install all the relevant applications onto your system locally. This simulates a production environment more closely than the alternative: using Locomotive. Locomotive is an all-in-one solution for using Rails that is simply a standard Mac OS X application.

There are benefits and tradeoffs with Locomotive. Locomotive enables you to test out Ruby on Rails with little commitment. Instead of going through the process of updating your Mac OS X system to use Rails, you can simply download the Locomotive application and then get up and running. This procedure is great if you aren't sure that Rails is for you and doesn't hinder your ability to move to a dedicated Rails install later on.

While Locomotive is easy to install and use, it does not allow for some more advanced uses of Rails that you might want to dive into as you become more proficient in using Rails. It is also not as up-to-date as a manual installation of Rails. If this is not an issue to you, you can skip to the Locomotive section a few pages away.

Before you begin these installation instructions, check a few things. First, ensure that you are running Mac OS X 10.4.8 or greater and that you have the Xcode development tools installed. You also need administrator privileges on your Mac.

> *These instructions might work in Mac OS X 10.3 Panther or versions of Tiger prior to 10.4.6, but I have not tested them on such environments. If you want more explicit instructions for installing Rails on Mac OS X Panther, see Scott Lewis' instructions at* http://scotfl.ca/2005/03/13/how-to-install-ruby-on-rails-on-mac-os-x-1038/.

Installing Xcode

The Xcode tools are available for free from the Apple Developer Connection (ADC) (http://developer.apple.com/). All you have to do is create a free ADC account to acquire them.

1. After signing up with ADC, log in to your new account and go to the Downloads section of the website. There should be a download for Xcode 2.3 or greater on the main page (see Figure 2-1). Download the disk image.

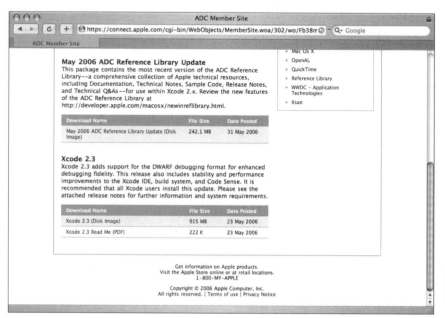

Figure 2-1.
Downloading Xcode from the ADC

2. After it is downloaded, double-click the disk image, if it is not already mounted, and run the Xcode Tools installer, as shown in Figure 2-2.

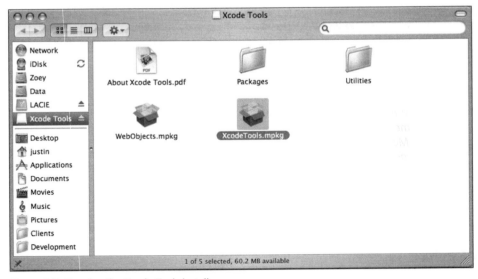

Figure 2-2. Running the Xcode Tools installer

3. When the Installer window pops up, click Continue, accept the license agreement, and set the installation destination to be your Mac's main hard drive (where your System folder is). Mine is shown in Figure 2-3.

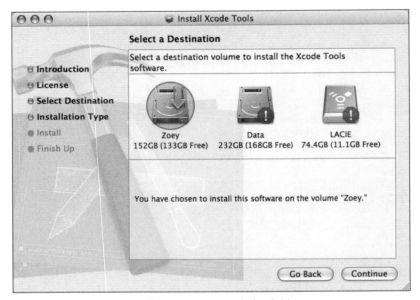

Figure 2-3. You need to install Xcode on your main hard drive.

4. Next, you have the option to customize your installation (for what you are doing, go ahead and just click Continue). At this point, the installation commences. Depending on your machine's speed, the process can take anywhere from a few minutes to an hour or more. Go grab a cup of coffee or a soda while it performs the installation.

After the installation is complete, you shouldn't have to restart your machine.

> *You might be wondering exactly why you need the developer tools for Mac OS X if you are doing web development. Well, by default, Apple doesn't include some important command-line utilities such as make when you get your new Mac. Apple assumes that most people will not have a use for tools such as these.*
>
> *This is a good assumption, but a lot of these tools are requirements for building Ruby and the Rails framework. Luckily, Apple makes it pretty easy to install Xcode.*

With the requirements out of the way, you now have another decision to make. You can run a script to perform the downloading, compiling, and installing Ruby on Rails semiautomatically—or you can go through the different steps manually.

Semiautomatic Rails install

To do the semiautomatic install, the only effort you have to put forth is to download the script and enter your Mac OS X password a few times. If that is the route you want to take, visit this book's page at www.friendsofed.com (or try the support site at www.railssolutions.com), download the script, and save it to your desktop. After you download it, open up the Mac OS X Terminal application (found in /Applications/Utilities) and run the following command:

```
sh ~/Desktop/rs_railsinstall.sh
```

The install takes a few minutes. After you reach the end, you can skip to the installing MySQL portion of this chapter.

> *IMPORTANT: Installing your Ruby on Rails environment involves quite a few different pieces of software, all of which are downloaded from the Web automatically by the script and installed. If you find that the script gives you any problems, it is probably because the version (and therefore name) or location of one of the pieces of software might have changed. Consult www.friendsofed.com or www.railssolutions.com and look for the install script changelog to see whether it has changed recently; then try to download it again.*

Manual install

1. The manual install is for more-advanced users who want to walk through the installation manually. First, open up the Mac OS X Terminal application (found in /Applications/Utilities).

2. Now you create a folder to hold all the source code for the files you'll be working with. Type the following two lines (press Return after each).

```
mkdir src
cd src
```

By default, this folder is at the root of your home folder alongside Desktop, Documents, Music, and so on. It doesn't really matter where this folder actually lives; I created it in the home folder, but it can be on the desktop or in /usr/local/src, for example. All operations should take place there.

Setting the file path correctly

Next, you need to set your path so that it looks in /usr/local first for the tools you'll be using. This is an important step that you cannot skip! I say this because if you run into problems in a few pages, a majority of them can be related to not correctly setting your path.

3. To set the path, open the .bash_login file in your home directory. Open up a new TextMate window (or your preferred text editor) and select File ➤ Open.

4. In the TextMate Open menu, select Show Hidden Files, as shown in Figure 2-4.

5. Select .bash_login if it exists. If it does not exist, press the Cancel button and just create a new file by selecting File ➤ New.

Figure 2-4. Electing to show hidden files in your text editor can reveal a lot!

6. Add the following line to the very end of the file and then save it:

```
export PATH="/usr/local/bin:/usr/local/sbin:$PATH"
```

7. If you are saving a new file, save it as .bash_login at the base of your home directory.

8. To make sure that the changes to the file are picked up immediately, you now need to execute the file with the following command in the Terminal window:

```
. ~/.bash_login
```

There will probably be no response from the shell here—that's OK. This command enables you to execute the installation commands in the forthcoming pages without having to open up a new Terminal window. With all the prerequisites out of the way, you can move on to actually installing Ruby and the Rails framework.

Setting up Ruby on Mac OS X

Even though Mac OS X Tiger comes with a version of Ruby preinstalled, it is not the latest version and it doesn't include the readline library, which is essential for working with Rails' console application. With that in mind, you need to install readline first.

9. Type the following lines into Terminal one by one, pressing Return between each one. There might be a lot of information dumped onto your screen after specific commands, so just wait until it finishes before typing the next one.

```
curl -O ftp://ftp.gnu.org/gnu/readline/readline-5.1.tar.gz
tar xzvf readline-5.1.tar.gz
cd readline-5.1
./configure --prefix=/usr/local
make
sudo make install
cd ..
```

What you just did was download the readline libraries using the curl command, which is a Unix command that makes it easy to download files from the Web from the command line. It downloaded a file called readline-5.1.tar.gz. The next command extracted the readline-5.1 folder. The cd command changes into the readline-5.1 directory and is followed by a configure command that gets the code ready for compiling. The make command builds the source code, and the make install command installs it in the appropriate folder.

Next, you install Ruby itself. The next set of commands downloads Ruby, extracts the files from an archive, and then compiles and installs it.

10. Again, type the following lines into Terminal one by one, pressing Return between each one:

```
curl -O ftp://ftp.ruby-lang.org/pub/ruby/1.8/ruby-1.8.4.tar.gz
tar xzvf ruby-1.8.4.tar.gz
cd ruby-1.8.4
./configure --prefix=/usr/local --enable-pthread --with-readline-
dir=/usr/local
```

```
make
sudo make install
cd ..
```

Next, you turn your attention to RubyGems, which is the package manager that makes downloading and installing the actual Rails framework a simple one-line command. Like Ruby before, you need to manually compile and install the Gems package.

11. Type the following commands into Terminal one by one, pressing Return between each one:

```
curl -O http://rubyforge.org/frs/download.php/5207/rubygems-0.8.11.tgz
tar xzvf rubygems-0.8.11.tgz
cd rubygems-0.8.11
sudo /usr/local/bin/ruby setup.rb
cd ..
```

Installing the Rails framework on Mac OSX...finally!

This is probably the portion of the installation where not properly setting your path a few pages earlier comes back to bite you.

12. If you are confident that you have the path set correctly, type the following line into Terminal:

```
sudo gem install rails --include-dependencies
```

The gem install command downloads the relevant files for installing Rails, configures them for your system, and then installs them where appropriate—all without you having to do any heavy lifting!

Even with your path set correctly, you might see an RDoc failure error. This one is actually nothing to worry about. Just rerun the previous original command above—or don't. Things should be fine either way (really). RDoc is the documentation that comes with Rails, but I have always found it easier to just access it via the Web.

Installing FastCGI

FastCGI is an extension to CGI that speeds up the performance exponentially. This isn't necessarily required for a Rails installation, but it will make developing your Rails applications a much more enjoyable process because you won't be waiting around for the execution of your code.

13. First, you need to install the actual extensions with the following command sequence:

```
curl -O http://www.fastcgi.com/dist/fcgi-2.4.0.tar.gz
tar xzvf fcgi-2.4.0.tar.gz
cd fcgi-2.4.0
./configure --prefix=/usr/local
make
sudo make install
cd ..
```

14. Now install the Ruby-FastCGI bindings, like so:

```
curl -O http://sugi.nemui.org/pub/ruby/fcgi/ruby-fcgi-0.8.6.tar.gz
tar xzvf ruby-fcgi-0.8.6.tar.gz
cd ruby-fcgi-0.8.6
/usr/local/bin/ruby install.rb config --prefix=/usr/local
/usr/local/bin/ruby install.rb setup
sudo /usr/local/bin/ruby install.rb install
cd ..
```

15. Finally, you need to install the fcgi RubyGem so that your Rails application can talk to everything you installed previously. Luckily, it's a simple one-line installation, thanks to RubyGems.

```
sudo gem install fcgi
```

Installing Lighttpd

LightTPD is the web server that you will be using to use to test and deploy your Rails-based applications. It is an up-and-coming web server that has gained its appeal in the community because of its light footprint and its capability to handle heavy server loads more efficiently than Apache. Before you can install Lighty (as it's referred to), you need to install one of its prerequisites: the PCRE libraries. These libraries are required for Lighty to be able to read its configuration file as it supports regular expressions—PCRE is a type of Regular Expression.

16. Type the following lines into Terminal, pressing Return between each one, as before:

```
curl -O ftp://ftp.csx.cam.ac.uk/pub/software/programming/pcre/pcre-6.6.tar.gz
tar xzvf pcre-6.6.tar.gz
cd pcre-6.6
./configure --prefix=/usr/local CFLAGS=-O1
make
sudo make install
cd ..
```

17. With the libraries installed, you can actually install Lighttpd by using the following commands:

```
curl -O http://lighttpd.net/download/lighttpd-1.4.11.tar.gz
tar xzvf lighttpd-1.4.11.tar.gz
cd lighttpd-1.4.11
./configure --prefix=/usr/local --with-pcre=/usr/local
make
sudo make install
cd ..
```

You still need to create a configuration file, but you will do that when you start working on an actual application. For now, move on to the last few portions of the installation process.

Installing MySQL on Mac OSX

As mentioned before, MySQL is the most common database used in conjunction with Rails (and in fact, any development language) to develop web applications. Unlike before, you don't actually need to compile MySQL yourself. While it is possible, the MySQL parent company, MySQL AB, provides excellent precompiled versions of its database for a variety of platforms, Mac OS X included.

18. First, you need to download a copy of MySQL 5.0 for your specific architecture (PowerPC or Intel) from the MySQL download site (http://dev.mysql.com/downloads/mysql/5.0.html#Mac_OS_X).

19. After it downloads, double-click the disk image to mount it.

20. Locate the MySQL installer (a file named something like mysql-standard-5.0.21-apple-darwin8.2.0-intel.pkg) and run it, providing your username and password as needed.

21. Double-click MySQLStartupItem.pkg, authenticate, and let it install. This sets the MySQL server to run each time your machine starts up. It's easier to just automate this than to have to remember to manually launch the server from System Preferences every time you reboot.

22. Finally, double-click MySQL.prefPane and install it, deciding whether to make it available to just the current user or to all system users. This lets you start and stop MySQL via the System Preferences application.

23. After the install is complete, start the MySQL server using the newly installed Control Panel.

> *A word of warning: MySQL installs with a default user of root, which has no password. This is a major security hole that you need to patch. In your terminal, type the following:*
>
> `/usr/local/mysql/bin/mysqladmin -u root password _new_password_here_`
>
> *Obviously, you should replace _new_password_here_ with your password of choice! Make sure you don't forget it—you will be in trouble if you do.*

24. You should add MySQL to your path so that you can easily run the mysql client from Terminal without having to type its full path. Like before, edit your .bash_login file and make your PATH statement look like this:

    ```
    export PATH="/usr/local/bin:/usr/local/sbin:/usr/local/mysql/bin:$PATH"
    ```

25. Save your changes and close the file.

26. Finally, you need to install the MySQL bindings for Ruby and Rails. Type the following line into Terminal:

    ```
    sudo gem install mysql -- --with-mysql-dir=/usr/local/mysql
    ```

27. You are prompted to select a gem for your specific platform. Select the mysql 2.7.1 (ruby) option, as shown in Figure 2-5 (option 2).

```
Terminal — ruby — 90x19
Zoey:~ justin$ sudo gem install mysql -- --with-mysql-dir=/usr/local/mysql
Password:
Attempting local installation of 'mysql'
Local gem file not found: mysql*.gem
Attempting remote installation of 'mysql'
Updating Gem source index for: http://gems.rubyforge.org
Select which gem to install for your platform (powerpc-darwin8.6.0)
 1. mysql 2.7.1 (mswin32)
 2. mysql 2.7 (ruby)
 3. mysql 2.6 (ruby)
 4. mysql 2.5.1 (ruby)
 5. Cancel installation
> 1
```

Figure 2-5. Select the right Ruby gem for your platform.

You should now have a working Ruby on Rails development environment!

Locomotive

If running through all the previous commands seems daunting to you, Ryan Raaum has created a free, all-in-one solution called Locomotive (http://locomotive.raaum.org/).

1. To install it, first download the Locomotive disk image, mount it on your desktop, and drag the Locomotive folder into your /Applications folder.

2. Next, start Locomotive by navigating into the folder and running Locomotive.app. Locomotive enables you to import existing Rails projects and create new projects.

Its main window displays a list of all the Rails projects it is managing, as shown in Figure 2-6, and enables you to start and stop those applications. You edit your application's files outside Locomotive. One word of warning: when using Locomotive, you must use its console to type commands. Access it from the Rails ➤ Open Terminal menu option. If you try to just open a Terminal window outside of Locomotive (just launching it from the Dock, for example), it won't have a reference to the Locomotive bundles and can cause you problems down the road.

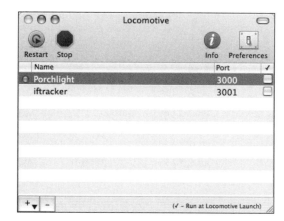

Figure 2-6. Locomotive main console window

Extra tools for Mac OSX

Whether you built Rails from scratch or using Locomotive, there are a few other tools that you and other Mac OS X Rails developers will find useful.

- **CocoaMySQL**: When you need to create or manually edit data in your MySQL database, it's a lot easier to work with a graphical user interface (GUI) such as CocoaMySQL instead of manually typing SQL update queries via a command line. Using CocoaMySQL, you can perform 90 percent of the database-related tasks afforded to you as a Rails developer through its interface. The application is free and can be found at http://cocoamysql.sourceforge.net/.

- **TextMate**: Most Mac users who are also Rails developers are using TextMate (http://macromates.com/) as their text editor of choice. If you have watched the Rails screencasts on http://rubyonrails.com/, the editor that the author is using is, in fact, TextMate. TextMate's main advantage for Rails developers is its liberal use of macros and code snippets, which makes a developer's life much easier. TextMate costs about $50.00, but it is worth every penny. If you are on a tight budget, a freeware text editor such as Bare Bones' TextWrangler (http://barebones.com/products/textwrangler/) works just as well.

Installing Rails on Windows

Installing Ruby on Rails for Windows is a bit easier than it is for Mac OS X solely because you don't have to manually compile the software yourself. The process is fairly similar, however. Before you can move forward with installing on Windows, make sure that you have Administrator privileges on your Windows account. If you are the single user on the machine and not connected to a corporate network, you probably have Administrator privileges. If you are connected to a corporate network, ask your system administrator.

> *If you don't have administrative access to your Windows PC, InstantRails might be the only option for you. It bundles Rails, MySQL, and a web server in a single application that you can run on your machine. Skip over a few pages to read more about it.*

Installing Ruby on Windows

1. First, you need to install Ruby itself. This is simple: just download the one-click installer from the Ruby Installer project page (http://rubyinstaller.rubyforge.org/) and run through the Setup Wizard.

2. After installation is complete, you need to ensure that the path to ruby\bin is in your path variable. You can do this by opening Start ➤ Run, typing cmd, and pressing Enter.

3. In the window that pops up, type path. Make sure that your path contains c:\ruby, as shown in Figure 2-7.

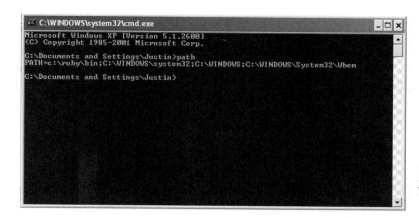

Figure 2-7. Make sure that your PATH variable is set correctly for Rails to run.

If it isn't set correctly for some reason, you can edit it manually. Skip steps 4–7 if your path did set correctly.

4. From the Windows desktop, right-click My Computer and select Properties.

5. In the System Properties window, click the Advanced tab.

6. Click the Environment Variables button.

7. Finally, in the Environment Variables window, highlight the path variable in the System Variables section, as shown in Figure 2-8, and click Edit. Add or modify the path lines with the paths you want the computer to access. Each different directory is separated with a semicolon.

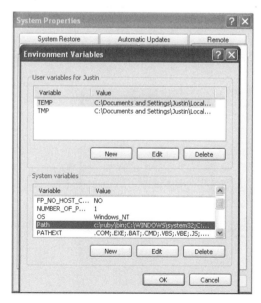

Figure 2-8. Edit the path variable to set it correctly.

What is so great about the one-click installer is that it includes RubyGems preinstalled—so you don't have to worry about installing it yourself. All that's left is to install Rails itself. In the command prompt window type gem `install rails --include-dependencies`.

Installing MySQL on Windows

The most complicated part of the Windows installation is installing and configuring MySQL. First, download and run the latest Windows Essentials (x86) version of MySQL from the MySQL download site (http://dev.mysql.com/downloads/mysql/5.0.html). At the end of the wizard is a MySQL Server Instance Configuration Wizard that you should run.

8. Select Detailed Configuration, as shown in Figure 2-9, and then click Next.

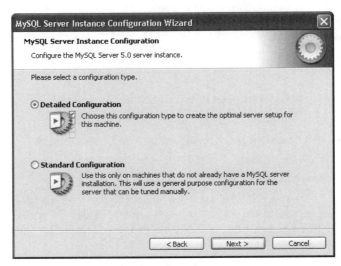

Figure 2-9. Choose Detailed Configuration.

9. Choose Developer Machine, as shown in Figure 2-10, and then click Next.

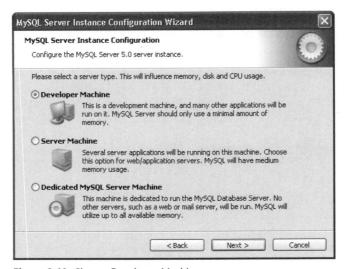

Figure 2-10. Choose Developer Machine.

10. Choose Multifunctional Database, as shown in Figure 2-11, and then click Next.

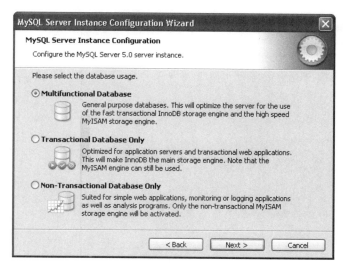

Figure 2-11. Choose Multifunctional Database.

11. Leave the next screen unchanged (see Figure 2-12) and then click Next.

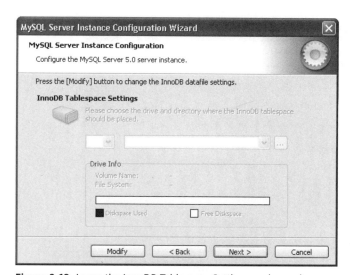

Figure 2-12. Leave the InnoDB Tablespace Settings unchanged.

12. Choose Decision Support (DSS)/OLAP, as shown in Figure 2-13, and then click Next.

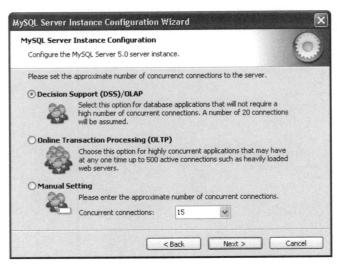

Figure 2-13. Choose Decision Support (DSS)/OLAP.

13. Choose Enable TCP/IP Networking and leave Enable Strict Mode checked, as shown in Figure 2-14. Click Next.

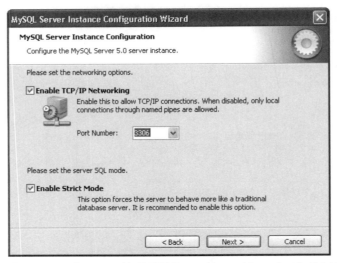

Figure 2-14. Choose Enable TCP/IP Networking and leave Enable Strict Mode checked.

14. Choose Best Support for Multilingualism, as shown in Figure 2-15, so MySQL will use Unicode for stored data. If you are planning to support only English and western European languages, you can use the Standard Character set to save some hard drive space.

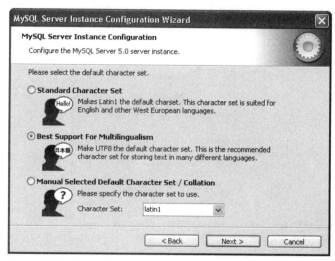

Figure 2-15. Choose Best Support for Multilingualism.

15. Make sure that both Install As Windows Service and Include Bin Directory in Windows PATH are checked, as shown in Figure 2-16, before clicking Next.

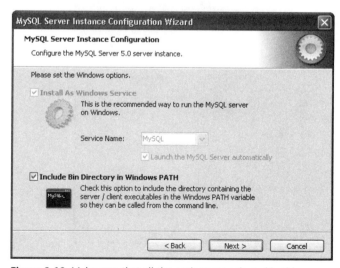

Figure 2-16. Make sure that all the options are selected in this screen.

16. Create a password for the root account and leave Enable Root Access From Remote Machines unchecked, as shown in Figure 2-17.

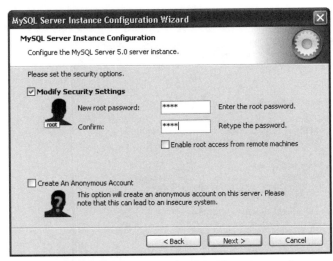

Figure 2-17. Create a root password and enable root access from remote machines.

17. Click Execute. If everything went OK, you should have blue check marks for all installation steps, as shown in Figure 2-18. You can now click Finish to exit the MySQL installer.

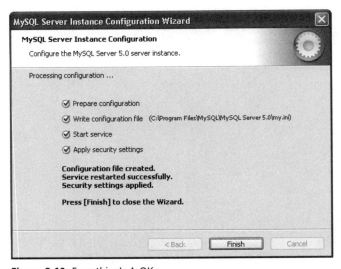

Figure 2-18. Everything's A-OK.

18. The next step is to ensure that your MySQL instance is working properly. Open a command prompt again and type the following line:

```
mysql.exe -h 127.0.0.1 -u root -p
```

You are asked to type your password; if everything is fine, you should see the message Welcome to the MySQL Monitor and the MySQL prompt.

InstantRails—Rails for Windows

Similar to the Locomotive project for Mac OS X, InstantRails is an all-in-one solution put together by Curt Hibbs for developers using Ruby on Rails (http:// instantrails.rubyforge.org/), as shown in Figure 2-19.

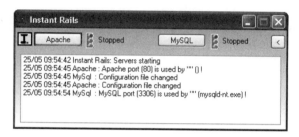

Figure 2-19. InstantRails

Instead of using Lighttpd for the web server, InstantRails bundles Apache as well as Ruby, Rails, and MySQL—all preconfigured and ready to go. To install InstantRails, follow these steps.

19. First, create a folder to contain the InstantRails installation files. This folder cannot contain spaces. I suggest c:\rails.

20. Next, visit the InstantRails site and download the latest ZIP file. If the archive isn't automatically unzipped, unzip it into the directory you created in your previous step.

21. Finally, go to the directory into which you installed the application and run InstantRails.exe. You might be asked whether or not to unblock Apache. Unblock it. A small window should appear. This is where all your active projects will exist. If you need access to Rails' console in future chapters, it can be accessed via InstantRails by clicking the I (I-beam) button in the top-left corner of the window. From the menu, select Rails Applications ➤ Open Ruby Console Window. Whenever you want to enter commands in a console window, you must use the console started from the InstantRails menu. It doesn't work otherwise.

Extra tools for Windows

When you installed Ruby, it should have bundled the SciTE text editor (www.scintilla.org/SciTE.html), which is a good freeware text editor for Windows. SciTE features automatic syntax highlighting, sessions, and code folding.

Besides SciTE, you might also want to get SQLyog (www.sqlyog.com/) for working with MySQL with a GUI. SQLyog makes it easy to create and delete databases, edit the data structure of an existing database, and manipulate data. SQLyog's community edition is open source and freely available from their Web site.

If you are a fan of the Eclipse development environment or if you long for a development environment that is more advanced, check out RadRails (www.radrails.org/). RadRails includes a built-in web server, web browser, database browser, and support for Rails generators. Best of all, it's free! I didn't choose to use it in this book because I wanted to keep things as simple as possible.

Ready? Let's do it!

Whether you are using Windows or Mac OS X, you should now have a fully functional Rails development environment to work in. The rest of this book is platform-independent, so it shouldn't matter which development environment you chose. If there are differences along the way, they will be pointed out.

Ready to start riding the Rails?

3 RUBY FOR RAILS DEVELOPERS

Before you dive into developing Rails applications, you should take the time to get acquainted with the foundation of Rails: Ruby. All the code that you will be writing in the forthcoming chapters is in Ruby, so it's only natural to give you a gentle introduction to the language. After all, you don't try to build a house if you've never used a hammer before.

This introduction assumes that you have a little bit of knowledge of programming. If you've ever done any work with PHP, JavaScript, BASIC, or other similar programming languages, you are in good shape. If not, there are many excellent tutorials online that can get you caught up to speed, such as *Introduction to Programming* by JoAnne Allen (http://www.wired.com/webmonkey/98/37/index3a.html?tw=backend).

Basic Ruby syntax

Ruby is a very clean and readable programming language. Unlike languages such as PHP, it is not littered with curly braces and hard-to-understand method names. When Yukihiro Matsumoto created Ruby, he designed it with ease of development in mind.

Instead of trying to explain the idioms and structure of Ruby code, let's walk through a few basic examples first. Type the following code into a new text document and save it as helloPerson.rb:

```
def helloPerson(name)
  result = "Hello, " + name
  return result
end

puts helloPerson("Justin")
```

Open up the Mac OS X Terminal or a Windows command prompt, go to the directory in which you stored the file (using the cd command you discovered in Chapter 2) and type ruby helloPerson.rb. You should see an output of Hello, Justin. Congratulations! You just wrote and ran your first Ruby application. While it's nothing spectacular, it does offer a few things to discuss.

The first line of the Hello Person application is the method definition. Methods are actions that you want to perform: calculating a value, printing out your name, or saving data to a database. Any action can be a method. Between the parentheses is a parameter called name. Parameters are values that help the method accomplish its task. You don't have to provide a value for all parameters because some can be set as optional. In Rails, many methods have an optional parameter called options = {}. Although you can provide data to this argument that will be passed to the method, the method still executes if you don't.

Methods can trail with a ? or !. A trailing ? defines a method as a query. For example, if you want to check whether the value in the name parameter is defined, you can use the nil? method:

```
name.nil?
```

The returned result is either true or false.

Adding a trailing ! to a method means that it modifies the receiver. For instance, String provides both a strip method and a strip! method to remove the leading and trailing spaces from the value that it receives. The difference between the two is that strip returns a modified copy of the string, and strip! modifies the receiving string itself.

The second line begins with an instance variable that simply contains the result of prepending the word Hello to the name parameter. Variables are simply placeholders for values that you don't know when you initially run an application. Variables can contain text strings, numbers, or even objects.

Unlike other programming languages, you don't have to explicitly define the type of variable you are working with. Ruby is capable of determining it based on the value it receives.

The third line simply returns the value of the result variable. Methods do not always require a return value.

The fourth line simply lets the Ruby interpreter know that the method helloPerson is now complete. All methods must end with an end statement.

The last line is the actual action that the helloPerson.rb file is performing. The puts method is a standard Ruby method that prints a value onto the screen. On this line, you merely return the resulting value of the helloPerson method onto the screen.

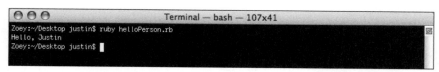

Figure 3-1. After running the Ruby script, you see a single line of output in your Terminal or command prompt window.

Ruby variables

The Ruby language has four types of variables: local variables, class variables, instance variables, and global variables. You already dealt with local variables in the previous example. They are merely used inside a specific Ruby method and cannot be accessed outside of it. For example, using only local variables, this code is allowed:

```
def returnFoo
  bar = "Ramone, bring me my cup."
  return bar
end

puts returnFoo
```

But this code is not allowed:

```
def returnFoo
  bar = "Ramone, bring me my cup."
  return bar
end

puts bar
```

It is not allowed because bar is not visible outside of the returnFoo method. To solve this problem, Ruby has global variables, which can be accessed anywhere in a Ruby application. They are prefixed with a dollar sign ($). In general, you should not use global variables in your application because most of the time you can use either a local or instance variable. Using global variables makes your application harder to debug since the source of your error could be anywhere in your application—the variable could have been defined in any of your Ruby files! How do you find it if you have 100+ files?

An instance variable is unique to each instance of a class and begins with an at sign (@). Instance variables are what you will probably use the majority of your time when developing in Rails because you usually work with specific instances of classes.

For example, if you had a class called Apple that defined the features and characteristics of an apple, each time you wanted to manipulate the characteristics of that apple, you could create it as a new instance variable.

```
@apple = Apple.new
@apple.seeds = 15
@apple.color = "Green"
```

These values are unique within this specific instance of the Apple class. You could create another instance variable that references a second Apple and give it completely different attributes.

```
@apple2 = Apple.new
@apple2.seeds = 22
@apple2.color = "Red"
```

Both apples can exist in the same context because they reference two different objects.

Classes and objects

Classes are the basis of object-oriented programming; they define the structure and actions that should be performed on a specific instance of that class. Here's a sample class definition that contains two methods:

```
class Course
  def initialize(dept, number, name, professor)
    @dept = dept
    @number = number
    @name = name
    @professor = professor
  end

  def to_s
    "Course Information: #@dept #@number - #@name [#@professor]"
  end
  def
    self.find_all_students
    ...
  end
end
```

In Ruby, everything is an object. In the real world, an object is anything you can see or touch. In programming terms, it's somewhat similar. An object is an actualized version of a class. Classes begin with the keyword class, followed by the class name. In Ruby, the class name must start with an uppercase letter.

The first method in the preceding Course class is called initialize, which is a special Ruby method called a constructor. The constructor is the first thing called each time you convert your class into a real Ruby object. The initialize method takes the parameters that define the variables that are a part of the class: dept, number, name, and professor.

Let's look at it in terms of building a house. Before you can begin construction, you need to have some sort of blueprints that outline the layout of the house, the square footage, and so on. Basically, this is what a class is: it's a blueprint of your object. When you take the blueprints and actually build the house, you have created an object. The house is just like an object.

Looking at the previous example, the find_all_students method is prefixed with the self keyword. Defining a method as self means that it is a class method and can be called on the actual class itself instead of an object. In other words, it is not specific to a particular course.

```
Course.find_all_students(@course.id)
```

Nonclass methods, or regular methods, can be called on realized versions of the class (that is, specific courses). By default, your class's methods are public, which means that anyone can call them. This behavior can be manipulated by setting your methods as either protected or private. Declaring all your methods as private would defeat the concept of information hiding.

Let's look at an example of a body.

```
class Body
  def leftEye
  end
```

```
        def rightEye
        end

    private
        def heart
        end

        def leftLung
        end

        def rightLung
        end
    end
```

The leftEye and rightEye methods are declared as public since a body's eyes are visible to an observer. The heart, leftLung, and rightLung methods are declared as private because the organs they represent are hidden in the body. If you declared them as public, it would be the equivalent of having those organs exposed on a physical body.

To understand the concept of protected, let's look a different example.

```
    class Employee
        def name
        end

    protected
        def employeeID
        end

    private
        def salary
        end
    end
```

In the Employee class, the employee's name should be public so that everyone can see the name. The salary should be private so that only the employee can see it. The employee ID should not be public information, but if you create subclasses of Employee such as CEO or Manager, you want those classes that inherit from the base Employee class to have access to the ID. That's where protected should be used.

Now, let's relate this knowledge back to the student example.

```
    class Student
        def login_student
            puts "login_student is running"
        end
    private
        def delete_students
          puts "delete_students is running"
```

```
    end
  protected
    def encrypt_student_password
      puts "encrypt_student_password is running"
    end
end
```

Using these methods, you can now do a few things. Let's create a new Student object and try to use the protected and private methods you created.

```
@student = Student.new
@student.delete_students # This will fail
```

Try running this code snippet; you should receive an error that tells you that you cannot run the private method delete_students. If you comment out the private line in the Student class definition and run the same code again, it will work successfully because Ruby sets all methods to be public by default. If you want to use the delete_students method, you need to reference it inside the actual Student class definition. For instance, you could call the delete_students method inside any of the methods of the class definition and it would run just fine. Modify the login_student method to look like the following:

```
def login_student
  puts "login_student is running"
  delete_students
end
```

Then change the @student.delete_student line at the bottom of your code to read as follows:

```
@student.login_student
```

Now run your code sample and you should see the output of both the login_student and the delete_students methods. Since delete_students is private, you can call it from within another method in the Student class, but not from outside that class.

Next, let's try to use the protected method. Replace the @student.login_student line with the following line and run your code.

```
@student.encrypt_student_password
```

Again, you get a warning that you cannot run a protected method in this way. You can, however, run it inside the Student class itself. Modify the login_student method to look like the following:

```
def login_student
  puts "login_student is running"
  delete_students
  encrypt_student_password
end
```

And change the @student.encrypt_student_password line back to @student.login_student and run your code sample. You should now see the output of all three methods on your screen.

Inheritance

One of the coolest features of object-oriented programming is inheritance, which is the process of taking a base object and extending its existing functionality with new methods and data attributes. For example, you can inherit from the previous generic Course class and create a new class called GradClass with data unique to graduate courses.

```
class GradCourse < Course
  def initialize(dept, number, name, professor, semester)
    @dept = dept
    @number = number
    @name = name
    @professor = professor
    @semester = semester
  end

  def find_all_fall_semester
  end

  def to_s
    super + " [Offered in [#@semester]]"
  end
end
```

The first line still defines the class name; after the name of the class is a less-than sign, followed by the parent class name. This tells Ruby that the GradClass class inherits all the data and functionality of the Course class. The constructor for the new class takes all the same parameters as its parent, but it also adds the semester parameter that will define whether a course is offered in the spring or fall semester.

The class also offers a new method called find_all_fall_semester. This method and the semester data attribute are visible only to GradCourse objects or any objects that inherit from GradCourse.

An interesting part of the new subclass is that you inherited the default to_s method, but enhanced it. You took the output from the Course class's implementation and appended the semester information to it. The super keyword is what causes the parent classes' data to be inherited into the new implementation.

Polymorphism

As mentioned before, since Ruby is an object-oriented programming language, it also supports polymorphism. Polymorphism describes the behavior of an object that varies depending on the input.

Let's say you have a base object called Person that has two subclasses: Student and Teacher. The two subclasses inherited the features of the Person class, in addition to each having its own unique characteristics.

Each subclass has a method that enables the person to enroll in a class. Teachers and students enroll in different ways. If a student enrolls in a class, it is to take the course; if a teacher enrolls, it is to teach the course.

You can define this situation as follows:

```
class Person
  # Generic features
end

class Teacher < Person
  # A Teacher can enroll in a course for a semester as either
  # a professor or a teaching assistant
  def enroll(course, semester, role)
    ...
  end
end

class Student < Person
  # A Student can enroll in a course for a semester
  def enroll(course, semester)
    ...
  end
end
```

This code sample shows the generic Person class and then has the Teacher and Student classes inheriting from Person. Both the Teacher and Student classes have a method called enroll with a different method signature. In the case of the Teacher, you are passing in the course name, the semester in which it will take place, and the role the Teacher plays in the course (instructor, teaching assistant). The Student is registering only for a specific class at a specific semester.

Now when you create a Teacher object and a Student object, and then call the enroll method, the correct version of enroll is called depending on which object you are working with. That's the power of polymorphism.

Calling objects

After you take the time to create classes and subclasses, you probably want to convert them into objects that you can work with in your applications. This process is called *instantiation*. Let's create a few courses.

```
@course1 = Course.new("CPT","380","Beginning Java Programming","Lutes")
@course2 = GradCourse.new("CPT","499d","Small Scale Digital
Forensics",➡
"Mislan", "Spring")

p @course1.to_s
p @course2.to_s
```

What you just did was create an instance variable called @course1 that contains information about a Course. @course2 is another instance variable, but it contains information about a GradClass object. The instantiation of a class into an object takes place by calling the class name and appending .new to it. Afterward, the information is passed into the constructor so that you have data to work with in the class.

The last two lines call the to_s method to print out data about the new objects. Notice that the @course2 variable has the semester data as well as previous Course data.

Arrays and hashes

An easy way to think about arrays and hashes is that they are variables that store more than one value. The primary difference between the two is that arrays reference each item of data using a numeric ID, and hashes use an object as a key. Most of your Rails development will involve the use of arrays because they are much easier to work with. Even so, hashes are covered because there might be times when you will find them more beneficial in your work down the road. Let's look at a code sample.

```
fruit = ['Apple', 'Orange', 'Squash']
puts fruit[0]
fruit << 'Corn'
puts fruit[3]
```

The first line defines a new array called fruit that contains three values. The second line outputs the first value in the array: Apple. Arrays in Ruby start at an index value of 0. The third line appends a new value to the end of the fruit array using the << method. The last line outputs that new value.

Hashes use braces instead of brackets to let the Ruby interpreter know what is being created. You must also supply two pieces of information when you define a new entry in the hash.

```
fruit = {
  :apple => 'fruit',
  :orange => 'fruit',
  :squash => 'vegetable'
}
puts fruit[:apple]
fruit[:corn] = 'vegetable'
puts fruit[:corn]
```

The first value you provide, which is known as the key, must be a unique value for that particular hash. Accessing values is done by referencing the key instead of the object's numeric identifier, as you did in an array.

In line 7, you append a value to the hash by simply setting a new key and providing a value for it.

Decision structures

Decision structures are an integral part of any programming language. Unlike PHP, there are no braces surrounding the body of each statement. Instead, the end of a line is signaled by an end keyword (just like classes and methods). There are two main types of decision structures that you will use when working on your Rails application: while and if. The if statement, which is a staple of any programming language, enables the programmer to test a value against an infinite number of possibilities and thus return a specific value based on the criteria met. Let's look at an example.

```
age = 40
if age < 12
  puts "You are too young to play"
elsif age < 30
  puts "You can play for the normal price"
elsif age == 35
  puts "You can play for free"
elsif age < 65
  puts "You get a senior discount"
else
  puts "You are too old to play"
end
```

This if statement merely checks to see whether the value of age fits any of the criteria. The first criterion is if the age value is less than 12; it's not. The next statement uses the elsif keyword instead of if. This statement enables you to continue a single if statement across multiple value checks.

You set the value of age to be 40 so it will print out You get a senior discount because the value of age is less than 65.

while

The other type of decision structure you need to become familiar with is while. This structure is useful when you want to continually loop through a set of commands while a specific situation is true or false. For example, suppose you participate in a football match (or a soccer match, as referred to by Americans) and want to continue kicking the ball until the clock reaches 90. If you were to describe that using Ruby code, it might look something like this:

```
clock = 0
while clock < 90
  puts "I kicked the ball to my team mate in the " + count.to_s + "
minute of the match."
  clock += 1
end
```

All this code did was output that you kicked the ball in a certain minute of the match. Each time after it printed the line, it incremented the clock variable by one. After the value of clock was equal to 90, the printing stopped.

Iterators

An iterator loops through a collection of values like an array. In most programming languages, the for loop is the main iterator used. It is available in Ruby, but there is a much better solution: each.

```
fruit = ['Apple', 'Orange', 'Squash']
fruit.each do |f|
  puts f
end
```

An each iterator begins with appending the each keyword followed by do and an instance variable |f| that defines the specific item in the array being worked with. Like decision structures, the value is contained between the each and end statements. The previous example simply prints out the name of the fruits in the array on a new line.

If you need access to the index of each object in your array, Ruby also includes each_with_index.

```
fruit = ['Apple', 'Orange', 'Squash']
fruit.each_with_index do |f,i|
  puts "#{i} is for #{f}"
end
```

This example contains two values between the goalposts: f and i. When you print out your data, you tell Ruby that f contains the array value, and i contains the index of that value.

How does using an each loop differ from a for loop? One major difference is that you don't need to pass along the size of your array since the each loop is smart enough to know when it has reached the end of your array or hash. Second, an each loop reads more naturally than a for loop. As mentioned before, Ruby is designed to be elegant. Compare the previous code sample to the following:

```
fruit = ['Apple', 'Orange', 'Squash']
for i in 0...fruit.length
  puts fruit[i]
end
```

Which do you think is more readable?

Exception handling

Exception handling is the process of protecting your users from the atypical events that might occur during the execution of your application. It's undeniable that at one time or another your user will do something that can cause your application to behave irregularly, or a server error will cause erratic behavior in your application. For example, if your network connection is lost during an action, you need a way to protect the application from bad data that might come as a result. By wrapping code that you anticipate could cause problems in an exception block, you can set rescue actions that are executed in the event certain exceptions are thrown.

```
begin
  @user = User.find(1)
  @user.name
rescue
  STDERR.puts "A bad error occurred"
end
```

An exception block is preceded by a begin keyword, which is followed by the code that you want wrapped. When you want to intercept a specific exception, you put that code under a rescue block. This may not make much sense right now, but once you start working with Rails, you can actually put exception handling into action.

Summary

Obviously, I have not covered Ruby from top to bottom, but what this chapter should have given you is enough of a start with the language to be able to get your feet wet with writing Rails applications. A great online reference for Ruby is the RubyCentral class and library reference (www.rubycentral.com/ref/). It provides a quick reference to all the methods that are a part of the Ruby language. I find myself constantly going there to look up a method I need.

If you are looking for a more in-depth introduction to Ruby, the Why's Poignant Guide to Ruby is a great online introduction to the language. It's unlike any other programming tutorial on the Web with its use of cartoons to help illustrate facets of Ruby. You can find it at http://poignantguide.net/.

Now that the basics are out of the way, it is now time to start building your first Rails application.

4 GETTING STARTED WITH RAILS

Now it's time to get your hands dirty and create your first Rails application. This chapter focuses on the basics of using Ruby on Rails: creating projects, adding models and controllers to your application, and writing some basic code that gets your application off the ground and running. Before you begin, let's go over what exactly you will be building.

Throughout the course of the book, you will be spending the majority of your time working on a classified ad application similar to craigslist. The application, cleverly titled railslist, will enable users to post their classified ads on the site, assign them to a category, add photos, and create their own user accounts to track their listings. Users will also be able to search through listings to find what they are looking for. The architecture of the application is shown in Figure 4-1.

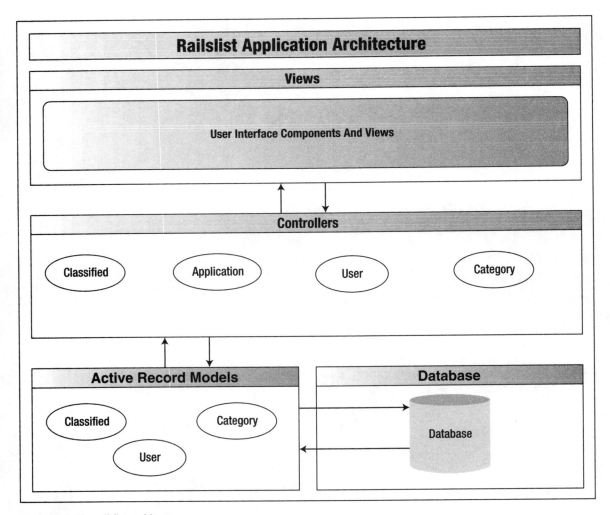

Figure 4-1. The railslist architecture

The application has a basic architecture and will be built using three ActiveRecord models to describe the types of data that is stored:

- Classified, which describes an actual listing
- Category, which is used to group classified ads together
- User, which is used for user accounts

Each time you create an ActiveRecord model object, it is built from a row in the MySQL database. You need to be concerned only with creating the database fields and assigning some validation rules to the models; ActiveRecord handles all the heavy lifting.

Besides the models, there are three controllers—User, Category, and Classified—which enable you to work with each of the model objects. You could use a single controller for the application, but it would not follow the Model-View-Controller (MVC) paradigm well.

The Classified controller enables you to perform the basic create, read, update, delete (CRUD) functionality on your classified ads and enables users to contact the seller to purchase an item. The Category controller enables you to manipulate categories that you can then associate with classified ads. Finally, you have the User controller that enables users to sign up for accounts and then log in to that account. The controllers are where you will write most of your Ruby code (you got the foundation you need to do that in the previous chapter).

The user front-end will be the views that you create for each of the actions in the controller. In terms of the actual users of the railslist application, the front-end is the only thing they are concerned with.

Luckily, Rails makes everything you want to do incredibly easy to accomplish.

The goal of building railslist is to introduce you to as much of the Ruby on Rails framework as possible. As you work through the book, my goal is to show you how easy it is to iteratively develop an application from something very basic into something that can easily be used by anyone around the Web.

There are a few basic steps that are followed each time you create a new Rails application:

1. Use the rails command to create the basic skeleton of the application.
2. Create a database on the MySQL server to hold your data.
3. Configure the application to know where your database is located and the login credentials for it.
4. Start the web server inside the Rails application.
5. Build and test the application.

I'll discuss more of the internals of the application as you proceed through the book.

You'll be writing a lot of code in this chapter and subsequent chapters. If you aren't too keen on all that typing, you can visit this book's website and download all the sample code. There's a separate folder for each chapter that contains the completed code as it stands at the end of that chapter.

Let's get started.

Creating a Rails project

The first task that any Rails developer has to do when starting a new project is create the application, which can be done by using one of the many command-line tools available when the framework is installed. The command-line tools can be used with the Mac OS X Terminal application (found in /Application/Utilities/) or the Windows command prompt (Start ➤ Run ➤ cmd).

1. The rails command is used to create the skeleton of a new Rails application. Open up a new Terminal or command prompt window and navigate to the directory in which you want to store your application. It doesn't matter where it goes, but I suggest somewhere in the home folder for Mac users and at the root of the c:\ drive for Windows users.

2. After you select a directory, type rails railslist at the command prompt and press Enter. Your output should look similar to Figure 4-2.

3. Type cd railslist and press Enter.

4. Type ls on Mac OS X or dir on Windows.

Figure 4-2. The output when you use the rails command to create a new application skeleton

If you're using Locomotive or InstantRails to work through this book, all you need to do is use walk through each application's specific project creation wizards to create your new application. You can also skip the forthcoming "Configuring the web server" section because your web server is built in.

The rails command created a lot of directories that are a part of the application. Let's go through each directory and define its purpose.

- **app**: Home to all MVC code.

- **components**: Miniapplications that can bundle controllers, models, and views together. (This subject is covered in Chapter 13.)

- **config**: Database configuration, routing configuration, and environment settings.

- **db**: Database schema files and Rails migration files.

- **doc**: Documentation for an application.

- **lib**: Application-specific custom code that doesn't belong in controllers, models, or helpers (for instance, background processes that work in conjunction with an application are put here). For example, if you were running a stock market tracker, you could write a background process that would ping your stock quote provider for data and put it in this directory.

- **log**: Error and access log files for an application.

- **public**: Cascading Style Sheets (CSS), JavaScript, and other static files.

- **script**: Generator scripts, debugging tools, and performance utilities.

- **test**: Files for testing an application, including unit, fixture, and integration test code. (This subject is covered in Chapter 5.)

- **tmp**: Holds cache files, session information, and socket files used by the web server.

- **vendor**: Where Rails plug-ins are installed. (This subject is covered in Chapter 13.)

Configuring the web server

Rails bundles a web server called WEBrick in the script folder, which makes the barrier to entry as low as possible for any platform. Since WEBrick is built using Ruby, anyone who has the Ruby language installed (as shown in Chapter 2) can run it. Included in the script directory is a tool called server. By default, server launches the WEBrick web server that is bundled with Ruby, but if it detects Lighttpd, it instead creates a default lighttpd configuration file and uses Lighttpd instead of WEBrick.

6

> If you're a Mac user, you might ask why I had you go through the process of installing Lighty if Rails is bundled with a web server. The reasoning is that I want you to have experience with a production web server such as Lighttpd when developing your applications so that you can have your development environment as close to production quality as possible. Since a majority of Rails applications are deployed using Lighttpd, it only makes sense to show you how to use it in conjunction with developing with Ruby on Rails.
>
> Unfortunately, it is not yet easy enough to configure Lighttpd to work with Windows and Ruby on Rails, so I recommend using WEBrick if you are developing on that platform. The Rails code you write works the same way in both environments.

That said, to launch WEBrick or Lighttpd, go back to the Terminal or command prompt window you used to create your Rails application and type ruby script/server and execute the command. You should get an output that looks like this:

```
Zoey:~/railslist justin$ ruby script/server
=> Booting lighttpd (use 'script/server webrick' to force WEBrick)
=> Rails application started on http://0.0.0.0:3000
=> Call with -d to detach
=> Ctrl-C to shutdown server (see config/lighttpd.conf for options)
```

What the server just did was create a basic lighttpd.conf file in the application's config directory and then launch lighttpd using that file if you are using Lighttpd. If you are on Windows, WEBrick was launched instead. There is no configuration file for it since it is a fairly basic (yet functional) browser.

You will use the lighttpd.conf file in Chapter 13 when you deploy the application to a production server.

Viewing the application

Open up a web browser and go to http://localhost:3000. You should see a Rails welcome screen like the one shown in Figure 4-3.

Figure 4-3. Default Rails application page

This is the default page for your Rails application. It gives you some pointers on how to get started in developing your Rails application and some links for documentation and support. More importantly, the page shows that your server is working properly. Let's follow its suggestions on how to get started and create the MySQL database.

Creating the database

Your database server should still be running if you are running either Mac OS X or Windows. If you aren't sure that it is running, you can check it via the following methods:

- **Windows**: Open the Windows Control Panel and go to Administrative Tools. Open the Services application and find the MySQL service. If it does not say it is started, double-click it and push the Start button.

- **Mac OS X**: Open the System Preferences application and go to the MySQL preference pane. Click the Start MySQL Server button if it does not already say that the MySQL server instance is running.

When working with Rails, you need to define a separate database for each environment in which you run the application. In this case, it is three environments: development, test, and production. The development database is what you will work with most of the time, but having a production copy on the local machine can be beneficial if you want to test how the application works in a simulated production environment. The test database will be used by Rails' testing framework (covered in Appendix B).

The easiest way to create and manipulate the databases is by using the graphical user interface (GUI) tools you learned about in Chapter 2. For Mac users, it is CocoaMySQL (http://cocoamysql.sourceforge.net/); for Windows users, it is SQLyog (http://www.sqlyog.com/). If you didn't install the applications before, I recommend downloading and installing them now. The installation process is straightforward for both applications. SQLyog has a basic setup.exe file to walk you through the installation, and CocoaMySQL is an easy drag-and-drop install like most other Mac applications.

Windows

To create a database using SQLyog on Windows, launch the application and follow these steps:

1. In the Connect To MySQL window, enter localhost as the MySQL host address.

2. Enter root as the User Name and your MySQL password in the Password field.

3. Click the Test Connection button to ensure your login credentials work.

4. Under the DB menu, select Create Database.

5. Enter railslist_development in the Create Database popup window.

6. Under the Open Session window, double-click the new Rails Development session.

Figure 4-4.
Setting the name of the railslist databases on Windows.

Mac OS X

For Mac users using CocoaMySQL, the instructions are similar. After launching CocoaMySQL, follow these steps:

1. In the sheet that pops up, enter localhost as your host, root as your username, and the password to be what you set in Chapter 2. Leave everything else blank so it picks up the default values.

2. Click the Connect button.

3. Under Databases in the top-left corner, click the Add database button, as shown in Figure 4-5.

Figure 4-5.
Adding a database in
CocoaMySQL on Mac OS X.

4. A dialog box appears. Type railslist_development and click Add.

5. Repeat this process two more times, creating the railslist_test and railslist_production databases, respectively.

Using the command line

If the thought of using GUIs insults your inner geek, you can also create your database using the mysql command-line tool.

6

1. In Windows, go to Start Menu ➤ All Programs ➤ MySQL ➤ MySQL Server 5.0 ➤ MySQL Command Line Tool (Mac users should just open up a new Terminal window and type mysql –u root -p).

2. When prompted for your password, enter it.

The MySQL command prompt is not too exciting; it is just a blank screen with mysql> preceding it.

3. At the prompt, type the following three commands (shown in Figure 4-6):

```
create database railslist_development;
create database railslist_test;
create database railslist_deployment;
```

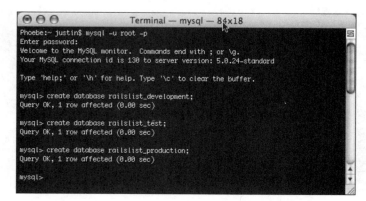

Figure 4-6. Creating the databases by using the command prompt instead is not too difficult.

You just created three blank databases that will be the home of the application data.

You might be wondering about creating the database tables—don't worry about this for now. Later in this chapter, you'll handle this easily using Rails!

Telling Rails about the databases

The final step of creating the databases is to tell Rails about them. Database information is stored in the database.yml file in the application's config directory.

4. Open the file in your text editor of choice and take a few moments to examine it.

The database.yml file is written using YAML. YAML, which stands for YAML Ain't Another Markup Language, is used to develop configuration files for scripting languages such as Ruby. Notice that the file is pretty human-readable, and configuration information is stored in key:value pairs. It defines the three execution environments and the database information for each one, respectively.

Since you took some care in the way you named the databases, the only area you need to change in the YAML file is the password for each database.

5. Change all three password fields to contain the MySQL password. When you're done, your file should look similar to Figure 4-7.

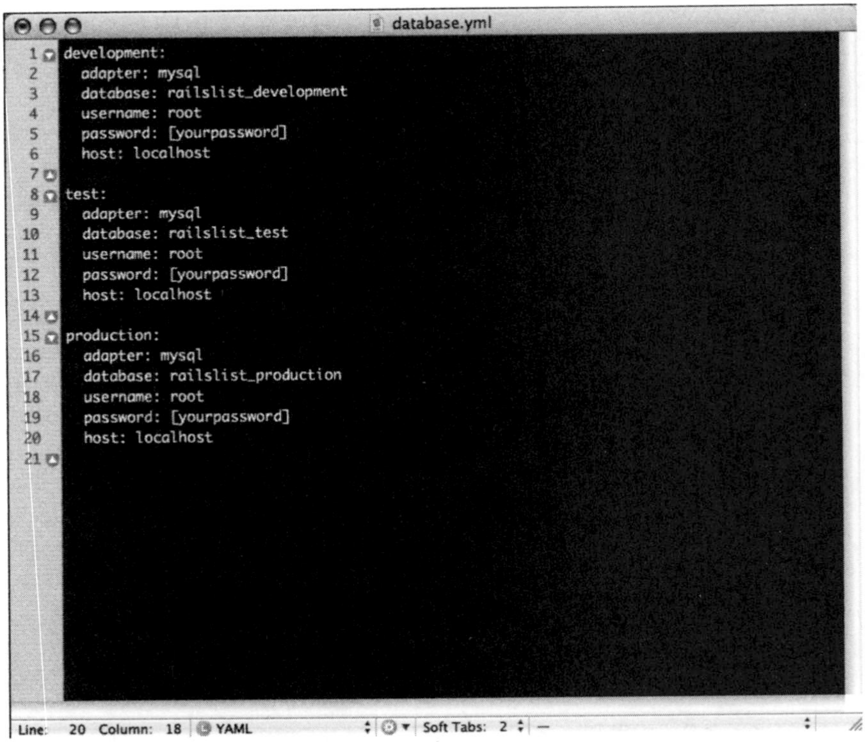

```
1  development:
2      adapter: mysql
3      database: railslist_development
4      username: root
5      password: [yourpassword]
6      host: localhost
7
8  test:
9      adapter: mysql
10     database: railslist_test
11     username: root
12     password: [yourpassword]
13     host: localhost
14
15 production:
16     adapter: mysql
17     database: railslist_production
18     username: root
19     password: [yourpassword]
20     host: localhost
21
```

Line: 20 Column: 18   YAML   Soft Tabs: 2 —

Figure 4-7. Updating your YAML file to point to your databases

Creating the model

With the database creation out of the way, you can start focusing on building the application. My recommended workflow (see Figure 4-8) is to first define the model classes because they are the business objects you'll be working with in your controllers. The model also gives you an idea of how to define the fields in your database.

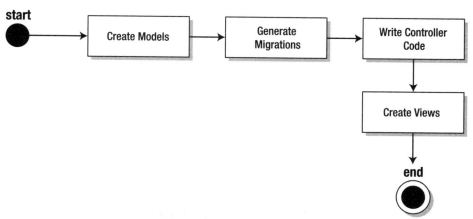

Figure 4-8. Recommended workflow for creating Rails applications

To create a model, you simply use the generate model command to create the basic skeleton. Generators, which are a major part of Rails development, enable you to call a single command and perform several tasks at once. Generators are found throughout Rails: creating models, controllers, database migrations, and more.

1. To use the model generator for this example, open up a command prompt or Terminal window, go to the directory in which the application is located, and then type ruby script/generate model Classified. You should see the following:

```
Zoey:~ justin$ cd ~/railslist/
Zoey:~/railslist justin$ ruby script/generate model Classified
      exists   app/models/
      exists   test/unit/
      exists   test/fixtures/
      create   app/models/classified.rb
      create   test/unit/classified_test.rb
      create   test/fixtures/classifieds.yml
      create   db/migrate
      create   db/migrate/001_create_classifieds.rb
```

You're telling the generator to create a model called Classified to store instances of classified ads. Each time you create a Classified model, you're pulling a row from the database table. Notice that you are capitalizing Classified and using the singular form. This is a Rails paradigm that you should follow each time you create a model.

When you use the generate tool, Rails creates the actual model file that holds all the methods unique to the model and the business rules you define, a unit test file for performing test-driven development, a sample data file (called fixtures) to use with the unit tests, and a Rails migration that makes creating database tables and columns easy. (Appendix B covers the unit test and fixtures files.) Right now, let's focus on the model itself and the migrations file.

Rails migrations

Web developers used to have it really hard having to know multiple languages. Besides the basic HTML and CSS knowledge, their tool belts usually included PHP, SQL, and JavaScript as a bare minimum. Rails aims to eliminate two of those languages from the tool belt by making it incredibly easy to write SQL and JavaScript using Ruby. (Rails' solution for complex JavaScript, called RJS, is covered in later chapters.) For now, let's focus on the Rails way of making SQL and database management a snap: migrations.

Migrations were created because the developers of Ruby on Rails realized that data models for an application can change over time and that deploying those changes can sometimes be a difficult task. They also didn't want to have to work with complex SQL queries that could sometimes take line upon line of code.

A migration file contains basic Ruby syntax that describes the data structure of a database table. Let's describe the Classified model using the migration created when you generated it.

2. Go to your `railslist` directory and open up the `001_create_classifieds.rb` file in the db/migrate folder.

> *If you are using TextMate on Mac OS X, drag your entire* `railslist` *folder onto the* TextMate *icon. A project window displays, which contains all your application's files in a single window. I find this a much easier way to work.*

3. After the file is open, look at the first line. Notice that a migration is just another class that inherits from ActiveRecord, which is why you can use many of the luxuries of Rails to manipulate the data structure. A migration file starts with two methods: `self.up` and `self.down`. With Rails you can migrate to specific versions of the data model at any point in time. The code in the `self.up` method is executed when migrating forward while `self.down` is executed when migrating backward (that is, creating a new version of the database or rolling back to a previous version).

An easy way to think about it is that `self.up` is the action you want to perform in the migration file, and `self.down` is the exact opposite. It is just like using the Undo command in Word or some other application—you're just undoing the changes you made. So, for example, if you want to create a table called classifieds, you create it in the `self.up` method and then destroy it in `self.down`. Let's look at how you do that.

4. Replace the default code in your 001_create_classifieds.rb migration file with the following and save your changes:

```
class CreateClassifieds < ActiveRecord::Migration
  def self.up
    create_table :classifieds do |t|
      t.column :title, :string
      t.column :price, :float
      t.column :location, :string
      t.column :description, :text
      t.column :email, :string
      t.column :created_at, :timestamp
      t.column :updated_at, :timestamp
    end
  end

  def self.down
    drop_table :classifieds
  end
end
```

When you think about a basic classified ad, it contains only a minimal amount of data: a title for the item, a price for the item, a location for the item, a description of the item, and a way to contact the seller. You just created it in this migration. The self.up method calls create_table, which lets Rails know that it should create this table and then add any columns that are defined between the create_table structure.

> *Rails tables should always be named the pluralized version of your model's name. In the case of the Classified model, the table was named classifieds. If you had a model called Food, you would create a table called foods. Rails is even smart enough to know common pluralizations for words like People, so it will create a table called persons. If you have trouble figuring out the pluralized version of your model, you'll be pleased to know that Geoffrey Grosenbach has created Pluralizer to assist you. It can be found at http://nubyonrails.com/tools/pluralize.*

Migrations support all the basic data types: :string, :text, :integer, :float, :datetime, :timestamp, :time, :date, :binary and :boolean:

- :string is for small data types such as a classified title
- :text is for longer pieces of textual data, such as the description
- :integer is for whole numbers
- :float is for decimals
- :datetime and :timestamp store the date and time into a column
- :date and :time store either the date only or time only
- :binary is for storing data such as images, audio, or movies
- :boolean is for storing true or false values

You are making use of many of these data types in the table. Code was written to create a column for each of the pieces of data you want to store as well as two special columns: created_at and updated_at. They are two special database columns that Rails can modify on its own. The created_at column is modified only when the row is created with the current time stamp. On the other hand, updated_at is modified with the current timestamp each time the row's data is manipulated.

Looking back at the self.up method, the create_table call is followed by do |t|, which enables you to easily define the columns that are a part of this table inside the create_table call. The t between the goalposts is stuck at the beginning of each column definition, so Rails knows for sure that this column belongs to the classifieds table. The basic structure of a column definition is t.column :column_name, :data_type.

The self.down method is incredibly simple because it has only one line. All it does is remove the classifieds table from the database. If you're familiar with basic SQL, it is the same as drop table classifieds.

Now that you have created the migration file, you can execute it against the database.

5. To do this, go to a command prompt and go to the railslist directory, in which the application is located, and then type rake migrate.

```
Zoey:~/railslist justin$ rake migrate
(in /Volumes/Data/Users/justin/railslist)
== CreateClassifieds: migrating ======================================
-- create_table(:classifieds)
   -> 0.1674s
== CreateClassifieds: migrated (0.1678s)
======================================
```

Rake is a Ruby build program similar to the Unix make program that Rails takes advantage of to simplify the execution of complex tasks (such as updating a database's structure, for example). Over the course of reading this book, you will become very familiar with executing tasks via Rake.

The database now has a table in which to store the classified ad data, and you didn't have much work to do to accomplish this. Just for comparison, this is what the SQL query looks like if you want to create your table by hand-writing the SQL statement:

```
CREATE TABLE classifieds (
`id` int(11) DEFAULT NULL auto_increment
PRIMARY KEY, `title` varchar(255), `price` float,
`location` varchar(255), `description` text, `email` varchar(255),
`created_at` datetime, `updated_at` datetime) ENGINE=InnoDB
```

I don't know about you, but I'd rather write a few lines of Ruby than try to match the syntax and data types of that SQL statement.

The next time you want to modify the data model, you can create a new migration file and then run rake migrate again. Each time you run the migrate command, it starts at the first migration file (based on the number at the beginning of the filename) and checks to see whether it has been executed. If it has been run, it skips to the next file until it finds a starting point to begin executing. After it finds that point, it runs that migration and all migrations after that until it reaches the end.

Creating the controller

Aside from defining and running the migration, you won't work with the model just yet. Instead, you'll focus on writing the basic code to manipulate the model. That code is stored in a controller class, as you learned in the discussion of MVC in Chapter 1. As outlined before, Ruby on Rails is built using the MVC paradigm, which separates the business objects from the code that manipulates them and hides it all behind a user interface that is visible to your users.

1. To create a controller, open up a command prompt and go to the directory in which the application is located; then type ruby script/generate controller Classified.

```
Zoey:~/railslist justin$ ruby script/generate controller Classified
        exists  app/controllers/
        exists  app/helpers/
        create  app/views/classified
        exists  test/functional/
        create  app/controllers/classified_controller.rb
        create  test/functional/classified_controller_test.rb
        create  app/helpers/classified_helper.rb
```

   Creating controllers is just as easy as models because they both use the generate command-line tool. Besides the controller itself, generate also creates a classified folder under views that will be where you store the RHTML views (the pages that the user actually sees), a functional test in the test folder for test-driven development, and a helper file that interfaces with your views (more on that in future chapters).

2. Let's first take a look at the classified_controller.rb file. It is located under app/controllers.

```
class ClassifiedController < ApplicationController
end
```

   Controller classes inherit from ApplicationController, which is the other file in the controllers folder: application.rb. The ApplicationController contains code that can be run in all your controllers and it inherits from Rails' ActionController::Base class. You don't need to worry with the ApplicationController yet, so let's go back to classified_controller.rb and define a few method stubs.

6

3. Modify the file to look like the following and save your changes:

```
class ClassifiedController < ApplicationController
  def list
  end

  def show
  end

  def new
  end

  def create
  end

  def edit
  end

  def update
  end

  def delete
  end
end
```

These are all the methods that will be a part of the ClassifiedController. First, concentrate on the reading methods: list and show. The list method gives you a printout of all the classifieds in the database, while show displays only further details on a single classified ad.

4. Modify your code so that the show and list methods look like the following and then save again:

```
def list
  @classifieds = Classified.find(:all)
end

def show
  @classified = Classified.find(params[:id])
end
```

You added only a single line of code to each method, and that's all you need so far. The @classifieds = Classified.find(:all) line in the list method tells Rails to search the classifieds table and store each row it finds in the @classifieds instance object. The show method's @classified = Classified.find(params[:id]) line tells Rails to find only the classified ad that has the id defined in params[:id]. The params object is a container that enables you to pass values between method calls. For example, when you're on the page called by the list method, you can click a link for a specific classified ad, and it passes the id of that ad via the params object so show can find the specific ad. You can then output that ad's information to the screen (more on this later).

Creating the views

Let's see what happens when you try to execute the list method via the web browser.

1. Open up a browser and go to http://localhost:3000/classified/list. You'll probably see the message shown in Figure 4-9.

Figure 4-9. You created some application code, but you don't yet have anything to display the data!

Rails lets you know that you need to create the view file for the new method. Each method you define in the controller needs to have a corresponding RHTML file, with the same name as the method, to display the data that the method is collecting. Unfortunately, Rails can't read your mind, so it can't create a view file for each of the controller's methods. It's not a big deal, though. Do the following:

2. Create a file called list.rhtml using your favorite text editor and save it to app/views/classified.

3. After creating and saving the file, refresh your web browser. You should see a blank page; if you don't, check the spelling of your file and make sure that it is the exactly the same as your controller's method.

4. A blank screen is rather boring, so put some code into the `list.rhtml` file.

```
<% if @classifieds.blank? %>
  <p>There are not any ads currently in the system.</p>
<% else %>
  <p>These are the current classified ads in our system</p>

  <ul id="classifieds">
<% @classifieds.each do |c| %>
    <li><%= link_to c.title, {:action => 'show', :id => c.id} -%></li>
  <% end %>
    </ul>
<% end %>
  <p><%= link_to "Add new ad", {:action => 'new' }%></p>
```

This is a lot to digest, so let's go through it line by line. The first line is enclosed in `<% %>`, which lets Rails know that this is Rails code that should be interpreted. The code to be executed is to check whether the @classifieds array has any objects in it. The `.blank?` method returns `true` if the array is empty and `false` if it contains any objects.

The next line outputs a line of HTML if the @classifieds array is blank. The third line is a continuation of the line 1 if statement and gives the else clause (that is, if @classifieds is *not* blank).

The first two lines after the else clause print some basic HTML tags. After that, things get interesting. You have an each iterator that loops through each item in the @classifieds array. Each loop prints out a list item (`<li></li>`) that contains a link to the item.

Notice that the list item line contains `<%= %>` instead of `<% %>`. By appending the = sign to the escape clause, you tell Rails that you want to display the output of this Ruby code. The code between the `<%= %>` tags is a `link_to` method call. The first parameter of `link_to` is the text to be displayed between the `<a>` tags. The second parameter is what action is called when the link is clicked. In this case, it is the show method. The final parameter is the id of the classified item that is passed via the params object.

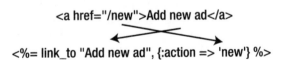

Figure 4-10.
A link is converted into a standard HTML tag, with the title and href values mapped accordingly.

> By using `<%= %>`, Rails puts each output on its own new line, which can cause a bit of clutter in your HTML source. If you are a tidy person, you can use `<%= -%>`, which keeps the code on the same line as the previous line of code.

5. Refresh your browser window; you should see a single line that says there are no ads in the system and an Add new ad link. (This link currently doesn't go anywhere, but you'll be creating the page it targets in the next section, so never fear.) If not, check your code syntax to make sure that everything looks exactly as it does here.

Creating the first objects

Having an application that doesn't have any classifieds is boring, so you need to start populating the application with some real data.

1. Go back to your classified_controller.rb file in app/controllers and edit the new method to look like this:

```
def new
  @classified = Classified.new
end
```

2. The line you added to the new method lets Rails know that you will create a new object in this view. Create the corresponding new.rhtml file in app/views/classified.

3. You'll create a basic input form to accept new classified postings. Add the following code to the new.rhtml file and save it:

```
<h1>Post new classified</h1>

<%= start_form_tag :action => 'create' %>

  <p><label for="classified_title">Title</label><br/>
  <%= text_field 'classified', 'title'  %></p>

  <p><label for="classified_price">Price</label><br/>
  <%= text_field 'classified', 'price'  %></p>

  <p><label for="classified_location">Location</label><br/>
  <%= text_field 'classified', 'location'  %></p>

  <p><label for="classified_description">Description</label><br/>
  <%= text_area 'classified', 'description'  %></p>

  <p><label for="classified_email">Email</label><br/>
  <%= text_field 'classified', 'email'  %></p>

  <%= submit_tag "Create" %>
<%= end_form_tag %>

<%= link_to 'Back', {:action => 'list'} %>
```

6

There are a few new Rails method calls in this template that should be discussed. The first one you will encounter is start_form_tag(). This method interprets the Ruby code into a regular HTML <form> tag using all the information supplied to it. This tag, for example, outputs the following HTML:

<form action="/classified/create" method="post">

Two lines below that is a text_field method that outputs an <input> text field. The parameters for text_field are object and field name. In this case, the object is classified and the name is title. The next new tag you encounter is submit_tag, which outputs an <input> button that submits the form. Finally, there is the end_form_tag method that simply translates into </form>.

After creating the form, you need to edit the create method so it can take the data submitted by the user and turn it into a row of data in the database.

4. Edit the create method in the classified_controller.rb to match the following:

```
def create
  @classified = Classified.new(params[:classified])
  if @classified.save
    redirect_to :action => 'list'
  else
    render :action => 'new'
  end
end
```

The first line creates a new instance variable called @classified that holds a Classified object built from the data the user submitted. The data was passed from the new method to create using the params object (which is why the text fields had their object set to classified).

The next line is a conditional that redirects the user to the list method if the object saves correctly to the database. If it doesn't save, the user is sent back to the new method. The redirect_to method is similar to performing a meta refresh on a web page: it automatically forwards you to your destination without any user interaction.

Since the create method called a redirect_to and render method for both of the if statement conditionals, you don't need to create a template for the create method because it will never have any output on the screen.

5. Go to your browser and visit http://localhost:3000/classified/new, enter some data into the form (as seen in Figure 4-11), and submit it.

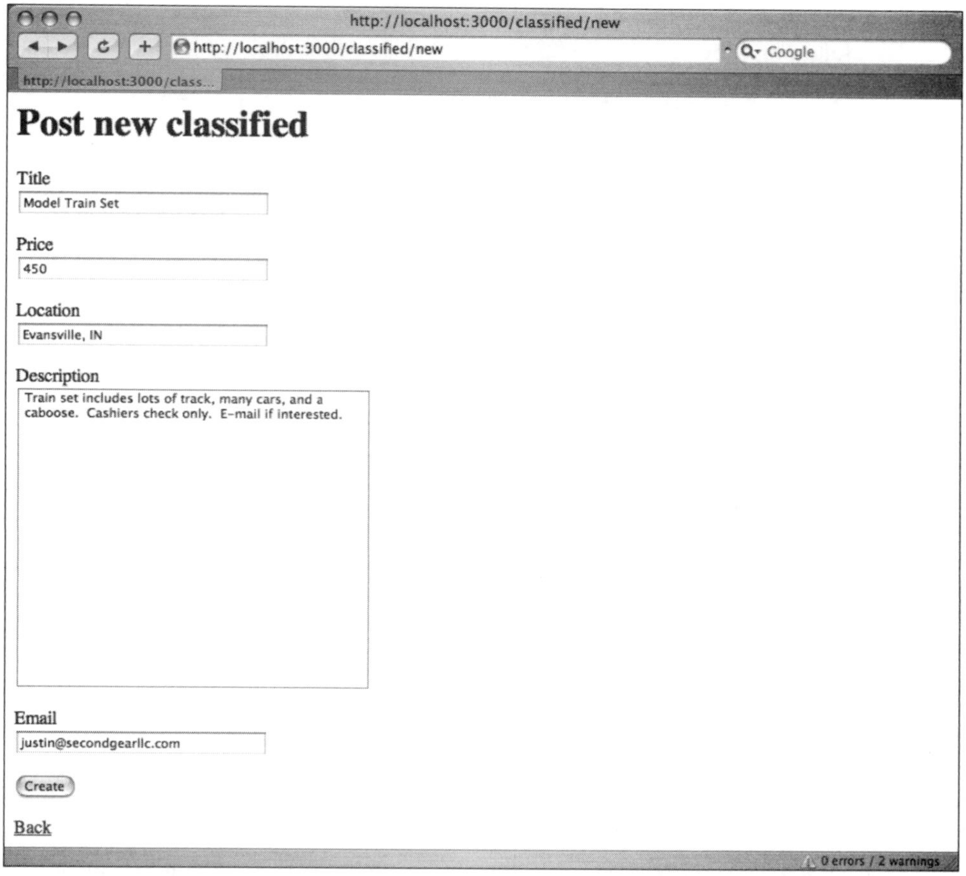

Figure 4-11. The form to create a new classified ad

> *Why should you bother learning new methods such as* start_form_tag, text_field, *and* submit_tag *instead of just writing straight HTML? Simplicity. Rails has made it very easy to create complex forms more rapidly by simply defining a keyword plus its parameters and then having Rails output the valid HTML for it. Take a look at the source code output by the form you just created and compare it with the code you wrote. You get a lot of payoff for less effort by using Rails' built-in form methods. Unfortunately, not all tags have Rails helpers, which is why you use regular* <label> *tags. Check out* http://www.rubyonrails.org/docs *for more information.*

The data should submit successfully and redirect you to the list page, in which you now have a single item listed. If you click the link, you should see another Template is missing error since you haven't created the template file yet.

6. Create a show.rhtml file under app/views/classified and populate it with the following code:

```
<h1><%= @classified.title %></h1>

<p><strong>Price: </strong> $<%= @classified.price %><br />
  <strong>Location: </strong> <%= @classified.location %><br />
  <strong>Date Posted:</strong> <%= @classified.created_at %><br />
  <strong>Last updated:</strong> <%= @classified.updated_at %>
</p>

<p><%= @classified.description %></p>

<hr />

<p>Interested?  Contact <%= mail_to @classified.email -%></p>

<%= link_to 'Back', {:action => 'list'} %>
```

There's not much new to this view other than the use of mail_to to display the e-mail address. It is similar to link_to, but instead creates a mailto: link. Also of note is the use of the created_at and updated_at fields. They are pretty ugly right now, but in later chapters you will do some things to make the display more appealing.

Updating existing ads

The final pieces of the basic implementation of railslist include allowing the user to edit and delete listings from the application. Let's tackle editing first.

1. Modify the classified_controller.rb edit and update methods to look like the following:

```
def edit
  @classified = Classified.find(params[:id])
end

def update
  @classified = Classified.find(params[:id])
  if @classified.update_attributes(params[:classified])
    redirect_to :action => 'show', :id => @classified
  else
    render :action => 'edit'
  end
end
```

Notice that the edit method looks nearly identical to the show method. Both methods are used to retrieve a single object based on its id and display it on a page. The only difference is that the show method is not editable.

The update method has a bit more going on, but it is strikingly similar to the create method you detailed before. The only difference is in line 3 of the method: if @classified.update_attributes(params[:classified]). The update_attributes method is similar to the save method used by create but instead of creating a new row in the database, it overwrites the attributes of the existing row (described in the @classified object) with the new data provided.

Now let's create the view for the edit method.

2. Create a new file called edit.rhtml and save it in app/views/classified. Populate it with the following code:

```
<h1>Editing Classified: <%= @classified.title -%></h1>

<%= start_form_tag :action => 'update', :id => @classified %>

  <p><label for="classified_title">Title</label><br/>
  <%= text_field 'classified', 'title' %></p>

  <p><label for="classified_price">Price</label><br/>
  <%= text_field 'classified', 'price' %></p>

  <p><label for="classified_location">Location</label><br/>
  <%= text_field 'classified', 'location' %></p>

  <p><label for="classified_description">Description</label><br/>
  <%= text_area 'classified', 'description' %></p>

  <p><label for="classified_email">Email</label><br/>
  <%= text_field 'classified', 'email' %></p>

  <%= submit_tag "Save changes" %>
<%= end_form_tag %>

<%= link_to 'Back', {:action => 'list' } %>
```

Other than line 1 printing the title of the classified ad and modifying the start_form_tag action to be update instead of create and defining an id, it is exactly the same form as the new method. You need to provide the user with an outlet for editing the classifieds, so let's edit the list.rhtml file.

3. Go to the <li></li> element and modify it to look like the following:

```
<li>
  <%= link_to c.title, {:action => "show", :id => c.id} -%>
  <small> <%= link_to 'Edit', {:action => "edit",
    :id => c.id} %></small>
</li>
```

All you did was add a link called Edit that takes the user to the edit form.

6

4. Point your browser to http://localhost:3000/classified/list and test the new functionality. The list page should now look like Figure 4-12.

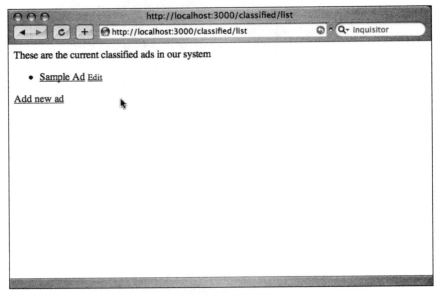

Figure 4-12. The list page, updated with the new edit link

Removing an ad

Removing information from a database using Ruby on Rails is almost too easy. Before you dive into the controller code, let's modify list.rhtml again and add a delete link.

1. Go to the <li></li> element and modify it to look like the following:

```
<li>
<%= link_to c.title, {:action => 'show', :id => c.id} -%>
<small> <%= link_to 'Edit', {:action => 'edit', :id => c.id} %></small>
<small> <%= link_to "Delete", {:action => 'delete',
  :id => c.id} %></small>
</li>
```

2. Open classified_controller.rb and modify the delete method as follows:

```
def delete
  Classified.find(params[:id]).destroy
  redirect_to :action => 'list'
end
```

The first line finds the classified based on the parameter passed via the params object and then deletes it using the destroy method. The second line redirects the user to the list method using a redirect_to call. This is almost too easy, and you should probably add a confirmation process to protect users against deleting items accidentally. Let's modify list.rhtml to confirm the deletions before proceeding.

3. Go back to the `<li></li>` element and edit it to be like the following:

```
<li>
<%= link_to c.title, {:action => 'show', :id => c.id} -%>
<small> <%= link_to 'Edit', {:action => 'edit',
:id => c.id} %></small>
<small> <%= link_to "Delete", {:action => 'delete', :id => c.id},
  :confirm => "Are you sure you want to delete this item?" %></small>
</li>
```

The main difference is that you added a `:confirm` parameter that presents a JavaScript confirmation box asking if you really want to perform the action. If the user clicks OK, the action proceeds, and the item is deleted.

Adding some style

Since this is a friends of ED book, and most of us are designers at heart, it is probably making you cringe that there isn't much style on the railslist application. Before wrapping up this chapter, let's work on implementing a layout and some CSS to the application. Ruby on Rails supports the use of layouts for defining a standard layout that is rendered for all actions.

Most websites make use of a layout or templating system. If you look at www.apress.com, as seen in Figure 4-13, you can see that on most pages there is a standard feature set: a logo at the top, navigation bar, and so on. In the main content area, the content changes depending on the book (or set of books) you look at.

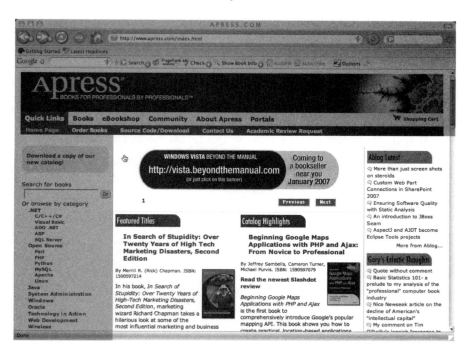

Figure 4-13.
In this screenshot, the darkened areas are part of the template. The lighter area is changing content per page.

Rails has built-in support for easily adding templating to your applications. The process involves defining a layout template and then letting the controller know that it exists and to use it. First, let's create the template.

1. Add a new file called standard.rhtml to app/views/layouts. You let the controllers know what template to use by the name of the file, so following a sane naming scheme is advised.

2. Add the following code to the new standard.rhtml file and save your changes:

```
<!DOCTYPE html PUBLIC "-//W3C//DTD XHTML 1.0 Transitional//EN"
"http://www.w3.org/TR/xhtml1/DTD/xhtml1-transitional.dtd">
<html xmlns="http://www.w3.org/1999/xhtml">
<head>
  <meta http-equiv="Content-Type" content="text/html;➥
charset=iso-8859-1" />
  <meta http-equiv="Content-Language" content="en-us" />
  <title>railslist</title>
<%= stylesheet_link_tag "style" %>
</head>
<body id="rails-list">
<div id="container">
  <div id="header">
    <h1>Railslist</h1>
    <h3>Classifieds powered by Ruby on Rails</h3>
  </div>
  <div id="content">
    <%= yield -%>
  </div>
  <div id="sidebar"></div>
</div>
</body>
</html>
```

Everything you just added were standard HTML elements, except line 7 and 15, which each have a single line of Rails code. Line 7 uses the stylesheet_link_tag helper method that outputs a stylesheet <link>. On line 15, the yield command lets Rails know that it should put the RHTML for the method called here.

Next, you need to let the Classified controller know about the new template.

3. Open up the classified_controller.rb file in app/controllers and add the following line just below the first line:

```
layout 'standard'
```

You are telling the controller that you want to use the layout in the standard.rhtml file.

4. If you go to http://localhost:3000/classified/list you should see that the template is now implemented, as shown in Figure 4-14.

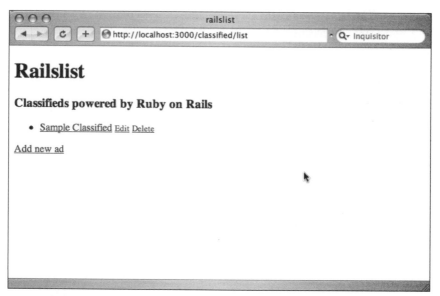

Figure 4-14. The template is now applied to the application.

By creating the stylesheet link using the Rails helper method, the fonts were converted to a sans-serif, even though you did not create a stylesheet for the application. This is because Rails defaults to linking to an internal stylesheet when it cannot find the actual CSS file you are referencing. Let's create the CSS file now.

5. Create a new file called style.css and save it in /public/stylesheets.

Anything you store in the /public directory is viewable by anyone who accesses the application from the web browser. So after you create the style.css file, you can access it via the Web at http://localhost:3000/stylesheets/style.css.

6. Add the following code to the CSS file and save your changes:

```
* {
  margin: 0;
  padding:0;
}

body {
  font-family: Helvetica, Geneva, Arial, sans-serif;
  font-size: small;
  font-color: #000;
  background-color: #fff;
}

a:link, a:active, a:visited {
  color: #CD0000;
}
```

```
a:hover {
  color: #F70000;
}

input {        margin-bottom: 5px;}

p { line-height: 150%; }

div#container {
  width: 760px;
  margin: 0 auto;
}

div#header {
  text-align: center;
  padding-bottom: 15px;
}

div#content {
  float: left;
  width: 450px;
  padding: 10px;
}

div#content h3 {
  margin-top: 15px;
}

ul#classifieds {
  list-style-type:  none;
}

ul#classifieds li {
  line-height:  140%;
}

div#sidebar {
  width: 200px;
  margin-left: 480px;
}
```

7. Refresh your browser and you should see your application displayed with a bit more style, as shown in Figure 4-15.

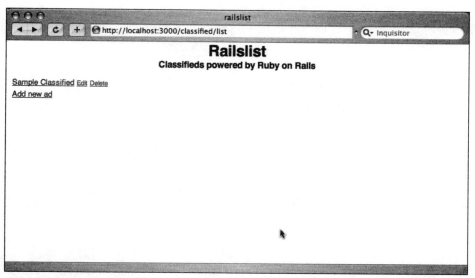

Figure 4-15. railslist in style!

Summary

This chapter covered a lot of territory. You started by creating the basics of your first Ruby on Rails application, which gave you a valuable hands-on introduction to the Rails way of doing things. You created your model and database migration, and then added a controller and methods with corresponding views to allow users to view and modify data. Next, you styled the application using a template and a stylesheet.

In the next chapter, you will begin to expand on your Rails knowledge by introducing model validations to the data model and learning some basic debugging skills.

5 **MORE ADVANCED RAILS**

You've now covered enough ground to have basic introduction to the functionality of Rails. Your railslist application is working at a basic level. You can create and view listings, update them with new information, and destroy them if necessary. You also have applied a default layout and stylesheet to your application. If you left the application in that state, it would be fine and functional, but not nearly as useful as it could be. For instance, there are no categories for items, so each item is listed on only a single listed page. This might be fine if you have only 10 listings, but if your application becomes popular, how can you handle tens of thousands of listings with that single page?

You're also not doing any sort of data validation, so users can just add any data they see fit to the application. They can also leave fields blank that might cause havoc when trying to render the pages. Let's try and address some of these issues in this chapter by using some of the other parts of the Ruby on Rails framework.

This chapter covers the following:

- Validating data on the server side
- Using migrations to add new data fields to the application
- Creating relationships between data models
- Customizing URLs
- Using transactions to improve data integrity
- Debugging controllers and views
- Using the Rails console to work with the application via the command line

Validating data

In a perfect world, all the data that users enter into forms would be perfect. They would know which fields to fill out automatically and would submit information in the exact format needed. Unfortunately, that is not the case. Users make mistakes. There are also users who enter bad data for malicious purposes. It is the developer's job to protect users and applications from those mistakes, which is why you validate data.

There are two ways to validate data in a Rails application. The first is on the client side using JavaScript. This is typically done by appending an onSubmit JavaScript event to the web form, which can catch many errors but also raises several issues. First, it increases the load time and complexity of the application. Second, it isn't foolproof. What if the user is using a browser with JavaScript turned off? Your validation won't even be triggered.

The second way to validate data is on the server side. Server-side validation works by sending a user's form data to the web server and testing it against various conditions. If those conditions are met, the action the user is trying to perform proceeds. If not, the user is returned to the form and told what the problem is and hopefully how to fix it. By performing server-side validation, you are ensuring that the database is protected from faulty data. You're also protecting the database from malicious data. You can use server-side validation to make sure that a user is not sending data that might be used as part of an SQL injection or cross-site scripting attack.

Server-side validation is what Rails offers. Even better, the framework makes it incredibly easy to implement this validation by using very little code.

Implementing validations in railslist

Think about your railslist Classified model for a moment. You are storing five pieces of user-submitted data (title, description, price, item location, and e-mail address) and you need to see whether the user entered all five. You also need to ensure that the user enters only a numeric value for the price. Finally, you want to make sure that the user provides a valid e-mail address. To do that, you can check the format of the e-mail address to make sure it includes a beginning, an at sign (@), and a fully qualified domain name.

The implementation of validations is done in a Rails model. The data you are entering into the database is defined in the actual Rails model, so it only makes sense to define what valid data entails in the same location.

1. Open up the `classified.rb` file in your app/models directory. At this point, it should look like this:

   ```
   class Classified < ActiveRecord::Base
   end
   ```

   Pretty bare bones so far. The validation definitions will go between the class and end lines. First, implement the required data validations.

2. Add the following three lines to your `classified.rb` file, before the closing end statement, and save your changes:

   ```
   validates_presence_of :title
   validates_presence_of :price
   validates_presence_of :location
   validates_presence_of :description
   validates_presence_of :email
   ```

   Like most everything in Rails, each of these lines is readable and descriptive. For the model to be valid, the user needs to have entered something in each database field. If nothing is entered, the line won't validate. Let's look at the validation in action.

3. Open up your web browser, navigate to the railslist application (http://localhost:3000), and create a new classified ad. When you fill in all the fields, it should create an item as normal.

4. Now try it again, except leave some fields blank this time. When you submit the form, instead of being forwarded onto the listing screen as usual, you are redirected back to your form with all your previous data still filled in. Your data did not pass the validation process.

This is all well and good, but unfortunately your users do not know an error occurred because you have not yet told Rails to display error messages. Let's remedy it now.

5. Open the new.rhtml file in app/views/classified and add the following line below the <h1> tag:

```
<%= error_messages_for 'classified' -%>
```

6. Save the file and go back to your browser.

7. Resubmit the form using the same data you entered before. You should now be notified that an error occurred, as shown in Figure 5-1.

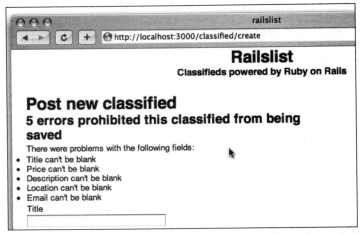

Figure 5-1. Now railslist displays some error messages to let you know what's going on.

This is what the default error handler provided by the Rails framework looks like. It lists the number of errors and what those errors are. The description is somewhat bare and to the point. If you want to modify the wording, you can.

8. Go back to the classified.rb file and change line 2 to look like the following:

```
validates_presence_of :title, :message => "cannot be blank. Make your➡
   title descriptive"
```

Now when you try to submit a classified ad with a blank title, your description will look similar to the way you defined it.

Next, ensure that the user can enter only a numeric value for the item's price.

9. Add the following line below your other validation rules in classified.rb:

```
validates_numericality_of :price
```

validates_numericality_of is another one of Rails' built-in validations. It ensures that the only data entered into a numeric field are numbers and periods (.). Like other validations, you can also modify the output of the error provided by adding the :message parameter.

> Another interesting parameter you could add is :only_integer, which checks to see whether the value entered is a whole number only (no decimal places).

10. Use the :message parameter to let the user know not to include the dollar sign. Change the line as follows:

```
validates_numericality_of :price, :message => "must be a numeric➥
value (do not include a dollar sign)"
```

11. Now try to post an ad, but include a price with a nonnumeric value, and you should see it fail.

You are also not checking to see whether the user is entering a positive value. This doesn't make much sense because you are dealing with financial values.

12. Add the following method to the Classified model again, just before the end statement. Rails automatically calls the method called validate before trying to save the values.

```
protected
  def validate
    errors.add(:price, "should be a positive value") if price.nil?➥
|| price < 0.01
  end
```

Because the validate method is automatically called, it throws another error if you are entering a null value or a price that is not a positive value.

Finally, you can validate the format of a user's e-mail address. Since interested parties need to contact the seller to complete the transaction, it is important to make sure that the user enters a valid e-mail address. The best way to ensure this is to use validate_format_of, which compares a user submitted value with a regular expression.

13. Add the following line to classified.rb, just before the last end statement:

```
validates_format_of :email, ➥
:with => /^([^@\s]+)@((?:[-a-z0-9]+\.)+[a-z]{2,})$/i
```

If you're not familiar with regular expressions, don't worry about trying to understand anything after :with =>. It's merely a common regular expression for e-mail addresses.

14. Now try entering an e-mail address without the at (@) sign; railslist tells you that the address is invalid.

> If you want to learn more about regular expressions, check out http://www.regular-expressions.info/.

Other common validations

Besides the three validations already discussed, there are a few more common ones that you will use in your Rails applications.

- validates_acceptance_of: If you provide users with a check box that they need to check (such as a terms-of-service agreement), this ensures that it is checked:

  ```
  validates_acceptance_of :eula, :message => "must be accepted"
  ```

- validates_confirmation_of: This validation is used primarily with storing passwords. Usually, when you want users to set their passwords, you have them enter it twice to make sure it is what they intend. This makes sure the first value is the same as the second:

  ```
  validates_confirmation_of :password, ➡
  :message => "should match confirmation"
  ```

- validates_length_of: Sometimes you might want to limit the number of characters that a user can enter in your field. This enables you to set the maximum:

  ```
  validates_length_of :first_name, :maximum => 30
  ```

- validates_uniqueness_of: When you create a user account, you want to make sure that each user has a unique name. validates_uniqueness_of ensures that the value the user enters does not match any of the other values presently stored in the database:

  ```
  validates_uniqueness_of :login
  ```

Adding categories with migrations

Up to this point, the application has only one model. However, Rails applications can have as many models as you need—they are used to define different types of data in the application. Models are also used to let Rails know how other models are related with each other. In this case, you tell the Classified model that it is associated with a Category model.

You can add another model that describes a category. Each category is capable of holding multiple categories, and each classified has a single category, as illustrated in Figure 5-2.

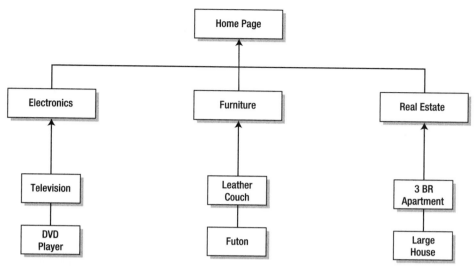

Figure 5-2. Each category in railslist can house multiple listings based on the type of item it is.

In the old days before Ruby on Rails, modifying the application's data model would be a complex task. It would require complex SQL queries to insert the new fields and even more complex routines to populate those fields if necessary. Not so with Rails, though. Migrations were discussed when you created the initial Classified model, and now you can use a single migration to both create a new model and to modify the existing one.

1. First, open up a Terminal or command prompt window and go to the railslist directory. Once there, type the following command to create the new model and press Enter.

```
ruby script/generate model Category
```

This command creates the model file itself as well as a migration file and the unit tests for the new model.

2. Go to the db/migrate directory and open up the 002_create_categories.rb file. Besides defining the category data, you also need to modify the classifieds table to hold a category reference.

3. Modify the file to look like the following and then save it:

```
class CreateCategories < ActiveRecord::Migration
  def self.up
    create_table :categories do |t|
      t.column :name, :string
    end

    Category.create :name => "Electronics"
    Category.create :name => "Real Estate"
```

```
        Category.create :name => "Furniture"
        Category.create :name => "Miscellaneous"

        add_column :classifieds, :category_id, :integer
        Classified.find(:all).each do |c|
          c.update_attribute(:category_id, 4)
        end
      end

      def self.down
        drop_table :categories
        remove_column :classifieds, :category_id
      end
    end
```

What this migration does is create a new categories table in the database that has a single column called name. It also adds a column called id that will act as the primary key. (The primary key is the unique attribute in a row that distinguishes it from all others in that table.) You also added a few starter categories to the database and a new column to the existing classifieds table that does enable you to associate a category's id field to a classified.

The most interesting portion of the code you just typed includes the last three lines of the self.up method. You want to set a default category for existing classifieds in the system, so you find all the items and then iterate through them setting the value to be 4, which is the id of the miscellaneous category (it was the fourth one you created).

In the self.down method, you made sure to undo the changes caused by this migration. In other words, you tell Rails to remove the new table and remove the category_id column from the classifieds table. That way, if you decide to migrate to a previous version of the database, the migration scripts remove any modifications you made.

4. Go back to your command prompt and run rake migrate. The new categories table and the category_id column are now added to the railslist database.

Creating associations between models

You now have two models in the railslist application, but you have not created any connection between those two models in the application. You can do this via associations. Active Record supports three types of associations: one-to-one, one-to-many, and many-to-many. These types of associations are called relationships. Let's examine what each of them means:

- **one-to-one**: A one-to-one relationship exists when one item has exactly one of another item. For example, a person has exactly one birthday or a dog has exactly one owner.

- **one-to-many**: A one-to-many relationship exists when a single object can be a member of many other objects. For instance, if you are designing a shopping cart, a product can be a part of multiple orders.

- **many-to-many**: A many-to-many relationship exists when the first object is related to one or more of a second object, and the second object is related to one or many of the first object. If you were designing a class schedule for a college, students and classes have a many-to-many relationship because a student can have many classes, and a class can have many students.

The relationship between the Classified and Category objects is a one-to-many relationship because a classified is associated with a single category, and a category can contain multiple classifieds, as illustrated in Figure 5-3.

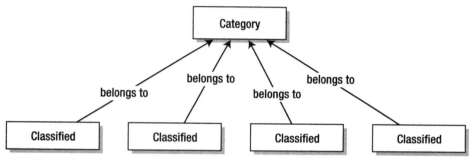

Figure 5-3. This diagram shows a has_many relationship for a category in the railslist application.

The Classified model has a belongs_to method because a classified belongs to a single category. How do you describe that in Rails? With ease, of course!

1. Open up the classified.rb model file and add the following at line 2:

belongs_to :category

2. Save your changes and then open the category.rb file that has been created in app/models. Add the following at line 2:

has_many :classifieds

Save those changes. Now you have a relationship that you can work with. When modifying the Classified model, you told Rails that it belongs to a single category. That is where the category_id field you created in the migration will come in. It will hold the row id of the category. The Category model defines the many part of the one-to-many relationship by saying that a single category can have many classifieds be a part of it.

Working with the new relationship

The first thing you need to do is modify the Classified controller to give a listing of all the categories in the new method.

1. Open `classified_controller.rb` and add the following line to both the new and create methods, just before the closing end statements:

```
@categories = Category.find(:all)
```

All this does is to grab all the categories from the database and puts them in an array called @categories.

Next, modify the new classified view to allow users to assign a category to the listing.

2. Open up the new.rhtml file in app/views/classified/ and add the following lines between the description and e-mail fields.

```
<p><label for="classified_category">Category</label><br />
<%= collection_select(:classified, :category_id, @categories, ➡
:id, :name) %></p>
```

Here you have encountered a new Rails method called collection_select, which creates an HTML select menu built from an array, such as the @categories one. There are five parameters, which are as follows:

- :classified: The object you are manipulating. In this case, it's a Classified object.

- :category_id: The field that is populated when the classified is saved.

- @categories: The array you are working with.

- :id: The value that is stored in the database. In terms of HTML, this is the <option> tag's value parameter.

- :name: The output that the user sees in the pull-down menu. This is the value between the <option> tags.

3. Now return again to the new classified listing page and you should see a drop-down menu that contains all the categories you created in the migration.

Now modify the edit.rhtml view with the same data.

4. Add a @categories array to the edit and update methods in classified_controller.rb.

```
def edit
  @classified = Classified.find(params[:id])
  @categories = Category.find(:all)
end

  def update
    @classified = Classified.find(params[:id])
    @categories = Category.find(:all)
  ...
  end
```

5. Add the following two lines to your edit.rhtml file, just as you did for the new view:

```
<p><label for="classified_category">Category</label><br />
<%= collection_select(:classified, :category_id, @categories, ➡
:id, :name) %></p>
```

Now that you've displayed the drop-down menu in the edit view as well as the new view, the last step of implementing categories in the classified listings is to show the category in the single item view.

6. Open show.rhtml in app/views/classifieds and add the following line between price and location:

```
<strong>Category: </strong> <%= @classified.category.name %><br />
```

This is the first time you have taken full advantage of associations, which enable you to easily pull data from related objects. The format used is @variable.relatedObject.column. In this instance, you can pull the category's name value through the @classified variable using the belongs_to associations.

Controlling the categories

Before you move on, you should create a view to enable users to get a listing of classifieds based on a category.

1. Add the following method to classified_controller.rb:

```
def show_category
  @category = Category.find(params[:id])
end
```

2. Create a new file, show_category.rhtml, in the app/views/classified directory.

3. Add the following code to it and save your changes:

```
<h1><%= @category.name -%></h1>
<ul>
<% @category.classifieds.each do |c| %>
  <li><%= link_to c.title, :action => "show", :id => c.id -%></li>
<% end %>
</ul>
```

You are once again taking advantage of associations by iterating through a single category's many classified listings. But you are not yet finished; you now need to add a mechanism to the application for the users to access this list of categories.

To bring uniformity throughout the application, modify a few more views to show category links.

4. Modify the Category: line of show.rhtml so that the category listing shows a link.

```
<strong>Category: </strong> <%= link_to @classified.category.name,➡
  :action => "show_category", :id => @classified.category.id %><br />
```

Output a list of categories on the index page, so that users can access them directly.

5. Open list.rhtml and add the following to the top of the file:

```
<ul id="categories">
<% Category.find(:all).each do |c| %>
  <li><%= link_to c.name, :action => "show_category", ➡
:id => c.id %></li>
<% end %>
</ul>
```

Go to http://localhost:3000/classified/list and you should see a listing of categories at the top that you can navigate through, as shown in Figure 5-4.

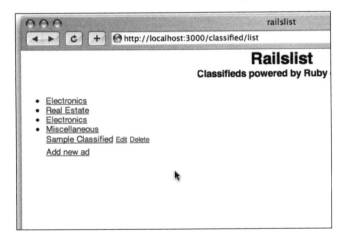

Figure 5-4.
You've added category navigation to the listing page, but it looks in need of some style.

This is functional, but it currently looks pretty horrible, so you need to add some style to the category navigation.

6. Add the following CSS styles to the style.css file in /public/stylesheets:

```
ul#categories {
  width: 700px;
  text-align: center;
  padding: 5px;
  background-color: #ececec;
  border: 1px solid #ccc;
  margin-bottom: 20px;
}
```

```
ul#categories li {
  display: inline;
  padding-left: 5px;
}
```

Refresh the page; you now have better-looking category navigation, as shown in Figure 5-5.

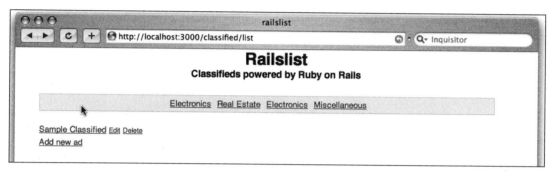

Figure 5-5. That's better!

Modifying URLs using routing

One of the often-overlooked aspects of designing a new web application is taking into account how clean your URLs are. In an online shopping site such as Amazon the URLs are long and confusing strings of text and numbers. If users want to easily return to a product listing they were looking at before, there is almost no way they can do it by committing the URL to memory. Instead, they have to search for the product again or create a bookmark in their browser.

One of the growing trends in web development over the past few years has been thoughtful URL design. Planning your URLs to be intuitive to users makes it easier for them to return to your products or e-mail a link to a friend without it being broken or wrapped onto two or more lines.

One of the best instances of this thoughtful design is by Apple, which follows a traditional URL design for its product pages. Want to check out the new iMac? Just visit apple.com/imac/. Want to learn more about iPhoto? The URL is apple.com/iphoto/. Users don't have to worry about drilling through several pages just to get where they want to be. Instead, they can just guess the URL—and they are most likely going to be correct.

Ruby on Rails allows for this thoughtful URL design using routing. Routing gives Rails developers an easy way to craft clean URLs without having to manipulate the configuration files of your web server. All the route does is redirect your application's incoming requests to the correct controller and action—it's like an internal forwarding service. Like migrations, Rails uses actual Ruby code to define the routing rules.

Defining your own routes

The routing rules for your application are stored in the `routes.rb` file in the `config` folder.

1. Open it up and inspect what is already there.

```
ActionController::Routing::Routes.draw do |map|
  map.connect ':controller/service.wsdl', :action => 'wsdl'

  # Install the default route as the lowest priority.
  map.connect ':controller/:action/:id'
end
```

The comments at the top of the file were omitted for brevity.

Think of routing as a map for your requests. The map tells the application where to go based on predefined parameters. Each route has a certain priority that is defined by the appearance of the route in the `routes.rb` file, ordered from top to bottom, so the last route you have defined is the lowest priority. In the case of this default configuration, the lowest route is `map.connect ':controller/:action/:id'`, which is what has been creating the URLs up to this point. `:controller` maps to the controller name, `:action` maps to the controller's action to execute, and `:id` is the actual database row to manipulate. Notice that all the URLs in the application have followed the same format so far, as illustrated in Figure 5-6.

Figure 5-6. Standard Rails URL format

The URL for showing a certain classified ad does indeed use the lowest priority route. These URLs are fine, but what if you want to modify how the URLs look so that users can go straight to `http://localhost:3000/classifieds/:id` instead? It's as easy as adding a new line to the top of the `routes.rb` file.

2. Add the following to line 2 and then save your changes:

```
map.connect 'classifieds/:id', :controller => 'classified',➡
  :action => 'show'
```

After `map.connect` is the URL you will use; in this case, it is `classifieds`, followed by the id of the classified. Next, you define which controller and action the route will be forwarded to.

Let's try it out! Go to `http://localhost:3000/classified/list`, click one of your classifieds, and notice the new URL, as shown in Figure 5-7.

Figure 5-7.
The ad URLs just became more compact.

The old `:controller/:action/:id` *route is still intact because it is the lowest priority. It is best to just leave it be and then create everything else above it. Without it, you cannot use the default* `controller_name/action_name` *route.*

Defining route en masse

The classified controller has eight methods thus far that all share a common attribute: a `:controller` parameter. You can save some typing by wrapping everything in another block.

1. Delete the new route you created and add the following code in its place:

```
map.with_options(:controller => 'classified') do |classified|
    classified.connect 'classifieds/new', :action => 'new'
    classified.connect 'classifieds/create', :action => 'create'
    classified.connect 'classifieds/edit/:id', :action => 'edit'
    classified.connect 'classifieds/update/:id', :action => 'update'
    classified.connect 'classifieds/delete/:id', :action => 'delete'
    classified.connect 'classifieds/categories/:id', ➡
:action => 'show_category'
    classified.connect 'classifieds/:id', :action => 'show'
    classified.connect '', :action => 'list'
  end
```

You just added a lot of code, so let's walk through it:

`map.with_options` enables you to define a common `:controller` for a set of routes and have it apply to all the routes within the code block. Below that line is a route for each of the controller's actions. Instead of using the `map.connect` line, you are using `|classified|` since that is what you defined as the iterator. This has a similar syntax to an `each` block.

The bottom route in the block is `''` (two single quotes,) which is the route for the root of your site, or `http://localhost:3000/`.

2. If you go to that URL, you would now expect to see a listing of all your classifieds, but unfortunately this is not yet the case—you need to take an extra step before the route takes effect. There is a file called `index.html` in the `/public` folder that will take precedence over your routes, so if you go to `http://localhost:3000`, you will get the default Rails page that you first saw when you first created your application skeleton.

3. Remove that file from the `public` folder and then refresh your browser. You should now see your classified listings.

Named routes

As you continue developing your application, you will probably have a few links that you use throughout your application. For example, you will probably often be putting a link back to the main listings page. Instead of having to add the following line throughout your

5

application, you can instead create a named route that enables you to link to a shorthand version of that link:

```
link_to 'Home', :controller => 'classified', :action => 'list'
```

1. Add the following line below the map.with_options block:

```
map.home '', :controller => 'classified', :action => 'list'
```

The name of the route is defined after the map keyword. Instead of using connect, you are using a unique name that you can define. In this case, the route is called home. The rest of the route looks similar to the others you have created.

Now you can use this in the controllers or views.

2. Open up show.rhtml under app/views/classifieds and modify this line:

```
<%= link_to 'Back', {:action => 'list'} %>
```

It should look like the following:

```
<%= link_to 'Back', home_url %>
```

3. Save your changes.

Instead of listing the :controller and :action to which you will be linking, you are instead putting the name of the route followed by _url. Your user shouldn't notice any difference. Named routing is merely a convenience for the Rails developer to save some typing.

Like I said, you can also modify the controllers to use named routes.

4. Open up classified_controller.rb in app/controllers and modify the create method to look like the following:

```
def create
  @classified = Classified.new(params[:classified])
  @categories = Category.find(:all)
  if @classified.save
    redirect_to home_url
  else
    render :action => 'new'
  end
end
```

Again, the user doesn't notice anything, but it does save the developer a bit of typing.

You can also use parameters in named routes. Let's create a named route for the show method.

5. Add this line to the routes.rb file above the maps.home route:

```
map.show 'classifieds/:id', :controller => 'classified', :action =>➡
'list'
```

6. Open up the `list.rhtml` file and modify the classified listings iterator (the code inside the `<ul>` with the id of `classifieds`) to look like the following:

```
<% @classifieds.each do |c| %>
  <li><%= link_to c.title, show_url(:id => c.id) -%>
  <small><%= link_to 'Edit', {:action => 'edit', ➥
:id => c.id} %></small>
    <small><%= link_to "Delete", {:action => 'delete', :id => c.id},
      :confirm => "Are you sure you want to delete this item?" %>➥
</small> </li>
<% end %>
```

The named route for show passes the parameter between a set of parentheses.

7. Test your application to make sure that everything is working okay. If not, check the code carefully against this chapter's code in the code download.

Basic debugging

Up to this point (assuming that you have been typing everything correctly), you shouldn't have run into any issues with the code you have developed. If you have experienced any problems, you probably mistyped something. Again, compare your work against the code download files for typos or other errors.

In the real world, however, it is rare that nothing will go wrong in your code. The Rails framework understands this and includes several tools that make it easy to debug your Rails applications. In this section, you'll look at them—specifically the following:

- Rails console
- breakpointer
- Debugging views

Rails console

The console is an extremely useful tool for development debugging of Rails applications. The console is based on Irb (Interactive Ruby), which is a command shell that is bundled with all Ruby installations. Using the console, you can create new (or manipulate existing) objects, find existing objects, and perform actions against them. You can perform the following tasks using console to show its power:

- Create a new classified object
- Save it to the database
- Read an existing classified
- Change its category
- Save those changes
- Delete the classified

First, you need to launch a console window. A copy of the console application is included with each Rails application in the script directory.

1. Open up a Terminal or command prompt window and go to your railslist directory. Once there, run the following command:

```
ruby script/console
```

You should be presented with a command prompt. It will look like this: >>. It's nothing too spectacular to look at, but it is quite powerful. You can use the console to create a new Classified object.

2. Type the following commands into your console window, pressing Enter at the end of each line:

```
@classified = Classified.new
@classified.title = "Rails Solutions: Rails Made Easy - Like New"
@classified.category = Category.find(:first, ➡
:conditions => "name = 'Miscellaneous'")
@classified.price = 40
@classified.location = "Chicago, IL"
@classified.email = "justin@secondgearllc.com"
@classified.description = "A great book for web designers to learn ➡
how to use Rails!"
@classified.valid?
@classified.save
```

You should see the overall output shown in Figure 5-8.

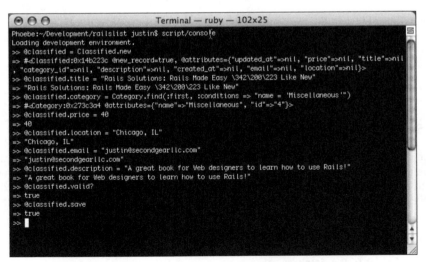

Figure 5-8. This is what the output of your commands should look like.

What you just did was create a new Classified object under the @classified instance variable. You then defined the attributes of the object. You set its title, category, price, and e-mail address. Of interest is the category in which you do a search for the category you are looking for by using a Rails find() method.

3. Finally, you check to see whether the item is valid and then save it.

4. Open your browser and go to your railslist application, and you should see a new item in the list containing the data you just entered in the console.

Reading existing data

Besides creating new objects, you can also read existing data in from the console. All the methods available to your controller are available via the Rails console, which includes the find() method. Let's test it out.

1. Type the following commands into the console:

```
@classified2 = Classified.find(:first)
@classified2.title
@classified2.price
@classified2.update_attribute(:price, 45)
```

What you just did was create a new instance variable called @classified2 that contains the first classified in the database. Next, you output the title of the classified and the existing price. The last thing you did was update the price attribute to be 45. update_attribute is a Rails method that enables you to easily update a single attribute for an object.

2. Go back to the browser and find the classified you just manipulated. Notice that the price change is now visible on the site.

3. Keep your browser there, but go back to the console window, type the following, and press Enter:

```
@classified2.destroy
```

4. You just deleted this classified from the database. Try to view it in your browser again—it's nowhere to be found.

breakpointer

When you work with code, sometimes you might want to inspect variables or test the execution of certain portions of the code while the application is running. This inspection is something that is done in almost all development environments. With each newly created Ruby on Rails application, a copy of the breakpointer application is included in the scripts folder. breakpointer, which runs in the background in a command prompt or Terminal window, serves as a go-between for the Rails application and the web browser for all requests from your application. All breakpointer does is look for the keyword breakpoint in the application. After it finds one, it stops the execution of the application and sends you to an Irb console.

After the console appears, it works just like the Rails console you outlined previously, but it contains the values from all your initialized variables so you can inspect them. You can also run methods against those variables. Let's see it in action.

1. First, open `classified_controller.rb` and put the keyword breakpoint in the update method right after the `@classified` declaration.

```
def update
    @classified = Classified.find(params[:id])
    @categories = Category.find(:all)
    breakpoint
    if @classified.update_attributes(params[:classified])
...
end
```

2. Next, open up a Terminal or command prompt window and go to the `railslist` directory. Once there, type the following command into the window:

```
ruby script/breakpointer
```

3. Your window should launch breakpointer and present you with a message about waiting for a breakpoint.

4. Open a browser and go into the railslist application.

5. Select one of the classifieds, edit it (modify some of the data), and click the Save button. The application's execution should grind to a standstill.

6. Hop over to the breakpointer Terminal/command prompt window and you should see a Irb prompt, as shown in Figure 5-9.

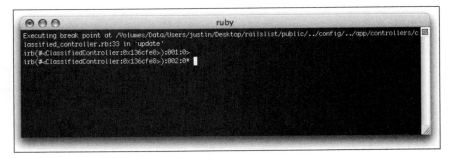

Figure 5-9. Ouput of the breakpointer application

The execution of the update method is stopped in its tracks. Anything that was executed up to the *breakpoint* keyword is available to you in breakpointer.

7. As an example, type in @classified and press Enter. You should see an output of the object's data.

```
=> #<Classified:0x2429ee4 @attributes={"updated_at"=>"2006-07-02
23:00:36", "price"=>"400", "title"=>"Apple iPod", "id"=>"1",
"category_id"=>"1", "description"=>"This is a new iPod Video",
"created_at"=>"2006-07-02 22:57:21",
"email"=>"justin@secondgearllc.com", "location"=>"Newburgh, IN"}>
```

8. Make sure that you have a valid object. Type in @classified.valid? and press Enter. Assuming that you entered nothing but valid data, the output is true.

After you finish working with the data and if you want to continue executing the code, just type exit and the code will continue. To stop the breakpoint service running, press Ctrl+C. Remember to remove the *breakpoint* from the code after you're done testing.

Debugging views

Controllers aren't the only areas that can be debugged in Rails; you can have debugging information output into views as well. Debugging info is useful when you are rendering an action and want to get more information about an object than just what is output by the view. For example, in the category listing, you are outputting only the title of the listing, but you can also show the other attributes.

1. Open the show_category.rhtml file from app/views/classifieds. Modify the listing output block to look like the following:

```
<ul>
<% @category.classifieds.each do |c| %>
<%= debug c %>
  <li><%= link_to c.title, :action => "show", :id => c.id -%></li>
<% end %>
</ul>
```

The only line you added was another output that used the debug method to output the values of each object in the @classifieds array.

2. View one of the categories; you should see an output similar to that shown in Figure 5-10.

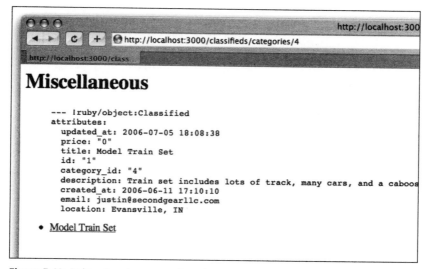

Figure 5-10. Debugging view on a categories page

As you can see, the other values in the object are all that the debug method outputs. It's nothing special, but it does offer a bit of convenience over having to execute a *breakpoint* and jumping between browser and breakpointer windows.

Summary

You covered several important topics in this chapter. You started by creating a new model and adding a migration to the application. Next, you created an association between the two models and discussed the types of relationships you can create. You also learned how to create customized URLs using Rails' routing functionality. Finally, you focused on debugging the application using the console, breakpointer, and debugging view.

In the next chapter, you will be formatting data to be friendlier to your users, which includes modifying the way dates and numbers are displayed.

6 FORMATTING DATA

When working with programming languages such as Ruby, one of the things you notice is that programming languages do not output friendly data when it comes to numbers and dates. Although they are readable by techies, it's clear that most of the time you want a date formatted to be more readable by the application's users and match a user's country and time zone instead of the default output given by a computer.

But with Rails, help is at hand. Rails has helpers, which enable you to easily format your data in a variety of ways. You can format a number stored in the database to be formatted as a currency. If you are working with dates, you can modify the date output to match standard human-readable date formats. If you want, you can also output the date using natural language like *5 days ago*.

Specifically, this chapter covers the following:

- Formatting numbers using NumberHelper
- Formatting dates using DateHelper

> *This chapter isn't a discussion of writing your own Rails helpers. Chapter 10 covers it in its discussion of user authentication and management.*

NumberHelper

NumberHelper is a built-in Rails set of helper methods that provides methods for converting a number into a formatted string of text. Using NumberHelper, a string of text can easily be converted into any of the following formats: phone number, percentage, money, or decimal precision. While in Railslist, you aren't storing any percentages or phone numbers; you can work with the money helpers. Let's implement that in the classified listing.

Open up the show.rhtml file under app/views/classifieds. Look for the line that contains the price. It should look like the following:

```
<strong>Price: </strong> $<%= @classified.price %><br />
```

Notice that you were just tacking a dollar sign ($) in front of the code for a classified's price, which doesn't take into account any sort of decimal places or cents, as well as assuming that the amount is U.S. dollars, not another currency, such as Euros. If you had a high-priced item in the classified system, the user might see something like the number shown in Figure 6-1.

Really Expensive Item
Price: $4000020.0
Location: Newburgh, IN

Figure 6-1.
This currency format isn't very intuitive.

It's hard to tell that you are selling an item that is $4,000,020.00. Let's format that field by using the number_to_currency helper.

1. Modify the line of code you highlighted before to look like the following and then save your changes:

```
<strong>Price: </strong> <%= number_to_currency(@classified.price)
%><br />
```

2. If you refresh your browser, the format of the number now looks like that shown in Figure 6-2.

Really Expensive Item
Price: $4,000,020.00
Location: Newburgh, IN

Figure 6-2.
This is much more readable!

Notice how much cleaner the number is to read. If you were running a U.K. version of railslist, you wouldn't want to display prices using U.S. dollars since you would have stored your prices in pounds.

3. To display your data using pounds, modify the line to look like the following and then save the file:

```
<strong>Price: </strong> <%= number_to_currency(@classified.price,
  {:unit => "&pound;", :separator => ".", :delimiter => ","}) %><br />
```

4. Refresh your browser again, and the output will look like Figure 6-3.

Really Expensive Item
Price: £4,000,020.00
Location: Newburgh, IN

Figure 6-3.
Displaying the currency in U.K. pounds instead of U.S. dollars.

To accomplish the transformation of the classified values into a currency format, you are using some of the built-in parameters for number_to_currency. :unit takes the HTML entity for the currency you are working with. In this case, you are using £ to display the pound sign. The next parameter is :separator, which defines the unit separator (in the preceding case, pounds and pence). The default is a period (.), but you can set it to be any character. The final parameter is :delimiter, which defaults to a comma (,).

> For a complete list of HTML entities that you can use (including other currencies such as Yen), check out http://www.w3.org/MarkUp/html3/latin1.html.

Other helpers

Besides number_to_currency, there are a few other number-related methods that you might find yourself using in your Rails application development:

- *number_to_human_size*: If you are working with file sizes, you can wrap the numeric value with this method to output the size of a file in bytes, kilobytes, megabytes, or gigabytes.
  - number_to_human_size(123) => 123 bytes
  - number_to_human_size(1234) => 1.2KB
  - number_to_human_size(12345) => 12.1KB
  - number_to_human_size(1234567) => 1.2MB
  - number_to_human_size(1234567890) => 1.1GB

- *number_to_percentage*: Formats a number as a percentage. If you use the :precision parameter, you can further format the level of precision (the default is three decimal places).
  - number_to_percentage(100) => 100.00%
  - number_to_percentage(99.5565, {:precision => 2}) => 99.56%

- *number_to_phone*: Formats a number as a phone number. This method enables a lot of variations about how you format the number. If you want to wrap the area code in parentheses, set the :area_code parameter to true. By default, the delimiter used for separating parts of the phone number is a dash (-). You can modify the separator by using the :delimiter parameter.
  - number_to_phone(1234567890) => 123-456-7890
  - number_to_phone(1234567890, {:area_code => true}) => (123) 456-7890
  - number_to_phone(1234567890, {:delimiter => " "}) => 123 456 7890
  - number_to_phone(1234567890, {:area_code => true, :extension => 987}) => (123) 456-7890 x 987

DateHelper

Besides cleaning up the formatting of the numbers using the NumberHelper methods, you can also perform similar actions with dates. If you look at the dates on the classified listing, notice that it's chaotic (see Figure 6-4.)

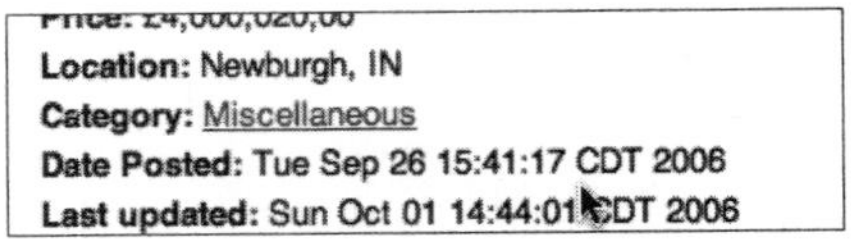

Price: £4,000,020,00
Location: Newburgh, IN
Category: <u>Miscellaneous</u>
Date Posted: Tue Sep 26 15:41:17 CDT 2006
Last updated: Sun Oct 01 14:44:01 CDT 2006

Figure 6-4.
The dates are also hard to read by default.

If you look at the date posted and last updated fields, it will probably take you a few seconds to decipher the format.

Tue	Sep	26	15:41:17	CDT	2006
Day Name	Month	Day's Date	Time	Time Zone	Year

Most people don't write out dates in this format. Rails understands this and provides a few methods that you can use to clean up the formatting of dates. Let's work with them now.

1. Go back to the show.rhtml file you opened earlier and look for the following two lines of code:

```
<strong>Date Posted:</strong> <%= @classified.created_at %><br />
<strong>Last updated:</strong> <%= @classified.updated_at %></p>
```

All you are doing in these two lines is outputting the date string as it is stored in the MySQL database. While the format may be friendly for the database, it could use a bit of work to be legible for users. There isn't a helper explicitly defined in Rails to do this, but with good reason. Ruby includes a method called strftime that enables you to easily format date and time values.

2. Modify the two preceding lines to look like the following and then save your changes:

```
<strong>Date Posted:</strong>
  <%= @classified.created_at.strftime("%B %d %Y") %><br />
<strong>Last updated:</strong>
  <%= @classified.updated_at.strftime("%B %d %Y") %></p>
```

3. Now if you go to your browser and look at the dates, notice that they are *quite* a bit more readable, as shown in Figure 6-5.

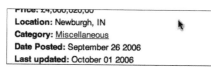

Figure 6-5.
You now cleaned up the dates as well!

The strftime method takes different format string parameters to define how you output the dates. In this case, the %B says to output the full month, %d is to post the day's date, and %Y outputs the full year.

> *You stripped the time out of the posting. It's not really relevant to the users to know exactly what time a classified was posted—only that it was posted on a specific day.*

There are several formatting codes you can use. The following are supported by Ruby:

Format	Meaning
%a	Abbreviated weekday name (Sun)
%A	Full weekday name (Sunday)
%b	Abbreviated month name (Jan)
%B	Full month name (January)
%c	Preferred local date and time representation set by the server
%d	Day of the month (01...31)
%H	Hour of the day, 24-hour clock (00...23)
%I	Hour of the day, 12-hour clock (01...12)
%j	Day of the year (001...366)
%m	Month of the year (01...12)
%M	Minute of the hour (00...59)
%p	Meridian indicator (AM or PM)
%S	Second of the minute (00...60)
%U	Week number of the current year, starting with the first Sunday as the first day of the first week (00...53)
%W	Week number of the current year, starting with the first Monday as the first day of the first week (00...53)
%w	Day of the week (Sunday is 0; 0...6)
%x	Preferred representation for the date alone, no time
%X	Preferred representation for the time alone, no date
%y	Year without a century (00...99)
%Y	Year with a century
%Z	Time zone name
%%	Literal % character

Defining date formats

It's probably safe to assume that you will want to use the same date format throughout your application. While it's not much effort to add the strftime string at the end of your dates, what if down the road you decide to change how you format the dates? That could potentially turn into a lot of work for you.

Wouldn't it be better to just define the format of the dates once and then use it whenever you want to display a date in the application? This is possible by creating your own date formatter. Date formatting is implemented in one of Rails' ActiveSupport classes that extend the functionality of Rails.

1. You define the date formats in the environment.rb file (found in railslist/config.) Open it up and add the following code to the bottom:

```
my_date_formats = {
  :us_date => '%B %d, %Y',
  :uk_date  => '%d %b %Y'
}

ActiveSupport::CoreExtensions::Time::Conversions::
  DATE_FORMATS.merge!(my_date_formats)
ActiveSupport::CoreExtensions::Date::Conversions::
  DATE_FORMATS.merge!(my_date_formats)
```

2. Save your changes.

What you just did was create a code block called my_date_formats with two different values inside. The first, :us_date, defines a date format of the order of *January 01, 2006*. The second, :uk_date, defines a date format that looks like *06 Jan 2006*.

The next two lines tell the ActiveSupport DATE_FORMATS module to include the custom date formats for use in the application.

3. Before you go forward, restart your Rails application so that the changes take effect. Remember that you need to restart the application any time you change the environment files. You can restart your application by killing your server (Ctrl+C) and then restarting it with another Ruby script/server command.

4. Now implement the date formats in place of the strftime methods you were using before. Go back to the show.rhtml file and modify the two date lines to look like the following:

```
<strong>Date Posted:</strong>
  <%= @classified.created_at.to_formatted_s(:us_date) %><br />
<strong>Last updated:</strong>
  <%= @classified.updated_at.to_formatted_s(:uk_date) %></p>
```

Instead of using strftime, you are using the to_formatted_s method and each of the date formats you defined earlier to format the dates.

6

5. Save your changes, go back to the browser, and do a refresh; you can now see how each of these is outputted (see Figure 6-6.)

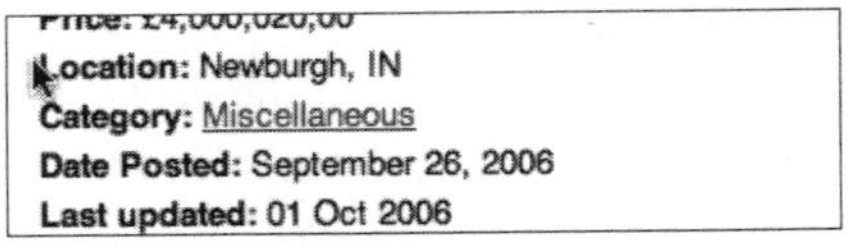

```
Price: £4,000,020.00
Location: Newburgh, IN
Category: Miscellaneous
Date Posted: September 26, 2006
Last updated: 01 Oct 2006
```

Figure 6-6.
You can fine-tune the format of the dates (and other data) as much as you want.

Using natural language

While it's nice to be able to format the dates literally, sometimes it's better to use natural language to describe when a date occurred. For example, if something happened yesterday, why not just be explicit and say *yesterday*? Rails includes methods to do this in the DateHelper. Let's implement them.

1. Go back to the show.rhtml file you have been working with and modify the date fields to look like the following:

```
<strong>Date Posted:</strong>
  <%= distance_of_time_in_words_to_now(@classified.created_at) %> ago➦
<br />
<strong>Last updated:</strong>
  <%= distance_of_time_in_words(@classified.updated_at, Time.now) %>➦
ago</p>
```

2. Save your changes.

You are using the two natural language methods. The first one you are using is distance_of_time_in_words_to_now. The only parameter you provide is the date you want to compare. The method's purpose is to compare the provided date against the current date and time. It then outputs the result using natural language such as *less than a minute; an hour; 10 days.*

The second method, distance_of_time_in_words, enables you to compare two dates instead of just one date against the current time. The first date provided is the start time and the second is the end time.

3. Refresh your application again to see how they render in a browser (see Figure 6-7.)

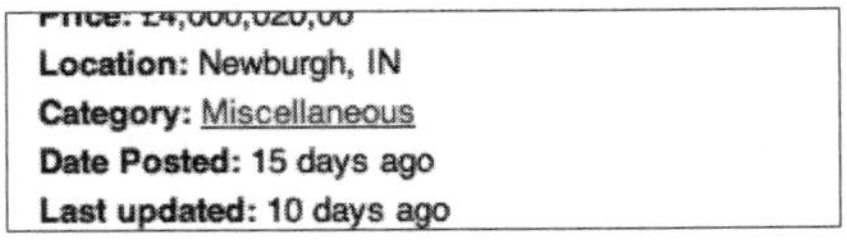

```
Price: £4,000,020.00
Location: Newburgh, IN
Category: Miscellaneous
Date Posted: 15 days ago
Last updated: 10 days ago
```

Figure 6-7.
Using natural language to express the dates.

Summary

In this chapter, you implemented the last bits of the Railslist application. You formatted the numbers and dates using the built-in helpers and defined your own date formats to be used throughout the application.

The next few chapters will discuss Ajax. They will cover what Ajax is and isn't, how Rails implements it, and where it's appropriate to use.

6

7 INTRODUCTION TO AJAX

One of the reasons why Rails has become so popular in such a short amount of time is its capability to make complex application development seem easy. This book has covered many instances thus far, but in my opinion, the best example is in terms of Ajax. If you have been following web development trends lately, you have no doubt heard about Ajax and its rise to prominence among web professionals because it enables the creation of a much more dynamic, desktop-like user experience. Whether you are new to Ajax or already using the technology, you will read about what Ajax is and how to implement it in Rails.

This chapter will discuss the following:

- A history of interactivity on the Web
- What Ajax is and where it's used
- How Rails implements Ajax
- Best practices for using Ajax

A history of web interaction

Prior to 1995, the Web was fairly basic. Servers sent web pages with nothing but HTML markup and images to web browsers. There was no interactivity. In 1995, Brendan Eich of Netscape wanted to change this, so he developed Mocha. Mocha was designed to bring interactivity to the Web by enabling users to run scripts inside web browsers. When Eich's creation finally made its public debut in December of 1995 with Netscape 2.0, it had a new name: JavaScript.

JavaScript's purpose is to enable you to add complex functionality to a web page without the overhead of having to compile any code (it's just interpreted by the browser, not compiled like many other programming languages). The web browser interprets the JavaScript code line by line and then outputs the result for the user. In languages such as C++ and Java, the code has to be compiled and run on its own. Since JavaScript eliminates the complex task of code compilation, it offers a low barrier of entry for programmers and nonprogrammers.

After Netscape 2 was released, Microsoft soon followed with its own implementation of JavaScript, called JScript, which shared many of the same features of JavaScript but in a totally different implementation. Because of the differences between JScript and JavaScript, Netscape and Sun worked to standardize the JavaScript language with the European Computer Manufacturers Association (EMCA). This standardization resulted in EMCAScript, which is what is today known as JavaScript.

> *Despite its name, JavaScript has absolutely nothing to do with Sun's Java development platform. While Sun did play a part in the development of JavaScript with Netscape, it is not a variant of Java. The name JavaScript was probably chosen over LiveScript (its original name after Mocha) for marketing reasons. Unfortunately, there was much confusion because web browsers can run Java applets and JavaScripts.*

In 1997, Netscape 4 and Internet Explorer 4 were both released with much fanfare. Both browsers promised improvements from previous versions and expanded JavaScript's functionality. The main selling point of both browsers was Dynamic HTML (DHTML). DHTML was not a technology, but a buzzword to describe the combination of HTML, CSS, and JavaScript working together.

Many sites began to implement DHTML because it enabled developers to animate things across the screen using JavaScript. Unfortunately, the ways in which IE and Netscape implemented the Document Object Model (DOM) were different, which required web developers to produce two versions of their scripts—one for each browser.

The DOM conceptualizes the contents of a web page in a tree format, as illustrated in Figure 7-1 (taken from the Firefox DOM Inspector). Using the DOM, you can access various elements of any web page in a uniform way. For example, you can get the contents of a form field via document.myForm.firstName.value. *For more on the DOM, check out Jeremy Keith's book,* DOM Scripting *(friends of ED 2005, ISBN: 1590595335).*

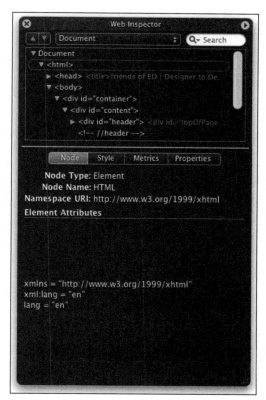

Figure 7-1. In the DOM, a web page is shown as a hierarchical structure, or "tree," of elements (called nodes in DOM-speak).

7

In 1999, Microsoft released IE 5, which included a new function call named XMLHttpRequest that enabled JavaScript inside a web page to get more data from the server without having to request an entirely new page. Netscape added this functionality to its browsers as well, but it was rarely—if ever—used until it got its new name in 2005: Ajax.

What is Ajax?

Ajax stands for *Asynchronous JavaScript and XML*. The term was coined by Jesse James Garrett of Adaptive Path in his article, "Ajax: A New Approach to Web Applications" (http://www.adaptivepath.com/publications/essays/archives/000385.php). Like DHTML in the late 1990s, Ajax is not a single technology; it is a suite of several technologies. Ajax incorporates the following:

- XHTML for the markup of web pages
- CSS for the styling
- Dynamic display and interaction using the DOM
- Data manipulation and interchange using XML
- Data retrieval using XMLHttpRequest
- JavaScript as the glue that meshes all this together

In layperson's terms, Ajax enables you to retrieve data for a web page without having to refresh the contents of the entire page. In the classic web architecture, the user clicks a link or submits a form. The form is submitted to the server, which then sends back a response. The response is then displayed for the user on a new page. There is nothing necessarily wrong with this model, but it's somewhat archaic and slow compared with how users interact with desktop applications.

Imagine that you're writing a book such as this one and are looking for a word in the document. You open the Microsoft Word Find panel, type in your query, and press Submit. The results are then showed instantaneously. If Word were like a non-Ajax–powered web application, you would enter the query you wanted to search for, and then your entire document would refresh with the word you were looking for highlighted. Obviously, this is not the way Word works. Ajax aims to make the Web give instant gratification in a similar fashion to desktop applications such as Word.

When you interact with an Ajax-powered web page, it loads an Ajax engine in the background. The engine is written in JavaScript and its responsibility is to both communicate with the web server and display the results to the user. When you submit data using an Ajax-powered form, the server returns an HTML fragment that contains the server's response and displays only the data that is new or changed (as opposed to refreshing the entire page).

For the budget-conscious, Ajax can save you money. Besides making the usability of your web applications easier to use for your users, the use of HTML fragments saves bandwidth. Instead of having to keep refreshing the entire page and reloading several kilobytes of data for each submission, you have to load only a few kilobytes. This process definitely cuts down on your bandwidth bill.

The *A* in Ajax stands for *asynchronous*. After you trigger the Ajax engine embedded in your application's page, it starts listening for input in the background while your users are interacting with the page. This interaction is done concurrently, so users are never staring at a blank page waiting for the server to do something. Instead, they are seeing the results of their actions almost instantly. This enables you to add very slick functionalities to web pages (more like that of a desktop application than a traditional web page experience) such as drag and drop, and customizable interfaces.

Where is Ajax used?

Ajax first started to be noticed when Google created Google Suggest (http:// labs.google.com/suggest). Google Suggest looks like a normal Google homepage, but instantly suggests terms as you began typing. Shortly thereafter, Google released Google Maps, which used Ajax technology to quickly display locations on a map.

After Google, many companies began to implement Ajax. One of the most widely used Ajax-powered sites is Flickr. Flickr (http://www.flickr.com) is a photo-sharing service that enables users to upload photos they have taken, adding their own titles and captions. Other Flickr users can add notes, comments, and tags to pictures. When you edit the title or description of the photo, the data is saved using Ajax, so the page doesn't need to be refreshed to see the changes. Flickr's Organizr (http://www.flickr.com/tools/ organizr.gne), which enables users to sort their photos into sets, is also written using Ajax.

Today, as Ajax goes mainstream, many major companies are implementing the technology in their websites and applications. Apple recently began experimenting with Ajax in its support section. To see whether your machine is still under warranty, you can enter your serial number in a form; it pings Apple's servers and returns the result instantly.

How does Rails do Ajax?

Before Ruby on Rails, constructing web applications that took advantage of Ajax was a time-consuming task that involved writing (and debugging) a lot of JavaScript code. This lack of simplicity is probably why the XMLHttpRequest feature sat dormant in browsers for so long. With the introduction of Rails, developers now have an easier way of working with Ajax. First, each Rails application comes bundled with two JavaScript libraries that make

Ajax development a bit easier. The first is the Prototype library by Sam Stephenson, which provides the foundation for Rails' Ajax implementation (http://prototype.conio.net/). The second library is Thomas Fuch's script.aculo.us effects library (http://script.aculo.us/), which includes several visual effects that can enhance the look and feel of your applications. These included effects enable you to draw attention to newly added elements of a page. Examples of visual effects include sliding elements in, fading them out, or using the Yellow Fade Technique popularized by 37Signals (among many others).

The second part of the Rails Ajax formula is JavaScriptHelper, which is an included Rails module that wraps all the functionality in the Prototype library behind Ruby methods. For example, if you want to create a form that automatically adds an item to a list of similar items, the JavaScript code looks like this:

```
<form action="/projects/1/project/add_category" id="newCategoryForm"➡
method="post"
  onsubmit="if (Field.present('category_name')) {
  new Ajax.Updater({success:'categoriesList',failure:'notice'},
  '/projects/1/project/add_category',
  {asynchronous:true, evalScripts:true, insertion:Insertion.Bottom,
  onComplete:function(request){
    categoriesManager.newCategoryComplete(request)
  },
  onLoading:function(request){categoriesManager.loading()},
  parameters:Form.serialize(this)}); }; return false;">
```

With JavaScriptHelper, this is all you need to write:

```
<% form_remote_for :category,
Category.new,
  :url => {:project => @project, :action => 'add_category'},
  :loading => "Element.show('category_busy');",
  :complete => "Element.hide('category_busy');",
  :condition => "Field.present('category_name')",
  :html => {:id => 'newCategoryForm'} do |f|
%>
```

As you can see, the JavaScriptHelper way is a lot cleaner and easier to understand. The third and final part of Rails' Ajax implementation is the Ruby JavaScript (RJS) template. Unlike regular RHTML templates, which render the results of an action, RJS templates provide instructions to Rails on how to modify an already rendered page. Using RJS, you can define how to insert the new HTML fragment and what sort of script.aculo.us effects (if any) to perform on the fragment.

By combining both JavaScriptHelper and RJS templates, you can almost totally eliminate the need to write any JavaScript code in your Rails applications.

When to use Ajax?

Like most things on the Web, there is a time and place for new technology to be used. Not every site needs to scrap its current offering and relaunch with everything dynamically rendered via Ajax calls. There is a common set of instances in which using an Ajax-powered implementation is a good idea.

- **Quick form submissions for small data**: When you visit a weblog, you are sometimes inclined to leave a comment on the article you just read. This is a small bit of data that can easily be appended to the article using Ajax. It is not the primary focus of the page and can quickly be rendered. Another example of a small piece of data is a tag. Tags are a new Web 2.0 phenomenon, which involves the use of single words to describe objects on the Web. For example, when I upload a new picture of my dog to Flickr, I can tag it with words such as dog, yorkie, bichon, romeo, bonnie. Each time I add a tag, it is sent to the server via Ajax, so I don't have to refresh the page.

- **Retrieving search results**: Like Google Suggest, getting search results is a great example of when Ajax is appropriate. As users type the query they want to find the answer to, the search results window is displayed with results that are related to the query. An example of this is Gmail's capability to match the e-mail address you type in the To: field to someone in your address book or previous contacts.

- **Filtering data**: If you have a large data set of 100 or more rows, you can easily filter it down to a smaller set based on the criteria entered using Ajax. This smaller set enables the users to quickly find what they are looking for without the hassle of having to refresh the page to get the results. This is similar to iTunes on the Mac or PC. When you search the Library for a song you want to listen to, iTunes removes any songs that don't match the search criteria each time you modify the search query.

7

What's the catch?

While Ajax solves many issues with user experience on the Web, not everything is perfect. There are a few cons to implementing Ajax technology that can make the user's experience less than stellar, including the following:

- **Accessibility**: If you are concerned with ensuring that the application is accessible to those with disabilities in compliance with the regulations (for example, the Web Accessibility Initiative's guidelines, http://www.w3.org/TR/WAI-WEBCONTENT/, or the U.S. Government's Section 508 standards, http://www.section508.gov/), implementing Ajax can be more time-consuming because you need to implement fallback methods for browsers that do not support JavaScript to a lesser or greater degree (screen readers, for example). This isn't impossible, but it does require thought in how you design the site.

- **Security**: Non-Ajax web applications typically conform to a policy that constrains them to connect only to the web server that delivered the base page. That is not the case using Ajax (the XMLHttpRequest object, to be more specific). A malicious scripter could create a script that could steal data stored in cookies or gain direct access to the originating server.

- **Usability**: Naysayers to the Ajax movement on the Web consistently bring up how the technology breaks the browser's Back button functionality. Like most things in web development, there are workarounds for it, but none of them is necessarily simple or intuitive to implement. It usually involves enabling a JavaScript that will roll back the changes the user has made.

None of these issues is incapable of being overcome. It just takes some extra thought and work to make sure that you take these issues into account. This is covered in the next chapter.

Summary

This chapter covered the basics of Ajax. You should be familiar with the concepts around this new technology and have a general idea of how Ruby on Rails makes it easy to implement Ajax without having to write hundreds of lines of complex JavaScript code. In the next chapter, you will learn how to convert parts of your railslist application to use Ajax. Instead of trying to post new classifieds using Ajax, you will create a second control that allows for the management of categories that is powered entirely by Ajax.

8 BRINGING FORMS TO LIFE WITH AJAX

The last chapter covered the basics of Ajax: its history, where it is used, and how Rails implements it. Ajax is such a broad topic, however, that I decided to spend two chapters discussing it. This chapter covers how you can implement Ajax in web applications. More specifically, the following topics are discussed:

- Creating an Ajax-powered form
- Using Ruby JavaScript (RJS) to enhance the style of your forms
- Creating a live search box
- Sending e-mail by using Action Mailer

Ajaxing your application

Based on the discussion of when Ajax is and isn't appropriate, it wouldn't make much sense to convert the classified posting form to be Ajax-powered. There are several data fields that need to be filled in by the user, and having such a large form on the listing page would be somewhat intrusive.

Instead, let's address one of the limits of your railslist application thus far: the fact that you have very few categories. When you added categories to the application, you added only four defaults, which are very limiting to the user.

One thing you can do to make things easier is enable categories to be created from within the railslist application itself. Even better, you can make it seamless and almost instant by using Ajax. Since you are defining only the name of a category and no other data, you can quickly add multiple categories using Ajax instead of having to go through the process of adding a category, saving it, having to refresh the page, and repeating. With Ajax, a user can add a new category and see it instantly appear—all without refreshing the page.

Creating the categories controller

The first thing you need to do is add a new controller to the application to manage the categories code. You could add this code to the existing classifieds controller, but I like to keep different aspects of an application as separated as possible. Not only is it easier to find a specific function intuitively but it also makes the code more manageable.

> You have already written a lot of the code for this previously, in the original controller. You are just moving it (refactoring it in geek speak) to the new controller.

1. Open up a Terminal or command prompt window and go to your railslist directory. Type the following command:

```
ruby script/generate controller Category
```

This command creates the new category controller under the app/controllers directory.

2. Open the `category_controller.rb` file in your text editor and stub out a skeleton to work from. Edit your file to look like the following listing:

```
class CategoryController < ApplicationController
  layout 'standard'

  def list
  end

  def show
  end

  def new
  end

  def delete
  end
end
```

This is pretty bare bones so far, but it gives you an idea about where you will go through this chapter. The first line is the class definition, as always. The second line of code lets Rails know to use the `standard.rhtml` layout file you created earlier, which gives the non-Ajax methods such as show and `list` the same style as the rest of the site.

Next, you create definitions for the four methods you will use to manage the categories. The `list` method gives you a listing of all the categories in the system. The show method shows you items from a specific category. The new method adds a new category to the application using Ajax, and delete removes a category via Ajax. Throughout this chapter, you will work to add functionality to each of these methods.

Write the code for the `list` method. All you need to do is get a listing of all the categories in the system and display them to the user. You can do that with a single line of code.

3. Modify your `list` method to look like the following:

```
def list
  @categories = Category.find(:all)
end
```

All the new line of code does is to use Rails' find functionality to get all the categories from the database and store them in the @categories array.

4. You need to create the view for this method, so create a new file called `list.rhtml` and save it under app/views/category.

5. Type the following code into the new file and save your changes:

```
<h1>Categories</h1>

<ul id="category_list">
<% @categories.each do |c| %>
```

8

```
<li><%= link_to c.name, :action => 'show', :id => c.id %>
<%= "(#{c.classifieds.count})" -%></li>
<% end %>
</ul>
```

You saw code similar to this before. All you are doing is iterating through the @categories array and outputting a `<li>` element containing a link to the category it is referencing for each item in the array. Additionally, you are outputting the number of classifieds in that specific category inside parentheses. Rails' associations make it easy to step through a relationship and get information like this.

6. Open up your browser and go to http://localhost:3000/category/list; Figure 8-1 shows the output of what you created.

Figure 8-1. Categories listing page in desperate need of some style

7. It is somewhat tacky at this point, so add a few style definitions to the style.css file in /public/stylesheets. Add the following rules to your stylesheet and then save your changes:

```
ul#category_list {
    padding: 20px;
    list-style-type: square;
}

ul#category_list li {
    line-height: 140%;
}
```

8. Next, add some code to the show method. This will be pretty easy since you already wrote it.

9. Open up your classifieds controller (classified_controller.rb) and go to the show_category method.

10. Copy the single line of code in it and paste it into the category controller's show method. Your method should now look like this:

```
def show
  @category = Category.find(params[:id])
end
```

Now, go back to the classified controller and remove the show_category method entirely. You no longer need it since you are moving the functionality into the new Category controller.

11. Next, you need to create a view for this file, but instead of reinventing the wheel, just use the show_category method view.

12. Go to app/views/classified, grab show_category.rhtml, and move it to app/views/category.

13. Rename it show.rhtml.

14. You need to change only a bit of the code in the new show.rhtml file. Open the file and modify the <li> line to look like the following:

```
<li>
  <%= link_to c.title, :controller => "classified", :action => "show",➡
  :id => c.id -%>
</li>
```

Now make sure that other parts of the application know that the show_category no longer exists.

15. Under app/views/classified, open list.rhtml. Modify line 3 to look like the following:

```
<li><%= link_to c.name, :controller => "category", :action => "show",➡
  :id => c.id %></li>
```

What you just did was modify the main classified listings page to show the category listings using the category controller's show method instead of the old show_category method under the classified controller.

16. Let's repeat this process for the show.rhtml file under app/views/classified as well. Modify the line that displays the category type of the item to look like the following:

```
<strong>Category: </strong> <%= link_to @classified.category.name,➡
  :controller => "category", :action => "show",➡
  :id => @classified.category.id %><br />
```

Finally, before moving on, clean up the URLs that are created by Rails to be something more meaningful.

8

17. Open up the routes.rb file under the config folder and add the following four lines below the classified controller routes:

```
map.with_options(:controller => 'category') do |category|
  category.connect 'categories', :action => 'list'
  category.connect 'categories/show/:id', :action => 'show'
end
```

18. Now test the application again. Refresh the category listing page (http://localhost:3000/category/list) and you should see the new URLs when you hover over a category link.

When you click one of the category links, you are taken to (for example) /categories/show/5 instead of category/show/5. It's a subtle change, but it makes the URL much more readable.

Adding a touch of Ajax

Now that you have the bare essentials of the new category controller out of the way, you can now focus on adding and removing categories by using Ajax. What you want to do is add the capability to type in the name of a new category and have it automatically appear in the unordered list in the list.rhtml view.

To get Ajax support in the Rails application, you need to include the necessary JavaScript files in the layout. Rails is bundled with several libraries that make using Ajax incredibly easy. The first is the Prototype library by Sam Stephenson (http://prototype.conio.net/); the other library is Thomas Fuch's script.aculo.us (http://script.aculo.us/). The script.aculo.us library's main focus is adding style and visual effects to the Ajax you build using Prototype. When you see a web page highlight a newly created item with a yellow fade or a <div> slide off the side of a browser window, script.aculo.us is probably responsible.

1. To add Prototype and script.aculo.us support to the application, open up the standard.rhtml layout file in app/views/layouts, add the following line just before the </head> tag, and save your changes:

```
<%= javascript_include_tag :defaults %>
```

This includes both the Prototype and script.aculo.us libraries in the template so their effects will be accessible from any of the views.

2. With that out of the way, open up the list.rhtml file in app/views/category and create the new form.

3. Add the following lines of code to the bottom of the file and save your changes:

```
<p id="add_link"><%= link_to_function("Add a category",
   "Element.remove('add_link');Element.show('add_category')")%></p>

<div id="add_category" style="display:none;">
  <%= form_remote_tag(:url => {:action => 'new'},➡
     :update => "category_list", :position => :bottom,➡
```

```
    :html => {:id => 'category_form'})%>
    Name: <%= text_field "category", "name" %>
    <%= submit_tag 'Add' %>
    <%= end_form_tag %>
</div>
```

The first line of new code is a link called "Add a category". Notice that you aren't using the trusty link_to method; instead, you use a new one called link_to_function. Why? The link_to method you have come to know and love does a great job at redirecting the browser to new actions as you click the links it provides, but not much else. The link_to_function method, on the other hand, enables you to harness the power of the Prototype JavaScript library to do some neat DOM manipulations. For instance, in this line of code you are removing the "Add a category" link and showing the add_category <div>.

The next line is the creation of the add_category <div>. Notice that you set its visibility to be hidden by default using the CSS display property. The preceding link_to_function is what will change this property and show the <div> to the user.

Next, you are creating the Ajax form using the form_remote_tag. This Rails helper is similar to the start_form_tag you have used in the past, but it is used here to let the Rails framework know that it needs to trigger an Ajax action for this method. The form_remote_tag takes the :action parameter just like its counterpart: start_form_tag.

You also have two additional parameters: :update and :position. The :update parameter tells Rails' Ajax engine which element to update based on its id. In this case, it's the <ul> tag. The :position parameter tells the engine where to place the newly added object in the DOM. You can set it to be at the bottom of the unordered list (:bottom) or at the top (:top).

Next, you create the standard form fields and submit buttons as before and then wrap things up with an end_form_tag to close the <form> tag. Make sure that things are semantically correct and valid XHTML.

4. Now write the controller code. Modify the new method in the category_controller.rb file to look like the following:

```
def new
  @category = Category.new(params[:category])
  if @category.save
    render :partial => 'category', :object => @category
  end
end
```

Just like other parts of the new Ajax code, there isn't too much terribly different about this method, either. You are creating a new Category object based on params[:category] and saving it to the database. The interesting part is the line after the if... line:

```
render :partial => 'category', :object => @category
```

Instead of redirecting to a new page, you are rendering a partial.

Partials

What's a partial, you ask? Imagine that you are at a gas station and you purchase a bottle of water for a total price of $1.03 after tax. You hand the salesclerk a one-dollar bill and three pennies. The three pennies are a fragment (or a partial) of a dollar. When a full dollar won't do, you can use pennies as partial bits of that dollar. Think of Rails partials as a code fragment that is dynamically called when it's needed without having to call a whole page in the process. One of the major benefits of partials is that they help you to eliminate code duplication in the application. Instead of having to copy the HTML involved with displaying information about a category into multiple views, you can instead put it in a single partial and call that from multiple controllers or views (similar to includes in other server-side languages such as PHP).

> *Partials aren't just good for rendering bits of an Ajax page; they also make a great tool for rendering common areas of a template such as headers or footers. If you have a complex template with thousands of lines of code, breaking it up into smaller bits can sometimes be beneficial. In this fashion, partials can be compared to the more common usage of Server Side Includes (SSIs).*
>
> *To render a partial in a view, just use* `<%= render :partial => 'partialname' %>`.

After you save a category, you want to render a partial called _category using the new @category object. You don't yet have this partial created, so go ahead and do that.

1. Under app/views/category, create a new file called _category.rhtml.

> *Take note that partials are all named with an underscore (_) at the beginning. It's one of the design decisions Rails makes for you.*

2. Type the following lines into your partial and save your changes:

```
<li id="category_<%= category.id %>">
  <%= link_to category.name, :action => 'show', :id => category.id %>
  <%= "(#{category.classifieds.count})" -%></li>
```

This line of code is just like what you use in the iteration of the list.rhtml method. In fact, you can replace the iteration with the partial.

3. Replace all the code between the `<ul></ul>` tags with the following bold line and save your changes:

```
<ul id="category_list">
  <%= render :partial => 'category', :collection => @categories %>
</ul>
```

What you are doing here is rendering each item in the @categories array using the new _category.rhtml partial. It's the exact same functionality as before, but with the code in one central, easy-to-update location.

4. Let's test things out at this stage. Go to http://localhost:3000/categories and add a new category. It should appear at the bottom of your list of preexisting categories (see Figure 8-2).

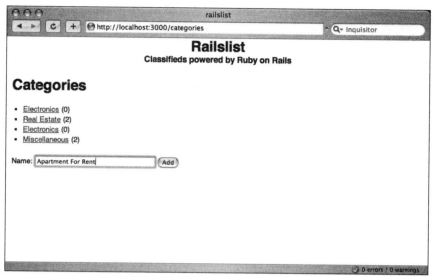

Figure 8-2. Ajax makes it easy to add categories to the application.

You can now easily add several categories without having to wait for the page to refresh after each category is added. Very nice!

Adding dynamic JavaScript functionality using RJS

The new category-adding functionality is pretty neat, but there are a few issues that are rather annoying. First, there is no visual cue for users to let them know that the new item has been successfully added. Second, after a new item is added, the form's data to add a new category is not cleared. You could write some JavaScript to solve both of those issues, but you don't have to.

Ruby on Rails (as of version 1.1) includes functionality called Ruby JavaScript (RJS) that enables you to write small bits of Ruby code that will call the Prototype and script.aculo.us JavaScript libraries included with Rails. RJS introduces a new type of template to the application called a JavaScriptGeneratorTemplate. It has a file extension of .rjs.

Let's use RJS to highlight the newly created category and clear the form.

1. Create a new file called new.rjs under app/views/category.

2. Add the following three lines of code to this file and save your changes:

```
page.insert_html :bottom, 'category_list', :partial => 'category'
page.visual_effect :highlight, "category_#{@category.id}"
page.form.reset 'category_form'
```

135

The first line of code tells RJS to insert the new category at the bottom of the element with an id of category_list using the _category partial, which is what the :update and :bottom parameters of the form_remote_tag are doing.

The second line tells RJS to highlight the newly created item using the script.aculo.us highlight effect. It determines the item to highlight based on the id of that item (constructed from category_ and the database id of the category).

Finally, you tell the category_form to reset itself.

3. Before you can test out the new RJS functionality, you need to clean up the form_remote_tag in list.rhtml. You no longer need the :bottom and :update parameters (since they're in the RJS template), so remove them. Your new form_remote_tag line should look like the following:

```
<%= form_remote_tag(:url => {:action => 'new'},➡
  :html => {:id => 'category_form'}) %>
```

4. Let's also add a line to the new method in category_controller.rb. After the if @category.save line, add the following:

```
return if request.xhr?
```

This code tells the controller to escape to RJS if a method is passed via Ajax. Without this line, the RJS template won't be called. The xhr? method checks to see whether you are sending an Ajax request (XmlHttpRequest, to be more specific).

Now refresh the categories listing page and add a new category. Notice that the new category appears highlighted in yellow. The yellow then fades, and the new category form resets itself after submission. Not only does it look cool, but it is also giving your visitors a better user experience.

What about validation?

Before RJS, validating Ajax submissions was a difficult process. As you know by now, Rails makes it easy to define data validations in your models such as validates_uniquesness_of or validates_presence_of, but it wasn't easy to test those conditions with Ajax. With RJS, that is a thing of the past. To illustrate this, let's prevent a user from adding a category with the same name twice.

1. First, open up your category.rb model file in app/models and add the following line to it (in bold in the following listing):

```
class Category < ActiveRecord::Base
  has_many :classifieds
  validates_uniqueness_of :name
end
```

2. Save your changes and close the file.

3. Go back to the new.rjs file and modify it to look like the following:

```
if @category.new_record?
  page.alert @category.errors.full_messages.join("\n")
```

```
else
  page.insert_html :bottom, 'categories', :partial => 'category'
  page.visual_effect :highlight, "category_#{@category.id}"
  page.form.reset 'category_form'
end
```

What you are doing is a bit of a hack since there isn't any sort of standard for performing Ajax validations in Rails, but it works well for what you want to achieve. When the RJS file is executed, it checks to see whether the @category object has been saved. If it hasn't, you can assume that there is a validation error of some sort and you display it in a JavaScript message box. The new_record? method in line 1 returns true if the object is not saved.

4. Refresh your page and try to create a new item with the same name as something you have already created. You should see the error message shown in Figure 8-3.

Figure 8-3. When you try to add another category with the same name as an existing one, this error pops up.

Deleting items with Ajax

Let's finish the implementation of the category controller by enabling the user to delete categories from the system.

> In a real-world system, not everyone should have the ability to perform a destruction action such as deleting a category. In Chapter 10, you will learn about security and user authentication. The chapter discusses how to secure your application so that only authorized users have the ability to delete a category.

The first thing you need to do is decide how to handle the situation in which a classified's category is deleted, resulting in classifieds that are no longer in a category. You have a few options, as follows:

- You can delete the classifieds from the system.
- You can set the category_id to NULL (this basically means "uncategorized").
- You can reassign the classified to another category (miscellaneous perhaps?).

The first option isn't a great idea because the classifieds contained under that category might be relevant to another category. More importantly, your users might be unhappy about their data loss! The third option isn't ideal, either, because you are changing the user's data in a way that they might not want So go with option two and just set the classifieds not be categorized. Users can be sent a mail alert; they can come and assign a new category to their classifieds.

To accomplish this, you need to set a parameter in the category model's has_many association.

1. Open the category.rb file under app/models and modify the has_many line to look like the following:

```
has_many :classifieds, :dependent => :nullify
```

The :dependent parameter tells Rails how to deal with any associated entities. In this case, you tell Rails to set the category_id of any associated classified to be NULL.

Next, modify the item listings to take into account the new business rule of a classified not necessarily needing a category.

2. Open up the show.rhtml file in app/views/classified and modify the category line to look like the following:

```
<% if not @classified.category.blank? %>
  <strong>Category: </strong> <%= link_to @classified.category.name,➡
  :controller => "category", :action => "show",➡
  :id => @classified.category.id %><br />
<% end %>
```

What you just did was add a conditional check that shows only the category if one is assigned to the classified. This prevents the application from crashing because it is trying to retrieve a nonexistent object.

3. Next, you will add a small delete button to the _category.rhtml partial in app/views/category. Add the following just before the </li> tag:

```
<small><%= link_to_remote 'Delete',➡
  :url => {:action => 'delete', :id => category} -%></small>
```

You use the link_to_remote method to create an Ajax-powered link that will delete the category. You pass the :action and :id parameters to link_to_remote to let it know what action to perform and on what object to perform said action.

4. With that out of the way, you can work on the category controller (category_controller.rb) delete method. Modify it to look like the following:

```
def delete
  @category = Category.find(params[:id])
  @category.destroy
  return if request.xhr?
  render :nothing, :status => 200
end
```

There is nothing much that you haven't seen before in this method. You find the category based on the :id parameter passed by link_to_remote and then destroy it. If you have an Ajax-supported Web browser, Rails uses the RJS template. If not, nothing is rendered.

> *Before the category is deleted, Rails goes through the classifieds table and searches for all instances of the* category_id *of the item you want to delete and replaces them with a* NULL *value. This is why you set the* :dependent *parameter in the model.*

5. Create a file called delete.rjs in the app/views/category folder and add this single line to it:

```
page.visual_effect :drop_out, "category_#{@category.id}"
```

All this line does is use the script.aculo.us dropout effect to remove the item from the list of items available.

6. Refresh the browser page and click one of the delete links. Notice that when you click a delete link, the item slides off the page. Very fancy!

Searching classifieds with Ajax

As the data in the application increases, it is more and more difficult for users to easily find what they are looking for. Sure, they can browse by category, but what if you are dealing with thousands of items per category? Every good website these days offers a search feature. You could go about developing standard search functionality (type query, submit, receive results), but that does not give you instant gratification. Fortunately, Ajax search does.

Similar to Google Suggest, you can filter search results as the user types in the query. To do this, you need to query the <input> box's value at a specified interval, query the database with it, and return the results. This workflow is similar to traditional search applications, except that results are returned without needing the page to refresh.

Rails makes it easy to query the text field using the observe_field helper method, in which observe_field binds itself to an <input> text box, grabs the value in that box, and then triggers a method in one of the controllers.

Let's implement this on the classified listing page. The first thing you need to do is convert the classified listing to use partials so it's easier to display the search results. It also prevents duplicate code in two places.

1. Create a new partial called _classified.rhtml under app/views/classified with the following code:

```
<li><%= link_to classified.title, {:action => 'show',➥
 :id => classified.id} -%>
  <small><%= link_to 'Edit',➥
    {:action => 'edit', :id => classified.id} %></small>
  <small><%= link_to "Delete", {:action => 'delete', ➥
 :id => classified.id}, ➥
 :confirm => "Are you sure you want to delete this item?" %></small>
</li>
```

2. Open `list.rhtml` in app/views/classified and remove the following code (everything in-between the second set of `<ul></ul>` tags):

```
<% @classifieds.each do |c| %>
  <li>
    <%= link_to c.title, {:action => 'show', :id => c.id} -%>
    <small>
      <%= link_to 'Edit', {:action => 'edit', :id => c.id} %>
    </small>
    <small><%= link_to "Delete", {:action => 'delete', :id => c.id},
      :confirm => "Are you sure you want to delete this item?" %>
    </small>
  </li>
<% end %>
```

You no longer need to iterate through the @classifieds array using the code you removed. Instead, you can just render a collection of partials from it.

3. Add this code in place of the code you just removed in `list.rhtml`:

```
<%= render :partial => 'classified', :collection => @classifieds %>
```

Creating the search box

You now need to create the search box.

1. Add the following bit of code to the same `list.rhtml` file you just edited right before the `<ul id="classifieds">` tag.

```
<%= text_field "classified", "title" -%>

<%= observe_field :classified_title,
  :frequency => 1.0,
  :update => 'classifieds',
  :url => { :controller => 'classified', :action=> 'search' },
  :with => "'search=' + encodeURIComponent(value)"
%>
```

You use the observe_field helper and tell it to retrieve its value from :classified_title (the text field) every second (the :frequency). You pass observe_field a URL just like the other Ajax methods you have used and tell it to update the HTML element with an ID of classifieds. In this instance, that is the unordered list of classifieds.

The :with parameter is a JavaScript expression that specifies the parameters to be passed for the XMLHttpRequest. You are using JavaScript's encodeURIComponent function so that it will automatically encode all the characters in the query. This prevents any text-encoding issues that may arise when using the search box with special characters.

Next, you need to create the search method in the controller.

2. Open the classified controller, `classified_controller.rb`, and add the following method to it:

```
def search
  @classifieds = Classified.find(:all,➡
    :conditions => ["lower(title) like ?",➡
      "%" + params[:search].downcase + "%"])
  if params['search'].to_s.size < 1
    render :nothing => true
  else
    if @classifieds.size > 0
      render :partial => 'classified', :collection => @classifieds
    else
      render :text => "<li>No results found</li>", :layout => false
    end
  end
end
```

The first thing you do in this method is compile an array with classified objects that meet the criteria. Notice that the `:condition` parameter is a bit different from before. MySQL databases store information as case-sensitive, so *Apple* is different from *apple*, which is different from *ApPle*. So you use MySQL's `lower()` function to set the value of all the titles in the database table to be entirely lowercase. You also convert the user's text input to be lowercase by using Ruby's downcase method. This way, the comparison logic works regardless of the case-sensitiveness.

You are also wrapping the `params[:search]` parameter in a set of percentage signs (%) so that MySQL can search for the query anywhere in the title. For example, if the user's query is rail, the query will return values such as guardrail, trail, or braille (think of the percentage signs as a wildcard that tries to match characters).

3. Test the search (see Figure 8-4). Type in a query and notice that the results are dynamically updated as you type. After you clear the text field, all the items are displayed once more.

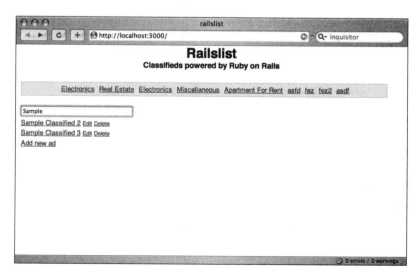

Figure 8-4. Ajax-powered live search makes it easier for users to instantly find what they are looking for.

141

Sending e-mail with Action Mailer

Action Mailer is the Rails component that enables applications to send and receive e-mail. With Action Mailer you can configure the application to enable interested parties to contact sellers via e-mail. Action Mailer works as a gateway between the Rails application and the e-mail server to facilitate sending data via e-mail. That data could be the results of a contact form, a welcome message for a new user who signs up for your service, or just a daily e-mail sent to your administrator with various statistics—the possibilities are endless.

You will create a web-based form on the classified listing page that enables you to send the classified's information to another user's e-mail address.

Configuring Action Mailer

Rails can do a lot on its own, but it cannot determine your mail server settings, so you need to do a bit of configuration before you can begin using Action Mailer. You can configure either globally or based on the environment in which the application is running. In this instance, let's work globally:

1. Go to the config folder and open environment.rb.

2. Add the following line to the bottom of the file:

   ```
   ActionMailer::Base.delivery_method = :smtp
   ```

   You are telling Action Mailer that you want to deliver e-mail using an SMTP server. You can also set it to be :sendmail if you are using a Unix-based operating system such as Mac OS X or Linux.

   Since you are using SMTP, you need to let Rails know about the SMTP server.

3. Add the following lines of code to the bottom of your environment.rb as well as replacing the placeholder values with your specific values:

   ```
   ActionMailer::Base.server_settings = {
   :address => "smtp.railssolutions.com",
   :port => 25,
   :domain => "railssolutions.com",
   :authentication => :login,
   :user_name => "username",
   :password => "password",
   }
   ```

> If you don't know the settings of your SMTP server, you can usually get that information from your system administrator or Internet Service Provider (ISP).

:address references the SMTP server you are trying to connect to, and :port is the port you connect through. By default, the port is 25. :domain is the actual domain name that Action Mailer should use to identify itself to the SMTP server. If you aren't sure what to put in this value, just use the domain name of your SMTP server. :authentication is the method of logging into the server, and :login and :password should be self-explanatory.

> *Action Mailer provides a wealth of features and configuration beyond the example here, so consult the documentation if you need to set more options for your SMTP server:* http://wiki.rubyonrails.org/rails/pages/ActionMailer.

Let's send some e-mail

Let's create the form to enable the user to send e-mail.

1. Open up show.rhtml in app/views/classified and remove the following line of code:

```
<p>Interested?  Contact <%= mail_to @classified.email -%></p>
```

2. In its place, put this code into the view:

```
<p>Interested?  <%= link_to_function('Contact the seller',➡
"Element.show('contact_seller')") %></p>

<div id="contact_seller" style="display:none;">
  <%= form_remote_tag(:url => {:action => 'contact',➡
    :id => @classified.id },➡
    :html => {:id => "contact_form"}) -%>
  Your e-mail: <%= text_field "contact", "email" -%><br />
  Message: <br />
  <%= text_area "contact", "message", {:rows => 10} -%><br />
  <%= submit_tag 'Contact seller' -%>
  <%= end_form_tag -%>
</div>
```

You have replaced the static e-mail link with a web form that will let interested buyers provide their e-mail addresses and short messages to the buyer. You now need to create a mailer to define the e-mail messages.

3. Like many things, there is a generator for this, so open up a Terminal or command prompt window, go to the railslist directory, and type in the following command:

```
ruby script/generate mailer ClassifiedMailer contact
```

Rails creates a new file under the models directory called classified_mailer.rb (as well as a bunch of other files you don't need to be concerned with at this point). It also creates a default method called contact, as you defined at the end of the generate command.

8

4. Open the classified_mailer.rb file and examine the contact method.

```
def contact(sent_at = Time.now)
  @subject    = 'ClassifiedMailer#contact'
  @body       = {}
  @recipients = ''
  @from       = ''
  @sent_on    = sent_at
  @headers    = {}
end
```

The contact method has a single parameter, sent_at, which defines when the e-mail is sent. The method also defines six standard parameters that are a part of every ActionMailer method:

- @subject defines the e-mail subject.

- @body is a Ruby hash that contains values with which you can populate the mail template.

- @recipients is a list of the people to whom the message is being sent.

- @from defines who the e-mail is from.

- @sent_on takes the sent_at parameter and sets the timestamp of the e-mail.

- @headers is another hash that enables you to modify the e-mail headers. For example, you can set the MIME type of the e-mail if you want to send either plain text or HTML e-mail.

The stub is a nice start, but you can modify it to better fit your needs. You want to be able to pass a classified object to the mailer so that you can easily populate the @body hash with values that you can then plug into the e-mail template. This enables the URL of a classified to be automatically included in the e-mail body.

5. Change your contact method to look like the following:

```
def contact(classified, buyer, sent_at = Time.now)
  @subject    = 'Railslist: A potential buyer has contacted you'
  @recipients = classified.email
  @from       = 'no-reply@yourdomain.com'
  @sent_on    = sent_at
  @body["title"] = classified.title
  @body["email"] = buyer[:email]
  @body["message"] = buyer[:message]
end
```

Notice that you added two new parameters to the method: classified and contact. The first accepts classified model objects; the second accepts the parameters of the contact form you created earlier. You modified the @subject and @from variables to have relevant data. You set the @recipient to be the value of the classified object's e-mail field.

The most interesting part of this method is how to use the @body hash. You created three key-value pairs: title, email, and message. You can now plug these values into the template.

6. Open contact.rhtml in app/views/classified_mailer and modify it to look like the following:

```
Hi there!

Just wanted to let you know that your classified, <%= @title -%>, ➥
has an interested buyer. Their e-mail address is <%= @email %>.➥
 They left you the following message:
<%= @message -%>

Thanks!

- railslist
```

An Action Mailer template is just text with standard Rails <%= %> placeholders scattered throughout. Notice that the name of each placeholder variable is the same as the key in the @body hash.

Now that Action Mailer is configured, and the method and template are created, let's write a method in the classified controller to handle the e-mail contact.

7. Open classified_controller.rb and add the following method to it before the last end:

```
def contact
  @classified = Classified.find(params[:id])
  ClassifiedMailer.deliver_contact(@classified,params[:contact])
  return if request.xhr?
  render :nothing => true
end
```

First, you are creating a classified object based on the classified the potential buyer is interested in. You then use ClassifiedMailer to send the e-mail. To deliver e-mail using the mailer's contact method, you have to add deliver_ to the beginning of the method name. You add a return if request.xhr? line so that you can escape to RJS (if the browser doesn't support JavaScript) and then tell the method to render nothing so it doesn't try to reload the template.

As the last step, create an RJS template that cleans up the form and alerts the user that the message was sent successfully.

8. Create a new file named contact.rjs under app/views/classified and add the following code to it:

```
page.alert 'Message successfully sent to seller.'
page.form.reset 'contact_form'
page.hide 'contact_seller'
```

You use RJS to alert the user that the message was successfully sent via a message box. Next, you reset the contact form and then hide the contact_seller <div>.

Let's test the new functionality. Select one of your existing classifieds and then try to send an e-mail from it using the new contact form. If you run into any issues when sending a message, make sure that the settings you added to environment.rb for your SMTP server

8

are correct. You might run into problems if your provider is stringent about whom or what can send mail. Check with your administrator to make sure that you can send mail via a web form like the one you created.

A bit of CSS style

Before you wrap up this section, let's add a bit of padding to the contact_seller <div>.

1. Add the following to the bottom of your style.css file in /public/stylesheets and save your changes:

```
div#contact_seller {
  padding: 10px;
}

div#contact_seller input {
  margin-top: 5px;
}
```

2. Test your application again. The form now has some room to breathe (see Figure 8-5).

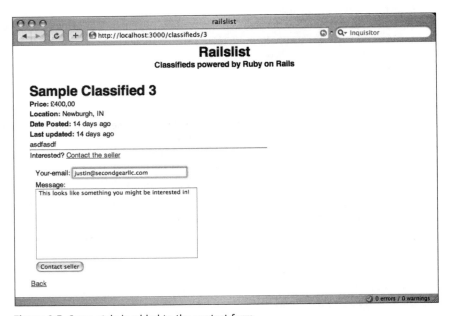

Figure 8-5. Some style is added to the contact form.

Summary

This chapter covered a lot of topics. You discovered how to use Ajax to add and remove data from the application and how to add styles and manipulate the DOM using Ruby JavaScript. The chapter covered how to create a live search box using observe_field. Finally, you were introduced to Action Mailer, which enables you to send e-mail from the application.

Hopefully, you now see the power that Ajax offers and how it can make your application behave more like a desktop application—with smoother and more dynamic functionality.

The next chapter will cover how to upload files to the application and how to send e-mail with attachments.

8

9 UPLOADING FILES AND SENDING ATTACHMENTS

Up to this point, you have been dealing only with character data: letters and numbers, in other words. Although this usually covers the majority of the data that you will be dealing with when working with any application, there are times when it is beneficial to enable the user to send and receive binary data such as images, audio files, or other types of complex data.

As always, Rails makes it easy to implement this sort of functionality in your applications.

This chapter covers the following:

- Uploading images and other files to your database
- Securing your application from malicious uploads
- Sending e-mail with attachments using ActionMailer

Uploading images to your database

Since you are building a classifieds application, it is safe to assume that sellers want to be able to provide a photo of the item they are selling. Not only does it provide a small bit of proof that the seller actually possesses the item but it also enables potential buyers to easily see what they are buying before they commit to the sale.

Traditionally, there are two methods of storing images in a Web application:

- Saving it to the server's file system in a directory
- Uploading it to a database

One of the major advantages of storing images on the file system instead of in a database is performance. The gains achieved from storing images outside a database are far greater than that of storing files in a database. MySQL and other database packages have improved their capability to handle noncharacter data such as images in the past few years, so the gap between storing files in the file system and database is far less than before. Even so, most professional developers suggest storing any nontext data in the file system instead of the database because it results in much better performance—accessing a database every time you want to access an image results in a performance hit.

On the upside, uploading files to a database enables easier portability of the application to multiple servers, requires less configuration on the server side, and makes it easier to migrate your application since you are required to keep track only of the database and the application code itself.

In railslist, you'll be storing your images in a database. Even though performance might be greater by storing the data in a file system, it can become much more complex to manage.

> *If you are interested in storing files in the file system instead of the database, check out the file_column plugin (http://www.kanthak.net/opensource/file_column/). Rails' plugin architecture will be covered in Chapter 12, so you might want to make note of that link for later.*

The first thing you need to do is add a new column to the classifieds table to store the classifieds' image(s).

1. In a Terminal or command prompt window, type the following command:

```
ruby script/generate migration AddPhotoColumn
```

2. Open the newly created 003_add_photo_column.rb file that was added under /db/migrate and modify it to look like the following:

```
class AddPhotoColumn < ActiveRecord::Migration
  def self.up
      add_column :classifieds, :content_type, :string,➡
 :default => "image/png"
      execute 'ALTER TABLE classifieds ADD COLUMN picture LONGBLOB'
  end

  def self.down
    remove_column :classifieds, :content_type
    remove_column :classifieds, :picture
  end
end
```

All you do in this file is to tell Rails to add two new columns to the classifieds table called picture and content_type. You are setting the picture column's type to be LONGBLOB, which is a MySQL-specific column type for storing large amounts of non-character data such as images. LONGBLOB is not a default migration type for Rails (there is a migration database called :binary for the BLOB datatype), hence having to use some actual SQL commands to add the second column. Since there is a chance that an image might be more than 65KB, using LONGBLOB is a better solution.

The content_type field stores the data type of the uploaded image, which gives the browser a hint of what type of file you are trying to work with so it knows how to render it.

3. Save the changes to your migration file and then run *rake migrate* in the Terminal or command prompt window. Your new column should now be created.

Let's continue with the quest of enabling a seller to upload an image when creating a new classified. The first thing you should do is update your new classified view.

4. Open up the new.rhtml file in app/views/classified and add the following code before the submit_tag line:

```
<p><label for="classified_picture">Picture</label><br />
<%= file_field 'classified', 'pictureimg' %></p>
```

This snippet of code introduces the file_field helper. The helper works just like a text_field helper, but instead returns an input tag of the "file" type instead of "text" (so it allows the user to upload a file instead of input text, as shown in Figure 9-1).

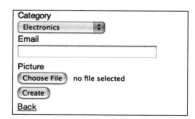

Figure 9-1. Clicking the Choose File button brings up a file browser in which you can select the image you want to upload.

9

151

5. Next, modify your start_form_tag to have the :multipart parameter set to true by changing the start_form_tag line to the following:

```
<%= start_form_tag ({:action => 'create'}, :multipart => true) %>
```

By setting the multipart parameter, you ensure that your action properly passes along the binary data from the file field to the database.

6. Next, open up the classified.rb in the app/models file and the following methods to it just above the protected keyword:

```
def pictureimg=(picture_field)
  return if picture_field.blank?
  self.content_type = picture_field.content_type.chomp
  self.picture = picture_field.read
end
```

Save your changes. The purpose of the pictureimg accessor method is to take the data from the file_field helper in our view and then associate the uploaded image's content type with our content_type field and the image itself with our picture field.

7. Now let's test your new picture upload functionality. Open your browser and try creating a new classified and adding an image to it—the new form should look like Figure 9-2.

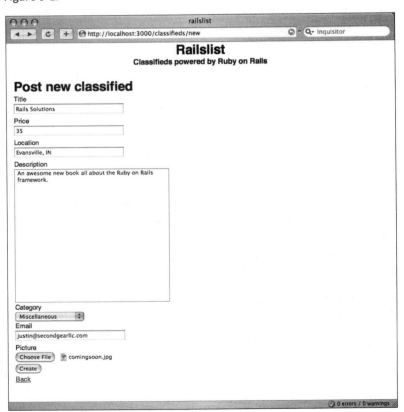

Figure 9-2.
Adding a new classified to your application with an attached image.

Of course, this great new functionality isn't much use yet because you can upload images, but you can't yet do anything else with them, like display them on the show pages! You'll remedy this next.

Reading files from the database

Although it can be beneficial to store images into your database, they are of no use to you if you cannot extract them to view on the Web. Since you are storing the actual data of an image in your database, you need to find a way to extract that data and rebuild it as an image. To accomplish this, you can use the send_data method, which is a part of ActionController and enables you to stream binary data—such as an image from the database—to the user and convert it into a readable format.

Think of send_data as an automatic puzzle solver. When you upload an image to your database, it converts the pixels into a bunch of 1s and 0s. When you retrieve those 1s and 0s from the database, they are all jumbled up like a puzzle when you first take it out of the box. With send_data, you can then put the pieces of the puzzle back together as an actual image and send it to the user's screen.

To work with send_data, you need to create a new method in the controller called image. The image method's sole purpose is to retrieve the data from the picture column and send it to the user's screen via send_data.

1. Copy the following method to classified_controller.rb:

```
def image
  @image = Classified.find(params[:id])
  send_data @image.picture, :filename => "photo.jpg",➥
  :type => @image.content_type, :disposition => "inline"
end
```

The send_data method has four parameters. The first is the actual column you are retrieving data from. The second is the name you want to give the file when it's saved to your database—you have set this hard-coded value to be photo.jpg. When an image is uploaded and inserted into your database, it always has the name photo.jpg (you can modify the name to be whatever you want, of course).

> *Of course, it makes more sense to enable readers to specify their own image name when uploading their classified ad, but you're going for simplicity here to make the upload code as simple to understand as possible.*

The :type parameter defines the HTTP content type that you will be returning. Finally, and most importantly, :disposition tells Rails to display the image in the actual web page instead of treating it as a downloadable file.

9

2. Next, open up the show.rhtml file under app/views/classified and add the following code just before the <hr />:

```
<% unless @classified.picture.blank? %>
<%= image_tag(url_for({:action => 'image', :id => @classified.id})) -%>
<% end %>
```

You are creating an image_tag with the src of the image being retrieved from the controller's image method. You are wrapping the tag in an unless decision statement because there might not be an image uploaded (or previously created classifieds do not have images). In this case, if the picture field has no data, the image_tag will not be included in the HTML code.

3. In your browser, look at the classified you created a few pages ago. You should now see the image you uploaded.

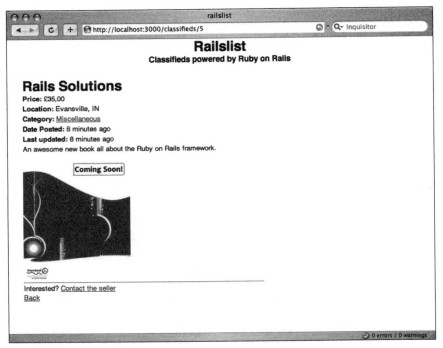

Figure 9-3. Showing an image of your products makes it much more appealing to the potential buyer.

Securing your data field

As a developer, you hope that your users will never make a mistake in the application and that they will provide perfect data 100 percent of the time. Unfortunately, that is not always the case. You already implemented validations for the other data fields, so now you need to implement it for your file upload field. In this case, you want to ensure that only JPEG, GIF, or PNG files are uploaded.

To do this, you need to check the content type of the uploaded file before you commit it to the database.

1. Go back to your `classified.rb` file and add the following validation rule below the belongs_to :category line:

```
validates_format_of :content_type, :with => /^image/, ➡
:message => "You can only upload pictures"
```

2. Save your changes.

You are using validates_format_of along with a regular expression to make sure that the content type passed with the image begins with *image/*. This enables you to be able to upload an image that has a content type like the following:

- `image/jpeg`: JPEG images
- `image/pjpeg`: Progressive JPEGs
- `image/gif`: GIF images
- `image/png`: PNG images
- `image/x-png`: Alternative content type for PNG images

A content type is simply a header that is sent with a file over the Web. It gives your browser a hint of what type of file you are trying to work with so it knows how to render it.

3. Open your browser and try out the new security function by trying to upload a PDF or other type of document to a new classified.

> *One thing not discussed is protecting the user from uploading huge files. For example, a user could upload a 2MB image straight from a digital camera. The best way to restrict the file size of an upload is in Lighttpd config. For more information on this, check out the Lighttpd manual (http://trac.lighttpd.net/trac/wiki/#ReferenceDocumentation).*

Updating the remaining views

Now that you have implemented image handling in your new classified and show views, you should implement the same code elsewhere in your application. For example, you need to create a way for users to modify or remove the image from their classified listing.

1. Open up the `edit.rhtml` file under `app/views/classifieds` and modify the `start_form_tag` to look like the following. You need to tell it to support the `:multipart` attribute as you did with the `create` form.

```
<%= start_form_tag ({:action => 'update', :id => @classified},➡
:multipart => true) %>
```

2. Add the following lines right before the submit_tag:

```
<p><label for="classified_picture">Picture</label><br />
<% unless @classified.picture.blank? %>
<%= image_tag (url_for({:action => 'image',➡
 :id => @classified.id})) -%><br /><br />
<% end %>

Change Photo<br />
<%= file_field 'classified', 'pictureimg' %></p>
```

3. Save your changes.

You are adding an <img> tag that contains the currently uploaded picture if it exists and then putting a file_field helper below it if the user wants to change the photo. If no picture currently exists in the database, the <img> tag is disregarded.

4. Try editing one of your classifieds and changing the image associated with it.

> *One thing not covered in this chapter is how to resize an image before it is uploaded. You need to install and use the Rmagick libraries to accomplish such a task. You can find out more about using Rails with Rmagick at* http://www.rubyonrailsblog.com/articles/2006/09/08/ ruby-on-rails-and-rmagick-crop-resize-rotate-thumbnail-and- upload-images.

Sending e-mail with attachments

In the last chapter, you were introduced to Rails' ActionMailer. You used it to enable potential buyers to notify an item's owner of interest in purchasing it. These e-mail messages merely contained text and didn't have any HTML formatting or images. In some cases, you might want to allow users to add an attachment to their e-mail. For example, if you want to e-mail a Web page to a user, you need to include the images as attachments.

You can include this functionality in your application. Add a button to the show form that enables a user to e-mail a classified to another person.

1. Open show.rhtml under app/views/classifieds and add the following link next to *Contact The Seller*:

```
<%= link_to_function('E-mail to a friend', "Element.show('email')") %>
```

2. Add the following block of code near the bottom of the file, just before the `<%= link_to 'Back', home_url %>` line:

```
<div id="email" style="display: none;">
  <%= form_remote_tag(:url => {:action => 'email',➡
:id => @classified.id}, :multipart => true) -%>
```

```
    E-mail: <%= text_field "user", "email" -%><br />
      <%= submit_tag 'Email classified' -%>
    <%= end_form_tag -%>
</div>
```

3. Save your changes.

4. Go to classified_controller.rb and add the following method to the bottom before the last end keyword:

```
def email
  @classified = Classified.find(params[:id])
  url = "#{request.env["SERVER_NAME"]}/classified/#{@classified.id}"
  if request.post?
    ClassifiedMailer.deliver_classified_with_attachment(➡
params[:user][:email], @classified, url)
  end
end
```

You create a @picture variable that holds the image file built from the send_data method. You then pass @picture along with your @classified and the user's e-mail address to ClassifiedMailer. You are using the same ClassifiedMailer ActionMailer class you created in the last chapter since most of the settings will be similar.

5. Open classified_mailer.rb in the app/models folder and add the following method:

```
def classified_with_attachment(email, classified, url, ➡
sent_at = Time.now)
  @subject    = 'RailsList: This item may be of interest to you'
  @recipients = email
  @from       = 'no-reply@yourdomain.com'
  @sent_on    = sent_at
  @body["title"] = classified.title
  @body["description"] = classified.description
  @body["price"] = classified.price
  @body["url"] = url
  unless classified.picture.blank?
    attachment :body => classified.picture, ➡
:content_type => classified.content_type
  end
end
```

6. Save your changes.

There's nothing you haven't seen before here except for the last three lines. You are using an unless decision structure that will attach the picture associated with a classified if it exists.

Let's also create an ERb template for the new method.

9

157

7. Under app/views/classified_mailer, create a new file called classified_with_ attachment.rhtml and populate it with the following code:

```
Hi!

Someone thought you might be interested in knowing ➡
about this classified.

Title: <%= @title -%>

Description: <%= @description -%>

Price: <%= @price -%>

You can view more information at <%= @url %>

Thanks!
- Railslist
```

8. Save your changes and then test the new "e-mail a classified" functionality.

   Notice that there isn't any sort of feedback telling the user whether or not a message was successfully sent. Let's add that notification.

9. Create a new file called email.rjs under app/views/classified. Add the following lines to it and save your changes:

```
page.alert 'Message successfully sent.'
page.hide 'email'
```

10. Refresh the classified page in your browser and try to send a classified e-mail again. You should now get an alert box letting you know that the message was successfully sent.

If you don't receive the successful message alert message, ensure that your SMTP settings are correct. There isn't much that can currently be done in terms of error handling with ActionMailer in Rails.

Adding some style

Let's now add some style.

1. Before you wrap up, add the following style to your style.css file in /public/ stylesheets:

```
div#email {
    padding: 10px;
    border: 1px solid #cecece;
    background-color: #ececec;
}
```

2. After you save your changes, refresh a classified listing's page to see your changes.

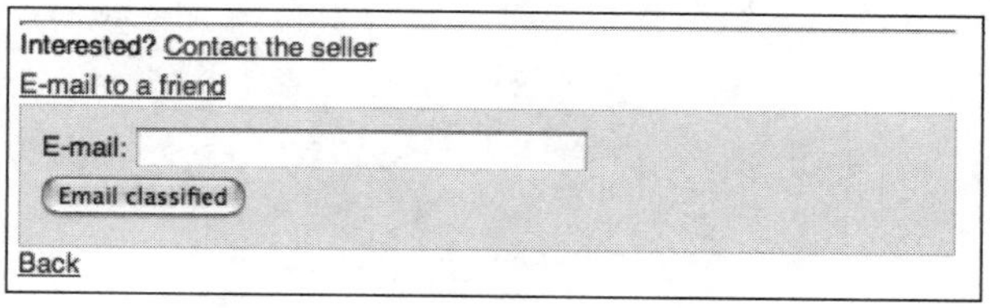

Figure 9-4.
CSS makes everything look better.

Summary

In this chapter, you learned how to upload files to your database so that you can have more than just text in your Rails applications. You learned how to secure the uploading functionality by restricting the types of data that is allowed to be uploaded. You also saw how to send an e-mail with attachments using Rails' ActionMailer framework.

In the next chapter, you will be working to secure your user's data by creating user accounts and having visitors log in to perform certain tasks.

9

10 USER AUTHENTICATION AND SESSION MANAGEMENT

Prior to this chapter, you allowed anyone to add, edit, and delete classifieds and categories. This is not really an ideal implementation because malicious users could delete someone else's classified or they might edit the details of it. A much better solution is to tie each classified to a user account, so only authorized users can edit classifieds—not just any casual browser who visits the site. The focus of this chapter is on allowing authorized users edit rights to a site.

This chapter discusses the following:

- Creating a new Rails model and database table to store user information
- Associating classifieds to a user account
- Implementing password protection into the application
- Implementing sessions to keep users logged in
- Discussing the security issues that surround sessions

Before you begin

Before you begin implementing the new user model, wipe the database clean. Previous versions of the application did not store any data about users, and there is not much sense in keeping that data now. Since you are gradually building this application throughout the book, you have thus far taken a different workflow approach to that of building a professional production application. Experienced Rails developers include vital data such as user accounts to start off with when planning the application, so everything they need is in place before the system is launched.

To delete the data from the database, you need to use SQLyog (Windows) or CocoaMySQL (Mac OS X) and remove all the rows from the classifieds table.

Mac OS X

To remove tables in MySQL, open up CocoaMySQL and follow these steps:

1. Open CocoaMySQL from the /Applications folder.
2. Log in to the MySQL server using the username and password you set in Chapter 2.
3. Select the railslist_development database from the pull-down menu in the Databases section of the CocoaMySQL window.
4. Select the classifieds table in the Tables section of the window.
5. Switch to the Content tab (see Figure 10-1) and then highlight all the rows. Click the Delete selected row(s) button.

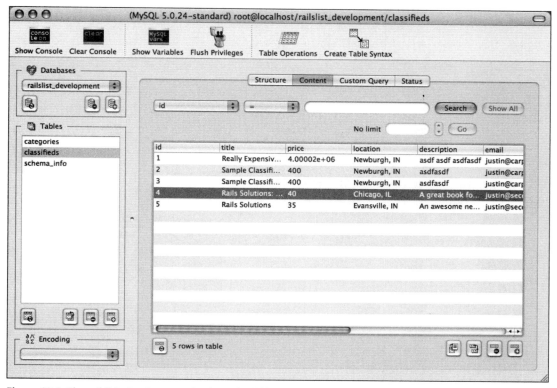

Figure 10-1. The railslist_development database should have only two data tables thus far. You need to remove all the data only from the classifieds table.

Windows XP

To remove tables in MySQL, open up SQLyog and follow these steps:

1. Under the Connect to MySQL Host window, select the MySQL server instance and click Connect.

2. Under the Open Session window, select the MySQL server instance.

3. In the left column, find the railslist_development database.

4. Right-click the railslist_development database and select the classifieds table. Next, select Truncate Table. This process removes all data from the database (see Figure 10-2).

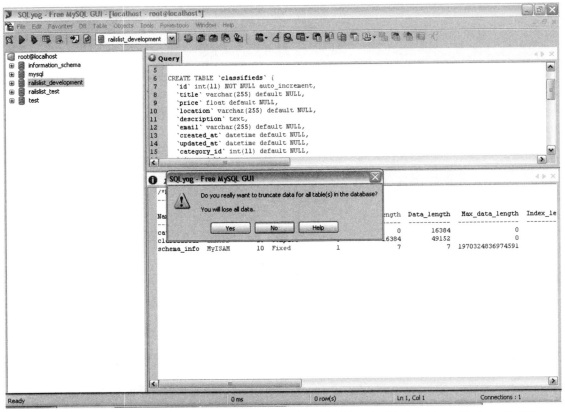

Figure 10-2. Deleting all the data from the database is a bit easier with SQLyog in Windows than with CocoaMySQL on Mac OS X.

Creating the user model

The first thing you should do before creating the actual model file is to decide what data you need to store to handle user accounts. Since the central focus of the application is outlining a classified listing's details, you don't need to store too much data about the user. You'll collect the following information when creating a new user account:

- Login name
- Password
- E-mail address

You need to create a new model to store the user information.

1. In the Terminal or command prompt window, navigate to the Railslist directory and type the following command:

```
ruby script/generate model User
```

This creates the model file user.rb and a migration file so you can manipulate the database. Let's edit that migration file, adding the database table information to it.

2. Open the 004_create_users.rb in db/migrate and edit it to look like the following:

```
class CreateUsers < ActiveRecord::Migration
  def self.up
    create_table :users do |t|
      t.column :login, :string
      t.column :password, :string
      t.column :email, :string
    end
    add_column :classifieds, :user_id, :integer
  end

  def self.down
    drop_table :users
    remove_column :classifieds, :user_id
  end
end
```

3. Save your changes. This code creates a new table in the database called users and populates it with three fields: login, password, and email. You are also adding a column called user_id to the classifieds table, which is for when you associate each classified with a specific user in the railslist application.

4. Run *rake migrate* in the Terminal or command prompt window.

Adding data model validations and associations

Since the application will have user accounts, you need to add some additional validation to the user model for everything to work.

1. Open up the model file user.rb under app/models.

   The model needs to define the following rules:

   - A user can have multiple classifieds.
   - A user must have a value for login, password, and e-mail.
   - A user's login must be unique.
   - A user's e-mail must be unique.
   - A classified is associated with one user.

2. Each of them is fairly easy to implement. Now modify the user.rb file to look like the following:

```
class User < ActiveRecord::Base
  validates_presence_of :login
  validates_presence_of :password
  validates_presence_of :email
```

10

```
      validates_confirmation_of :email
      validates_uniqueness_of :login
      validates_uniqueness_of :email
      has_many :classifieds
end
```

These are all validations and associations that you have seen in previous chapters.

> *One design decision you made was to limit an e-mail address to be able to be tied to only a single user account. If you want your users to be able to create multiple user accounts with a single e-mail address, you can remove the* validates_uniqueness_of *validation for the email field.*

The last rule you need to implement is to associate the classifieds to a single user account.

3. Open up the `classified.rb` model file and add the following line to it just below the belongs_to :category line:

```
belongs_to :user
```

Save your changes. Now that you have implemented these associations, you can retrieve user information easily. For example, you could get a list of all the classifieds for a single user like this:

```
@user = User.find(:first)
@user.classifieds
```

You could also get the user's login name from a classified ad with the following code:

```
@classified = Classified.find(:first)
@classified.user.login
```

It doesn't get any easier than that!

Adding a new controller

You need to add a new controller to the application to manage your user data. Although you could add the user management methods to another controller, it is best to separate application functions out logically.

1. Create the new controller via the Terminal or command prompt window by running the following command in the terminal/command prompt:

```
ruby script/generate controller User
```

Rails has generated a new user_controller.rb file under app/controllers.

2. Open that controller file and edit it to look like the following:

```
class UserController < ApplicationController
  layout 'standard'

  def signup
  end

  def login
  end
end
```

Here you have two simple methods: signup, which controls how users set themselves up with a user account, and login, which controls how a user logs in to the site.

Now that you have finished setting up all the background code that controls the user signups, you can turn your attention to the front end of the user account system. Let's implement the signup form first.

Creating a signup form

1. Create a new file called signup.rhtml under app/views/user and add the following code to it. It's just a simple HTML form with the three standard fields you'd expect for creating a user login: username, password/confirm password, and e-mail address.

```
<h3>Signup</h3>
<%= error_messages_for 'user' -%>

<%= start_form_tag({:action => 'signup'}) -%>
<fieldset>
<label for="user_login">Desired Login:
  <%= text_field :user, :login -%></label>

<label for="user_password">Password:
  <%= password_field :user, :password -%></label>

<label for="user_email">Your Email:
  <%= text_field :user, :email -%></label>

<label for="user_email_confirmation">Confirm Email:
  <%= text_field :user, :email_confirmation -%></label>

<%= submit_tag 'Create my account' -%>
</fieldset>
<%= end_form_tag %>
```

2. Save your changes.

Now add some Cascading Style Sheet (CSS) style to the user signup form.

10

3. Open up the style.css in /public/stylesheets, add the following CSS to the bottom and then save your changes:

```
fieldset {
  display: block;
  width: 255px;
  margin: 20px;
  padding: 10px;
  background-color: #eee;
}

fieldset > label {
  display: block;
  margin-bottom: 2px;
  font-weight: bold;
}
```

4. Test the signup page in the web browser (http://localhost:3000/user/signup/). Don't try to submit it yet—it doesn't work since you haven't added any code to the signup method in the user_controller.rb file.

5. Add it now—update the signup method so it looks as follows:

```
def signup
  case request.method
    when :post
      @user = User.new(params[:user])
      if @user.save
        redirect_to :controller => 'classified', :action => 'list'
      end
  end
end
```

This method is a bit different from the data-creation methods you used before. In previous examples, you created two methods, new and create, when you wanted to create data such as a classified. The new method would be called when the form was displayed, and the <form> action was set to create. In the signup method, you are consolidating the new and create methods into a single method using a Ruby case statement.

The entire reason behind having the two methods was because one called for an HTTP GET call and the second for an HTTP POST call. You can differentiate between those two by getting the value of Rails' request.method parameter. You pass that value to the case statement and execute a different code branch depending on the value of that parameter.

When :post is returned, the actual process of creating a user account happens. You don't need to do any processing for when :get is passed. You just show the user the signup form.

> *HTTP* GET *and* POST *are merely methods of the HTTP protocol that define how data is passed between the browser and web server. You use* GET *when you want to retrieve data from the server, and you use* POST *when you want to pass data to the server. By using* POST *instead of* GET *to pass data, you are not passing the form values in the URL. If you have created HTML forms before, you are probably familiar with the* <form> *tag's method parameter. It takes either* GET *or* POST, *depending on the form's purpose.*

6. Test out creating a new account.

If it is successfully created, you will be redirected to the classifieds listing. If you omit data or pass in bad values (such as not including an e-mail address), it returns the errors by using the error_messages_for Rails helper.

Securing the users

One issue that you have in the current implementation is that you are storing the passwords in the database as plain text, as shown in Figure 10-3. Users with access to the database can see the password for each user and easily log in to the account. If hackers got access to that data, they could create havoc inside your system.

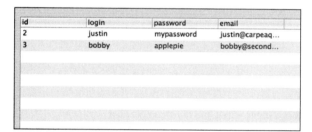

Figure 10-3. Plain text data is not very secure.

10

To make the application more secure, encrypt the password before it is stored in the database. There are several ways to do this, but here you learn how to encrypt it by using an SHA1 hash. SHA is a set of cryptographic hash functions that are available in many programming languages. SHA1 is the most commonly used one in terms of web applications. Another type of hash function you can use is MD5, but SHA1 is generally believed to be the more secure of the two. Both encryption algorithms work by taking your plain text password and then passing it through several levels of filtering and manipulation to convert your password into something that is not readable by a human and (hopefully) a computer.

> *To learn more about how SHA1 works, check out* http://nsfsecurity.pr.erau.edu/crypto/sha1.html.

1. Open up the user.rb model file in your text editor—it's located in app/models.

   You will override the password-creation method to encrypt the value provided by the user with SHA1.

2. Add the following method just before the last end keyword and save your changes:

```
def password=(value)
  write_attribute("password", Digest::SHA1.hexdigest(value))
end
```

What you just created was an accessor method for the password attribute. When you create an instance of the user model and then save the data to the database, the password value provided by the user is sent through this password method, and the returned value is saved to the database. When you name a method the same as a column in your database, Rails assumes that it is an accessor method and uses that method to read or write data values instead of the default Ruby methods. If you think back to the Ruby introduction in Chapter 3, you are overriding the default accessor method provided by Ruby with your own via inheritance.

3. Now try creating another user account. The password is encrypted before being saved to the database, as shown in Figure 10-4.

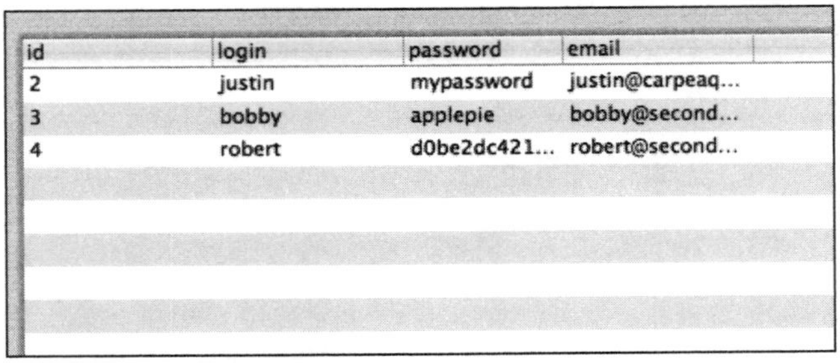

id	login	password	email
2	justin	mypassword	justin@carpeaq...
3	bobby	applepie	bobby@second...
4	robert	d0be2dc421...	robert@second...

Figure 10-4. Now that the password is encrypted, the third user account seen here is more secure.

Keep in mind that encrypting your password does not absolutely guarantee that a hacker cannot get your users' passwords. Encryption provides a very good barrier between your data and the hacker, but it is by no means unbreakable.

Creating a login form

While it is nice to allow users to create their own unique logins for the railslist application, it doesn't do much good if there is no functionality available for them to log in to their account. So, now create a login form.

You can also add the login form to the standard template's sidebar. If users aren't logged into the system, they are presented with a form to enable them to do so (or sign up for an account). If they are signed in, you can just offer them a greeting.

1. Open up the standard.rhtml file under app/views/layouts and modify the #sidebar to look like the following:

```
<div id="sidebar">
  <%= start_form_tag({:controller => 'user', :action => 'login'}, ➡
    {:id => "login_form"}) -%>
    <label for="user_login">Login:</label><br />
    <%= text_field :user, :login -%><br />
    <label for="user_login">Password:</label><br />
    <%= password_field :user, :password -%><br />
    <%= submit_tag 'Login' -%>
  <%= end_form_tag%>
  Need an account?  <%= link_to 'Signup today!', :controller => 'user', ➡
    :action => 'signup' %>
</div>
```

All you've done thus far is create a standard login form.

2. Look at it in your browser and notice that it is a bit out of place. Add some CSS styles to the bottom of the style.css file in /public/stylesheets to remedy it.

```
form#login_form {
  border: 1px solid #ccc;
  padding: 3px;
}

form#login_form label {
  font-size: 80%;
}

form#login_form input[type=text],
form#login_form input[type=password] {
  width: 150px;
}
```

3. Modify the #sidebar CSS rule to look like the following:

```
div#sidebar {
  width: 200px;
  margin-left: 480px;
  margin-top: 50px;
}
```

4. Try viewing the page again; the front page now looks like Figure 10-5.

10

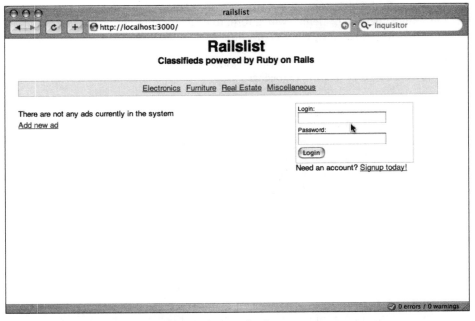

Figure 10-5. The sidebar now features a login form for the user accounts.

Adding the login code to the backend

Now that you have the form nicely styled, you can implement the actual login method in the User controller.

The logic behind the login method is that you will search the database looking for a user account with the login name and password provided. If the account exists and the values match, you allow the user to log in.

If you remember back to a few pages ago, you started encrypting login passwords by using SHA1, so you need to decrypt the password stored in the database and compare it with the user's input. You need to implement this code in the model, so do that first.

1. Open up the user.rb model file under app/models and add the following method to it just before the last end keyword:

```
def self.authenticate(login,password)
  find(:first, :conditions => ["login = ? and password = ?",➡
    login, Digest::SHA1.hexdigest(password)])
end
```

This method is fairly simple, save for the nasty-looking Digest::SHA1. hexdigest(password) parameter in the find method. It is telling Ruby to encrypt the value provided by the user so you can compare it with the stored password. Next, implement this method in the User controller's login method.

2. Edit the login method of app/controllers/user_controller.rb to look like the following:

```
def login
  if session[:user] = User.authenticate(params[:user][:login], ➥
params[:user][:password])
    redirect_to :controller => 'classified', :action => 'list'
  else
    redirect_to :controller => 'classified', :action => 'list'
  end
end
```

The login method's main purpose is to try and authenticate users based on the parameters they provide in the login form. If the values submitted are found in the database, you store the users' information into a session so that the users can remain logged in until they decide that they want to stop using the application for now (end the session.) This doesn't just happen by default—you will set this up next.

> *A session is a method of storing object data temporarily between different requests. A session makes it easy to work with logged-in users because you do not have to authenticate them each time they access a protected area of the application. Instead, you can authenticate them once and store their data in a session. A session is merely a container for storing a user's current state in a web application. Unlike a cookie, session information is stored on the server instead of the client's computer. You don't necessarily have to store only user data in a session. If you want, you can store a listing of all the classifieds in the application in a session. It doesn't make much sense, but Rails doesn't stop you from doing so.*

How to store session data

Even though Rails makes it easy to work with sessions, choosing the right type of session management is an important decision. Rails offers four different ways to store the session data:

- **Memory Store:** Rails keeps your session data in memory. Be aware that you can run into issues if your application has lots of users. Each session variable takes about 50KB of data on average. If you have 1000 sessions, that's ~50MB of memory overhead.

- **ActiveRecord Store:** Using ActiveRecord means that you are storing the session data in a table of the database. The database then automatically retrieves the session data using SQL queries. This is a more convenient method of managing sessions since it keeps all the session data in the database with the other data, but it is also more secure. There is a slight performance hit taken from Active Record, but it is not significant.

10

- **Drb Store:** This store uses distributed Ruby to store a user's session data. The performance is great, but it requires a bit more setup than the other stores.
- **PStore:** This is the default solution that is used in Rails. Using PStore, your session data is stored in small temporary files on your hard drive. These files are usually located in the tmp/sessions folder for the Rails app. The main downside of using the PStore is that you will have to do some session-pruning periodically because performance decreases as the number of sessions stored increases.

For these purposes, you will implement the ActiveRecord Store. The first step is to modify the environment.rb file to let Rails know what you are doing.

1. Open up environment.rb (it's in the config folder). Uncomment the following line:

   `# config.action_controller.session_store = :active_record_store`

2. Save your changes.

> If you want to use another store besides the ActiveRecord Store, check out http://wiki.rubyonrails.com/rails/pages/HowtoChangeSessionStore.

Next, create the sessions table. Since this type of session storage is built into Ruby on Rails, it's fairly easy to create this table.

3. Open up the Terminal or command prompt window and type the following command:

   `rake db:sessions:create`

   This command creates a new migration file, 005_add_sessions.rb, which contains the fields for the sessions table. Since you don't need to modify this migration file, go ahead and migrate the database so you have the new sessions table.

4. Run the rake migrate command from the Terminal or command prompt.

   Since you modified an environment file, you now need to restart the application so the change takes effect.

5. Kill the web server by typing Control-C in the command prompt or terminal window in which it is running.

6. After it has gone down, restart it by using the Ruby script/server command.

7. Now if users log in, their session data will be stored in the new sessions table—try logging yourself in!

> If you ever want to wipe all the values in your sessions table easily, there's a rake command for that too. Just open a Terminal or command prompt and type rake db:sessions:clear. *Easy enough!*

Working with the sessions

Now that you have users logged in and have created a session for them, it doesn't make much sense to show them the login form. Instead, welcome users to the application. Later on, you will also add a logout link so they can log out after they finish and aren't logged in forever.

1. Jump back to the `standard.rhtml` template; you'll wrap the form in a decision structure.

2. Before the `start_form_tag`, add the following line.

```
<% unless session[:user] %>
```

3. After the Need An Account signup link, add the following lines:

```
<% else %>
  <p><%= "Welcome #{session[:user].login}!" -%></p>
<% end %>
```

This decision structure tells Rails to show the login form unless there is already a session stored for the user. If there is already a session, welcome that user by the login name.

Locking railslist down

Setting up the application to enable a user to create an account and login is great, but it really doesn't serve a purpose unless you are locking down portions of the application to allow users to edit only their own data, not other people's.

Initially you should not allow other users to edit or delete another user's classifieds. Let's create a new helper method to accomplish this:

1. Open up the `application_helper.rb` file under app/helpers and add the following method to it before the last end keyword:

```
def can_edit?(classified)
  if classified.user == session[:user]
    return true
  else
    return false
  end
end
```

The can_edit? method returns true if the classified is owned by the user defined in the session. If not, it returns false. You can take this method and use it to hide the edit and delete links next to each classified in the listings. If the returned value of the can_edit? method is true, users see edit and delete controls for the classified. If it returns false, users don't see any controls—they can only view the classified, not change it.

10

2. Next, open up the _classified.rhtml file under app/views/classified and modify it to look like the following:

```
<li><%= link_to classified.title, {:action => 'show',➡
:id => classified.id} -%>
  <% if can_edit?(classified) %>
    <small><%= link_to 'Edit', {:action => 'edit', ➡
      :id => classified.id} %></small>
    <small><%= link_to "Delete", {:action => 'delete', ➡
      :id => classified.id},➡
  :confirm => "Are you sure you want to delete this item?" %></small>
  <% end %>
</li>
```

All you did here is wrap the edit and delete links with a decision structure using the new can_edit? method. If the value returned is true, the edit links work. Otherwise, users can't see the edit or delete buttons. Regardless, everyone—whether they have an account or are logged in—can still see the classified listings.

Next, you need to restrict the functionality, allowing users to add classifieds to registered users only. The first step you can take is to hide the "add new ad" link from nonlogged-in users.

3. Create another helper method called logged_in?. Add it to your application_helper file just before the last end keyword and save the changes.

```
def logged_in?
  return true if session[:user]
  return false
end
```

This method returns true if you have a session stored. Let's wrap the new add link with this code now.

4. Open up list.rhtml under app/views/classifieds and edit the "Add new ad" link to be like the following:

```
<% if logged_in? %>
  <p><%= link_to "Add new ad", {:action => 'new' }%></p>
<% end %>
```

5. Test railslist again—now you'll see the "Add new ad" link only if you are logged in, as shown in Figure 10-6.

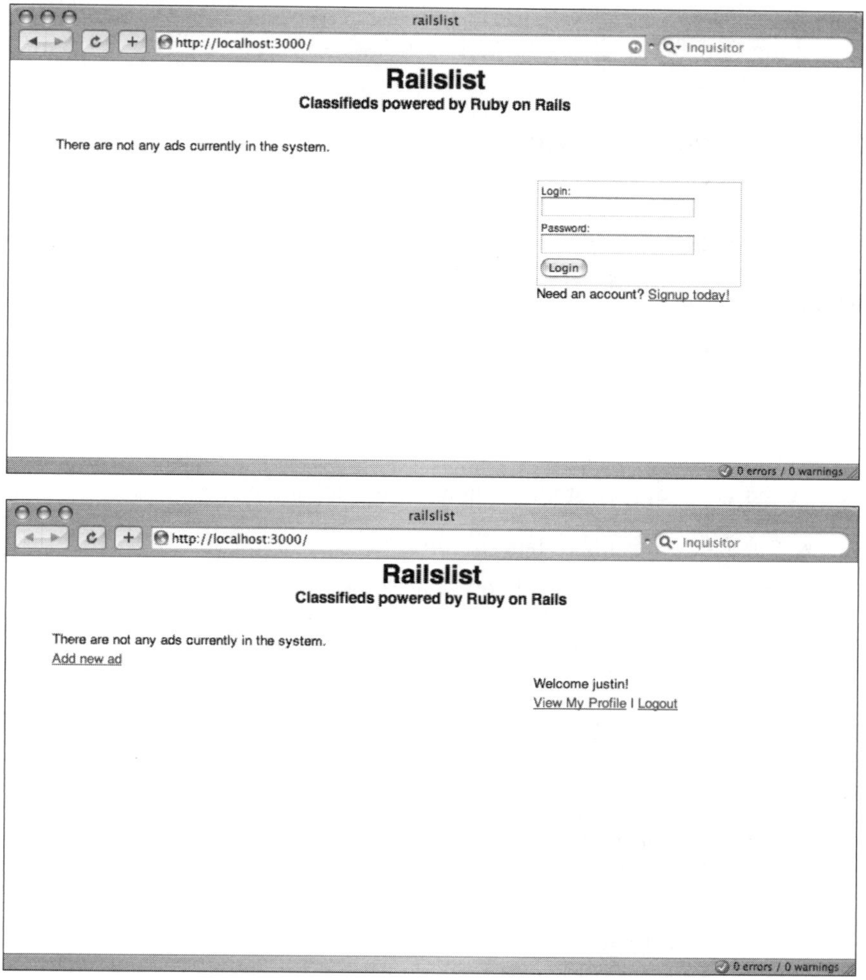

Figure 10-6. By default, the login box is shown in the right sidebar. If users are logged in, they get a welcome message in the sidebar and have access to the "Add new ad" link.

Next, you need to protect the actual methods from unauthorized users. Even though you have hidden the link from the views, users could still go to http://localhost:3000/classified/new and create a new ad without any authentication.

6. Edit the new method in classified_controller.rb to look like the following:

```
def new
  redirect_to :action => 'list' if session[:user].blank?
  @classified = Classified.new
  @categories = Category.find(:all)
end
```

Here you added a line that instructs Railslist to redirect users back to the classified listings page if they attempt to access the Post new classified page when a session does not exist (that is, they are not logged in).

Securing the categories controller

It would be remiss to not put some sort of access restrictions in the categories controller. If you were to leave the categories controller exposed in the wild, people who found the site on the Web could add their own categories to the application. You would no doubt have several ads for *V1@gra* or *Free H0me Mortgage* from the Spam bots that plague the Internet these days.

Since the categories controller is something that a nonuser shouldn't have any access to, you can create a filter that you can execute before any action is run in the controller. Rails includes a feature called *filters* that enables you to run a piece of code based on a condition in your controller or a specific method.

Rails supports three types of filters: before, after, and around:

- The before and after filters are run just before or just after a method.

- An around filter wraps around your method when it is run. The filter runs its first set of actions before the method executes and stops when it reaches a yield keyword. After it hits the yield keyword, the method's code executes. Upon completion, the rest of the filter is executed.

When restricting the categories controller, it makes the most sense to use a before filter so that you can see whether a user is logged in before providing access to the controller's methods.

1. Open your category_controller.rb file in app/controllers and add the following to the bottom just before the last end keyword:

```
protected
  def logged_in?
    unless session[:user]
      redirect_to :controller => 'classified', :action => 'list'
    else
      return true
    end
  end
```

This method, logged_in?, checks to see whether a session[:user] object exists for the user trying to access the category controller. If the session object exists, the user can work with the category controller. If it doesn't exist, the user is redirected to the classified controller's list method.

The second step of implementing a filter is actually letting the controller know that a method is a filter.

2. Add the following bold code to the category controller so that it matches the code listing and then save your changes:

```
class CategoryController < ApplicationController
  layout 'standard'

  before_filter :logged_in?, :except => [:show]

  def list
    @categories = Category.find(:all)
  end
  ...
end
```

The before_filter call lets Rails know that it should run the logged_in? method before any other method in the controller. There is a hierarchy of filters that you should be aware of. Filters are executed in the order in which they are read in the Ruby code, so if you have a bit of code like the following, the code executes the is_dog? method before the is_mammal? method:

```
before_filter :is_dog?
before_filter :is_mammal?
```

If you switch the order so the is_mammal? filter is listed first, it reverses the listing.

Now if you try to access the categories listing while not being logged in, you cannot access it.

You might be wondering why you are still letting any user create a category. You have earned a gold star for that astute observation! If you were to deploy Railslist as a publicly available application, you would want to use a permissions-based authentication system so only system administrators could add data like that. That process is beyond the scope of this introductory book, however.

10

Assigning classifieds to users

Back when you designed the user model, you set up an association stating that users could have many classifieds assigned to them. Now that you are restricting classified creation to logged-in, registered users, you need to make some modifications to the classified_controller.rb create method: you have to associate each new classified listing with a user account.

1. Add the following line to the create method below the @classified instance variable declaration in classified_controller.rb:

   @classified.user = session[:user]

2. Save your changes and create a new classified.

The classified should now be assigned to the user account, and you should be able to edit and delete it. If you were to log in with a secondary account and create another classified, edit controls would be hidden from any classified not owned by that new login.

Try adding a few classifieds to your system to see how everything works.

Removing the email field

Since you are storing the e-mail address along with the newly created user accounts' functionality, it doesn't make much sense to require users to provide an e-mail address each time they create a new classified. Instead, just grab the value associated with their account.

1. Open new.rhtml under app/views/classified and remove the following lines:

```
<p><label for="classified_email">Email</label><br/>
<%= text_field 'classified', 'email' %></p>
```

2. Open edit.rhtml under app/views/classified and remove these lines:

```
<p><label for="classified_email">Email</label><br/>
<%= text_field 'classified', 'email' %></p>
```

3. Save the changes to both files.

Now, you need to associate the email address with a classified in the controller.

4. Open classified_controller.rb in app/controllers and modify the create method to look like the following:

```
def create
  @classified = Classified.new(params[:classified])
  @classified.user = session[:user]
  @classified.email = session[:user].email
  if @classified.save
    redirect_to home_url
  else
    render :action => 'new'
  end
end
```

The only line you added is in bold (you associated the e-mail address stored in the user's session object with the email field of the @classified instance). Now users have a bit less information to enter each time they create a new listing.

Logging out

The last thing you need to implement for the basic user system is the ability to log out. Logging out sets the session to nil and removes any authenticated privileges users had when they were logged in.

1. First, you need to add a logout method to the user_controller.rb controller in app/controllers. Add the following method before the last end keyword and save your changes:

```
def logout
  reset_session
  redirect_to :controller => 'classified', :action => 'list'
end
```

Here you are introduced to the Rails method called reset_session. This method clears out all the data stored in the user's session. After you reset the session, you redirect the user back to the classifieds listings.

2. You need to add a logout link to the template as well, so open up standard.rhtml in app/views/layouts and add the bold line shown here:

```
<% else %>
<p><%= "Welcome #{session[:user].login}!" -%></p>
<p><%= link_to 'Logout', :controller => 'user', ➡
:action => 'logout' -%></p>
<% end %>
```

3. Save your changes and then go back to the web browser to test out the logout functionality, as shown in Figure 10-7.

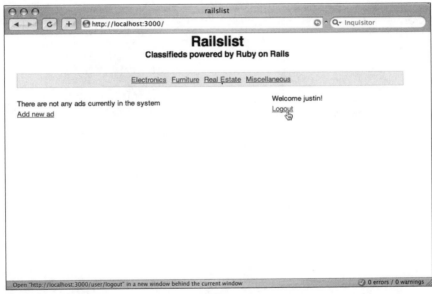

Figure 10-7. Clicking the logout link in the sidebar resets the users' session data and forces them to log in the next time they want to edit their data or create a new classified.

Summary

This chapter implemented some important functionality in the application. Most web applications have some sort of user authentication system, and Rails makes it incredibly easy to add that functionality. This is a very basic system that can be expanded further by adding functionality such as role-based permissions for users and other account privileges.

In the next chapter, you will complete the Railslist application by customizing and styling the views even more. You will add a tag cloud to the application so that users can see the most popular category visually. The chapter also introduces microformats and discusses how they can be beneficial to an application such as Railslist.

11 CUSTOMIZING RAILS VIEWS

At this point, the Railslist application is a fully functional web application powered by Ruby on Rails. If you wanted to, you could release it on the Internet right now and start signing up users and posting classifieds. If I let you do that now, though, I wouldn't be able to sleep at night. While the application works just fine, there is more you could do to make it look better and function more intuitively for users.

By the end of this chapter, the application will be more visually appealing, more user-friendly, and function more like a polished web application.

This chapter covers the following:

- Separating listings by date
- Creating a Rails helper method for the views to show edit controls
- Adding the Web 2.0 style to the application
- Implementing and using microformats to display contact information

Organizing listings

Right now you probably don't have that many listings in your Railslist database. You have been adding new classifieds each time you want to test something. If you opened the application up to an Internet full of real users, that wouldn't be the case. As more and more classifieds get listed, it will be increasingly difficult to visually separate classifieds on the listing page. Wouldn't it be nice if you separated them by the date they were posted? Let's do that now.

1. First, open up the `list.rhtml` file under app/views/classified. Before, you were listing the classifieds as a collection of partials in an unordered list. You were also using that list to do the live searching.

2. Because of that design decision, leave the <ul> tags, but remove the following line:

   ```
   <%= render :partial "classified", :collection => @classifieds %>
   ```

   This code line ensures that the live searching will continue working, but it will no longer be used to display the classifieds. To do that, you will use some different code. There is no easy way to sort items in a view by date, so you need to use a little bit of logic in the code.

3. Add the following code snippet to your `list.rhtml` below the </ul> tag; then you will walk through it:

   ```
   <% previous_day = "" %>
   <% @classifieds.each do |classified| %>
     <% if classified.created_at.strftime("%m/%d/%Y").to_s ➥
   != previous_day %>
       <h4><%= classified.created_at.strftime("%B %d, %Y") %></h4>
     <% end %>
     <p class="classified">
       <%= link_to classified.title, {:action => 'show', ➥
   :id => classified.id} -%>
   ```

```
<% if can_edit?(classified) %>
    <small><%= link_to 'Edit', {:action => 'edit',➡
:id => classified.id} %></small>
    <small><%= link_to "Delete", {:action => 'delete', ➡
:id => classified.id}, ➡
:confirm => "Are you sure you want to delete this item?" %></small>
    <% end %>
  </p>
  <% previous_day = classified.created_at.strftime("%m/%d/%Y").to_s %>
<% end %>
```

In the first line, you define a variable called previous_day. You will use it to store the previous created_at date's value as you iterate through all the classifieds in the system. After you start iterating through the @classifieds array, the first thing you do is compare the current classified's created_at column value to previous_day. You pass the value for created_at so it appears as *month/day/year*. This is done using Ruby's built-in strftime method. If the values of created_at and previous_day *do not* match, output a new <h4> tag with the date the classified was created. If the two dates match, just skip to the next line without outputting a new <h4> tag.

Output the actual classifieds information. It's similar to what you were using in the _classified partial, but you are wrapping everything in a paragraph tag instead of a list item.

Finally, you set the value of the previous_day variable to the current classifieds creation date so that you can compare the next classified to the date of the previous one.

4. Let's see how this new code looks. Open your browser and go to the classified listing page. You should see a much better organized layout, as shown in Figure 11-1.

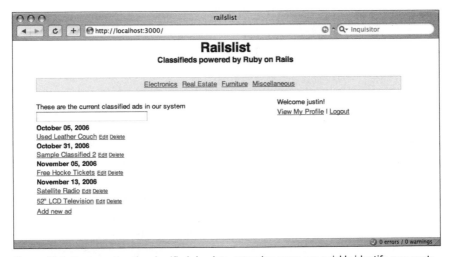

Figure 11-1. By separating the classifieds by date, returning users can quickly identify new posts.

Using helper methods in views

Helper methods are used to extract commonly used processing code into a single method definition that you can share throughout the application. You can also create helper methods that are restricted to a specific controller instead of the entire application.

You have already created a few helper methods in the application. In the last chapter, you created one called can_edit? that you added to the views to show and hide content, depending on whether or not users were logged into their account and had edit privileges. If users create a lot of classifieds in the system, the page can become somewhat cluttered with those links. Let's create a helper method to extract those links into a single method and then show or hide them only as the user hovers over the classified link. Let's use helpers now to clean up the classified listings page.

1. Open up the classified_helper.rb file under app/helpers.

   Since you are manipulating only the classifieds listing page, it's best to keep these methods under the helper for the Classified controller's views. The first method you need to create extracts the Edit and Delete links.

2. Add the following code to the bottom of the file—just before the last end keyword:

```
def admin_tools_for(classified)
  tag = [ ]
  tag << content_tag("span",
  link_to("Edit", {
    :action => "edit", :id => classified
  }, :class => "admintools") <<
  link_to("Delete", {
    :action => "delete",
    :id => classified.id,
  },
  :post => true,
  :confirm => "Are you sure you want to delete #{classified.title}",
  :class => "admintools"),
  :id => "classified_#{classified.id}")
end
```

   This method might look complex, but it's really simple. All you are doing is defining an array called tag and then adding the Edit and Delete links to it. You are wrapping those links in a span using the content_tag Rails method and giving that tag an id of classified_x, where x is the value of the id column in the classifieds database for that specific item.

   Let's add the helper to the list.rhtml view under app/views/classified.

3. Replace the code inside the can_edit? decision structure with the helper method. The code should look like the following after you finish:

```
<p class="classified">
  <%= link_to classified.title, {:action => 'show',➡
 :id => classified.id} -%>
```

```
<% if can_edit?(classified) %>
<%= admin_tools_for (classified) %>
<% end %>
</p>
```

4. Now load the classified listing page in the browser and then log in. You will see Edit and Delete links next to all your classifieds (but no one else's).

5. The new links are looking cool, but they could still use a bit of styling, so add the following Cascading Style Sheets (CSS) to the bottom of the style.css file and then save your changes:

```
a.admintools {
   font-size:   75%;
   margin-right: 3px;
   color:   #333;
}
```

Try the page again—now the links will be a bit smaller and have a different color to make them stand out more, as shown in Figure 11-2.

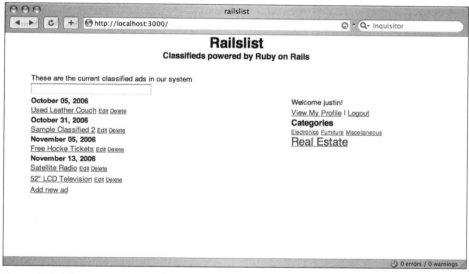

Figure 11-2. When a user owns a classified, the edit controls appear.

Adding Web 2.0 style

You added a search capability to the application using Ajax back in Chapter 8. The search functionality works just fine, but it could use a dash of spice to make it more usable and attractive. One issue with the search right now is that users don't get any notification that a search is in progress. It would be nice if you could show them a visual indicator that a search is in progress. Let's do that now.

1. Open up the list.rhtml template under app/views/classified in your text editor.

   You want to add a new <div> that will appear when the users' search query is triggered. The <div> merely shows a message letting users know that their search is in progress.

2. Add the following bolded line of code below the observe_field declaration:

```
<%= observe_field :classified_title,
  :frequency => 1.0,
  :update => 'classifieds',
  :url => { :controller => 'classified', :action=> 'search' },
  :with => "'search=' + encodeURIComponent(value)"
%>
<div id="loading" style="display:none;"><p>Searching...</p></div>
```

   You set the style of the new #loading <div> to be hidden by default so that if a search is not in progress, nothing will display. You can set its appearance in the observe_field method.

3. Add the following bolded lines into the observe_field method in list.rhtml and then save your changes:

```
<%= observe_field :classified_title,
:frequency => 0.5,
:update => 'classifieds',
:loading => 'Element.show("loading")',
:complete => 'Element.hide("loading")',
:url => { :controller => 'classified', :action=> 'search' },
:with => "'search=' + encodeURIComponent(value)"
%>
```

   The changes you made are highlighted with the previous bold text. You merely added two new parameters to the method. The first, :loading, tells the observe_field method an action to trigger as it's searching. In this case, it is showing the #loading <div>. The second parameter, :complete, is called after the search query is completed. You are telling :complete to hide the #loading <div> since you no longer need to show users that a search is in progress.

4. Open your browser and perform a search. You should notice that the *Searching...* text appears below the input field during your search.

5. It doesn't stand out as much as you want, so add the following CSS to the bottom of the style.css file:

```
div#loading {
  padding: 5px;
  background-color: #ffffcc;
  border: 1px solid #ececec;
}

div#loading p {
  font-weight: bold;
  font-size:  110%;
}
```

6. Now when you perform a search, the *Searching...* message is bold and displayed with a light yellow background, as shown in Figure 11-3. The search results then appear just below the search box.

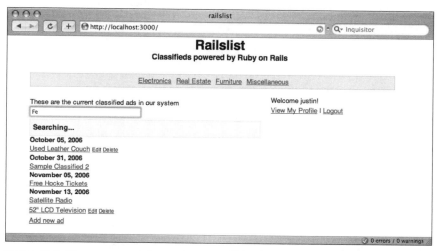

Figure 11-3. When you search for a value, you will be shown a Searching... message.

> *Unless you have several hundred or thousands of classifieds in your system, the message shouldn't appear very long because the search will be really quick.*

As a final bit to the search code, let's include add some styling to the search results so they can stand out a little bit more. Let's modify the classifieds styles in the style.css file. Make them look like the following and save your changes:

```
ul#classifieds {
  list-style-type: none;
}

ul#classifieds li {
  background-color: #ececec;
  padding: 5px;
  font-weight:bold;
  line-height: 140%;
}
```

Creating a tag cloud from the categories

Up until now, you have had the categories listed at the top of the classified listing. This is fine, but what if you start adding more than a few categories? It can get a bit confusing to sort through. Instead, you could move the categories listing to the sidebar of the layout and display it as a tag cloud, which will not only be fun but also more readable when there are lots of categories.

11

A tag cloud is a great way to see what the most popular items in a listing are by giving them a larger font than less-popular items in a list. Clouds are most often seen when used in conjunction with tags. One of the most popular uses of tags is on the del.icio.us social bookmarking site (http://del.icio.us). It has a tag cloud of the 100 most popular tags that have been used when posting bookmarks on the site (see Figure 11-4).

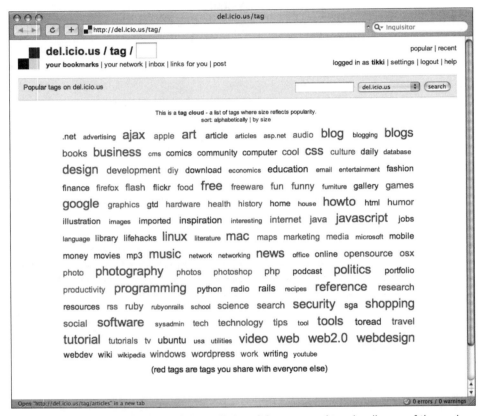

Figure 11-4. The del.icio.us tag cloud gives a listing of the most used tags by all users of the service.

Anyway, without further ado, let's implement this on the Railslist application. You first need to move the categories listing to the sidebar, as suggested previously.

1. Remove the following code from the list.rhtml view under app/views/classified:

```
<ul id="categories">
<% Category.find(:all).each do |c| %>
<li><%= link_to c.name, :controller => "category", :action => "show", ➥
:id => c.id %></li>
<% end %>
</ul>
```

2. Open up the `standard.rhtml` layout under app/views/layouts. Add the following code to the sidebar `<div>`, just before its closing `</div>` tag:

```
<h3>Categories</h3>
<% Category.find(:all, :order => "name ASC").each do |c| %>
  <%= link_to c.name, :controller => "category", :action => "show",➡
  :id => c.id %>
<% end %>
```

The biggest change to the code (beyond the HTML semantics) is that you are sorting the categories by their name so that they will be listed in alphabetical order. This is done using the `:order` parameter on the `find` method. *name ASC* tells Rails that you want to sort the method by the name column in the database and sort them ascending (A-Z). (If you want reverse-alphabetical order, you use *DESC* instead of *ASC*.)

3. Try the main page again in your browser; it should look like Figure 11-5.

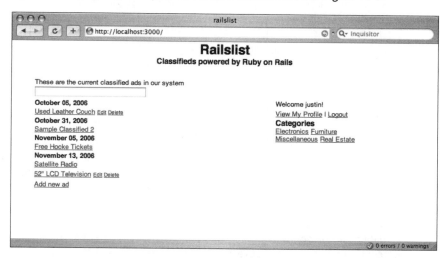

Figure 11-5. By moving the category listings to the sidebar, you have room to grow if the users begin adding more categories.

Now, let's create a tag cloud from the category listing. You can do this by emphasizing the most popular categories with a larger font size. The first thing you should do is define a helper method to render the cloud in the Railslist sidebar.

4. Open up the `application_helper.rb` file under app/helpers/.

You will put the `cloud` method in the Application helper because you are rendering the action in the layout. Since what is displayed in the sidebar propagates through all the other controllers, it makes more sense to store the `cloud` method there instead of in the Categories helper.

5. Add the following method to the application helper just before the last end statement:

```
def cloud(categories)
 return if categories.blank?
  output = ""
  mid = categories.collect {|i| i.classifieds.count}.max / 1.5

  categories.each do |c|
    size = 100 * c.classifieds.count / mid
    size = 75 if size < 75
    output << link_to(c.name, {:controller => "category", :action =>➡
 "show", :id => c}, :style => "font-size: #{size}%") << " "
end
  return output
end
```

This method is a bit more complex than anything else you have written thus far, so let's walk through it line by line.

The method definition, cloud, takes an array called categories as its parameter. Next, you define a variable called output that will hold the HTML that you will display in the browser window. The third line of the method involves a bit of math. You are creating a variable called mid that returns a new array. That new array gathers the number of classifieds under each category. For example, a computer category might have 4 classifieds, a furniture category might have 12 classifieds, and an auto category might have 2 classifieds. In this array, you are just storing those numeric values.

After those values are in the mid array, you use Ruby's max method to get the largest value of classifieds held by a single category and then divide that by 1.5. (The 1.5 was selected because I want the maximum font size to be 150 percent.) If you want something smaller or larger, you can manipulate that number by taking the desired number you want and dividing it by 100.

With the math out of the way, you iterate through all the categories that contain classifieds. First, define another variable called size that holds the font size (in a percentage value) for the current classified. That value is computed by multiplying the number of classifieds in that category by 100 and then dividing it by mid. The line below that sets the minimum font size value to 75 percent. Therefore you'll have a nice variation of fonts ranging from 75 percent up to 150 percent. If the value returned by size is less than 75, set the value to 75 so that the minimum font size for the category cloud is a legible 75 percent.

The last part of the iteration adds the current category to the output variable. The output contains a link to the category name and then sets the font size using inline CSS styling. You can choose to use external styles if you want, but by just using an inline style, you can modify the styles mathematically instead of using predefined sizes.

Now that you have the cloud method, let's add it to the template.

6. Open up the standard.rhtml template under app/views/layouts and remove the following code block:

```
<% Category.find(:all, :order => "name ASC").each do |c| %>
<%= link_to c.name, :controller => "category", :action => "show",➡
 :id => c.id %>
<% end %>
```

7. In its place, insert this single line and save your changes:

```
<%= cloud(Category.find(:all, :order => "name ASC")) %>
```

Now open up your Railslist application in a browser; you should see your own categories cloud, as shown in Figure 11-6.

Categories
Electronics **Real Estate**
Furniture **Miscellaneous**

Figure 11-6. The tag cloud you create from the categories uses different font sizes to show the more popular tags.

To get a better idea of how your tag cloud can develop, you could try adding 10 or 15 more categories to your Railslist application and then create new classified ads that are associated with those new categories. You would see something like Figure 11-7.

Down the road, if you start to notice that you have hundreds of categories and want to limit the size of your cloud to say 100, you can easily do that by modifying the call to your cloud method in the `standard.rhtml` layout file.

```
<%= cloud(Category.find(:all, :limit => 100)) %>
```

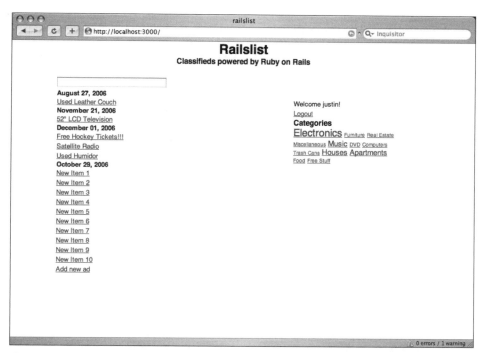

Figure 11-7. Notice that the tag cloud's size grows as you add more categories and items to it. The categories with the most classifieds have the biggest font sizes.

Adding microformats

Microformats is a web technology that will be exploding over the next couple of years. Put simply, a microformat is a set of open data formats to semantically describe data using standards that already exist. In layperson's terms, microformats are a simple and easy way to describe things such as contact information and calendar events in a common language. Microformats are built using XHTML tags and class attributes instead of proprietary formats built by a single company.

The contents of a microformat are designed to be machine readable *and* human readable. Imagine some different web applications that store music reviews. The reviews on different sites might grade the album in different ways. For example, look at the HTML for the following three reviews:

```
<p><strong>Chris Mills <em>(August 12, 2006)</em></strong> -
I loved the album. I give it a big thumbs up!</p>

<p><b>Justin Williams <i>(October 31, 2006)</i></b> -
The album was their best in ten years. 8 out of 10.

Ryan J. Bonnell (December 22, 2006) - <em>I think you should
go out and buy this CD immediately. Essential listening.</em>
```

Each one of these reviews is doing the exact same thing—telling you that the CD is a great listen and you should check it out. You can decipher it, but a computer can't—it would have trouble trying to parse all those reviews in a uniform manner because the HTML semantics are different for each review.

What you can do is use microformats to standardize the way you review albums on the website and then publish the reviews using a common format. In fact, there is already a microformat called hReview that will do just the trick. hReview (http://microformats.org/wiki/hreview) was designed by the father of microformats, Tantek Çelik. If you were to format the reviews using hReview, it would look like this:

```
<div class="hreview">
  <span class="reviewer vcard">
  <span class="fn">Chris Mills</span>,
    <abbr class="dtreviewed" title="20060812">August 12th, 2006</abbr>
  </span>
  <div class="item">
    <a lang="en" class="url fn" ➡
href="http://www.amazon.com/Dont-Believe➡
-Truth-Oasis/dp/B00097A5I6">
    Oasis - Don't Believe The Truth
    </a>
  </div>
    <div class="description"><p>
      I loved the album. I give it a big thumbs up!
    </p></div>
</div>
```

```
<div class="hreview">
  <span class="reviewer vcard">
  <span class="fn">Justin Williams</span>,
    <abbr class="dtreviewed" title="20061031">October 31st, 2006</abbr>
  </span>
<div class="item">
    <a lang="en" class="url fn" href="http://www.amazon.com/Dont-
Believe➡
-Truth-Oasis/dp/B00097A5I6">
    Oasis - Don't Believe The Truth
    </a>
  </div>
  <div class="description"><p>
    The album was their best in ten years.  8 out of 10!
  </p></div>
</div>

<div class="hreview">
  <span class="reviewer vcard">
  <span class="fn">Ryan J. Bonnell</span>,
    <abbr class="dtreviewed" title="20061222">➡
December 22nd, 2006</abbr>
  </span>
  <div class="item">
    <a lang="en" class="url fn" ➡
href="http://www.amazon.com/Dont-Believe➡
-Truth-Oasis/dp/B00097A5I6">
    Oasis - Don't Believe The Truth
    </a>
  </div>
  <div class="description"><p>
    I think you should go out and buy this CD immediately.
    Essential listening.
  </p></div>
</div>
```

Notice that the HTML for each of these reviews is exactly the same. The same tags and class attribute names are used for each review. If you render these three reviews on the Web, they are still readable by a human (see Figure 11-8), but they would *also* be able to be understood by a computer. An application or search engine that was aware of the hReview microformat could parse and aggregate all the hReview-formatted reviews off any music review sites that mark their data up with hReview and then display them to a user in a variety of different ways.

Being able to use data in a variety of ways is one of the main goals of the semantic Web and microformats in particular. One of the best examples (although on a larger scale than a microformat) is Really Simple Syndication (RSS). When a file is created using the RSS format, it uses the same set of tags so that an RSS aggregator such as NetNewsWire or FeedDemon can easily parse it and display its data to a user in a human-readable format. The same idea is being used with microformats.

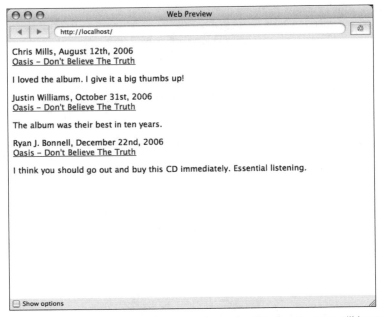

Figure 11-8. Even after formatting the reviews using hReview, they can still be read by a web browser—and thus by people. This is the beauty of using standard HTML to mark up the data.

One of the biggest implementations of microformats is Technorati, which has created a search engine specifically for searching for microformats posted on the Web (including hReview). You can check it out at http://kitchen.technorati.com/search.

Although still a relatively new technology, microformats have already been adopted in a lot of places. Another popular microformat is called hCard—an easy way to represent company and personal data that can then be read by a variety of different applications. hCard evolved from the vCard format that has been used for years in contact managers such as Microsoft Outlook and Apple Address Book. To better understand microformats, let's look an example comparing a person's contact information stored as a vCard versus an hCard. First, the vCard:

```
BEGIN:VCARD
VERSION:3.0
N:Justin;Williams
FN:Justin Williams
URL: http://secondgearllc.com/
ORG:Second Gear
END:VCARD
```

Now, let's look at the same data as an hCard:

```
<div class="vcard">
  <a class="url fn" href="http://secondgearllc.com/">
    Justin Williams
  </a>
  <div class="org">Second Gear</div>
</div>
```

Notice how legible the two formats are, yet how much more meaning can be extracted from the hCard—you are just using standard HTML elements such as `<div>` and anchor tags, which is something that has been used since the beginning of the Web. Microformats support the same fields as vCard, but instead use standard class attributes to define the data contained in the field, whereas a vCard uses colons to delimit the data.

When beginning an hCard, the outer container is always a `<div>` with a class attribute of vcard. Next, you define the website address of the organization, logically using the `href` attribute value of the anchor tag. This links to the organization address and is displayed in the browser as the same value as the vCard FN field. Also included alongside the `url` class name is the `fn` attribute, which stands for full name. It can be either a company name (for a business) or a person's name (for an individual). Finally, you create a second `<div>` tag that wraps around the organization's name represented by a class of org.

> While you're using only a few basic fields for the hCard implementation in Railslist, the entire hCard specification—including many other common fields—can be seen online at `http://microformats.org/wiki/hcard`.

If you were to view this on a web page, it would show up just like standard HTML. The power of microformats comes from how easily the information can be gathered and displayed (like the Technorati engine I mentioned before). The Firefox extension, *Tails* (`http://blog.codec.com/tasils-firefox-extension-03/`), provides a practical, real-world usage of a microformat. If browsing a website using Firefox with Tails installed, the extension will search the page and look for any embedded microformats. If it finds any on the page, it will display the formats as icons in Firefox's status bar, as shown in Figure 11-9.

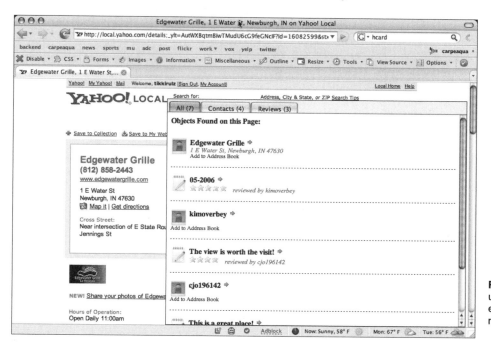

Figure 11-9. When using the Tails Firefox extension, extracting microformats is easy.

11

As you can see, microformats can be a helpful addition to any website. By adding them to your site, you are empowering Firefox extensions such as Tails or search engines such as Technorati to parse your data and enable people to use that data in a variety of different ways. Wouldn't it be great if you could surf any website and import a person's contact information into your address book with just a button click? With hCard and microformats, that might soon be a possibility. Even the new Apple .Mac Webmail service is using hCard for its address book, giving even more weight to the microformats movement.

> *Want to see how an hCard can quickly be created? Check out the hCard creator here:* `http://microformats.org/code/hcard/creator`. *For more information on microformats, check out* Microformats: Empowering Your Markup for Web 2.0, *by John Allsop (friends of ED, March 2007, ISBN: 1590598148.)*

Adding microformats to Railslist

So how can you leverage the hCard format in the Rails application? Let's create a profile page for each user who formats contact information as an hCard. You can then use Technorati to enable another user to download and save the information as a vCard.

First, add a link to a few views that will enable a user to view another user's profile.

1. Open up the `standard.rhtml` file under app/views/layouts and add the following bold code into the sidebar `<div>`:

```
<% else %>
  <p><%= "Welcome #{session[:user].login}!" -%></p>
  <p><%= link_to 'View My Profile', :controller => 'user', ➥
:action => 'show', :login => session[:user].login -%> |
    <%= link_to 'Logout', :controller => 'user', ➥
:action => 'logout' -%></p>
<% end %>
```

This link enables you to quickly view your own profile. Next, add a profile link to each classified listing to enable users to view the profile of each person who posts a classified ad.

2. Open up `show.rhtml` under app/views/classified and add the following link (highlighted in bold) right above the price listing:

```
<p>
<strong>Seller: </strong> <%= link_to @classified.user.login, ➥
:controller => 'user', :action => 'show', :login => ➥
@classified.user.login -%><br />
<strong>Price: </strong> <%= number_to_currency(@classified.price,➥
  {:unit => "&pound;", :separator => ".", :delimiter => ","}) %><br />
```

Now a user who looks at a classified listing can quickly view the user's profile page. The next thing you need to do is actually create the profile method and view it in the User controller.

3. Add the following method to the bottom of the user_controller.rb under app/controllers just before the end keyword; then save your changes:

```
def show
  @user = User.find(:first, :conditions => ➡
["login = ?", params[:login]])
end
```

This method simply creates an @user instance variable that is built from a user that has the login passed by the :login parameter.

4. Now, let's create a show.rhtml view under app/views/user. Populate the file with the following code (the bold code will be the hCard):

```
<h1><%= @user.login -%></h1>

<div class="vcard">
 <span class="fn"><%= @user.login -%></span>
 <a class="email" href="mailto:<%= @user.email -%>">
 <%= @user.email %></a>
</div>
```

This profile page puts the login name in an <h1> tag and then implements the hCard with the user's login name as the given name and includes the e-mail address.

5. Open up Railslist in a browser and click a My Profile link. You should notice two things: the page needs some CSS, and the URL (seen in Figure 11-10) is ugly.

```
🌐 http://localhost:3000/user/show?login=justin
```

Figure 11-10. Without routes, the profile page URLs are not as attractive as they could be.

To make the URL more "friendly," you need to add a route to the routes.rb file to rewrite everything after /show.

6. Open up routes.rb under the config directory and add the following route (the bold line) just above the classified listing route:

```
map.connect 'profile/:login', :controller => 'user', :action => 'show'
map.show 'classifieds/:id', :controller => 'classified', :action =>
'list'
map.home '', :controller => 'classified', :action => 'list'
```

Save your changes and then restart your server. Now if you click a Profile link, it has a much cleaner (and readable) URL, as shown in Figure 11-11.

```
🌐 http://localhost:3000/profile/justin
```

Figure 11-11. This looks much nicer!

11

7. Now let's take care of the CSS style for the profile. Add the following to the bottom of the `style.css` file:

```
div.vcard {
  margin:  5px;
  padding:  15px;
  border: 1px solid #ccc;
  background-color:  #ececec;
 font-size: 120%;
}

span.fn {
  font-weight:  bold;
  font-size: 110%;
  width:  100%;
  display:  block;
}

a.email {
  width:  100%;
  display:  block;
  padding-top: 5px;
}
```

If you refresh the page, it now looks a lot better (see Figure 11-12.)

If you look at the site using Firefox with the Tails extension installed (see Figure 11-12), you can easily extract the hCard and import it into the address book.

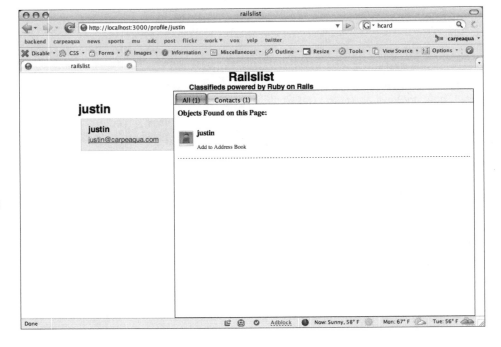

Figure 11-12. Using hCard in Railslist enables users to be able to extract a person's contact information from the profile page and optionally import it into their address book.

If you want to go further with microformats, you can use the rel-tag format in conjunction with the categories or the hListing format that is currently under review to be adopted as an official microformat. hListing is designed to create a standard markup for auction or classified listings. For more information on those two microformats, visit http://microformats.org/wiki/rel-tag and http://microformats.org/wiki/hlisting-proposal, respectively.

Summary

This chapter covered a variety of topics related to cleaning up the formatting of the Railslist application's views. You organized the listings based by date to make the pages more readable, cleaned up the display of the search results, added a cloud of categories to the sidebars that help users can see the most-used categories in the system, and implemented microformats to help build a more semantic Web.

Now that you have completed the Railslist application, all it needs is a *Beta* tag so that it will match all the other Web 2.0 applications available today!

11

12 USING RAILS PLUG-INS AND ENGINES

Over the course of reading this book, you have learned a lot about Ruby and the Ruby on Rails framework. You have used your knowledge to implement the Railslist sample application using 100 percent custom code. What if I told you that you did too much work and that you could get a lot of what you already did for free?

While it's incredibly simple to build a basic Rails application from scratch (especially compared with the old method of nonframework development), there are ways you could have saved some time using a few bits of Rails functionality that haven't yet been covered. In this chapter, you will rebuild the core of the Railslist application using these new techniques.

This chapter covers the following:

- Using Rails scaffolding for rapid application development
- Using plug-ins in the application
- Using engines in the application

Building applications with scaffolding

Scaffolding is one of the most touted features of Ruby on Rails. Scaffolding gives you basic create, read, update, delete (CRUD) functionality in your newly created controllers so you can instantly start working with your application.

In many other Ruby on Rails books on the market, one of the first few things a new developer learns about Rails is its scaffolding functionality. Usually, this is done to show how easy it is to build a functional application with little work. The problem with that approach is that it teaches many new Rails developers to rely on scaffolding code.

The problem with relying on this code is that it almost always needs some sort of modifications. By introducing you to writing your own Rails code before showing you the shortcuts, I think you will gain a greater understanding of how the code works, so you will be better equipped to make modifications when necessary and to deal with any errors and exceptions that arise.

Creating a new application with scaffolding

1. Start by creating a new Rails application in your chosen directory. Navigate to it using the Terminal or command prompt window; then enter the following command.

   ```
   rails railslist2
   ```

   This command creates the basic foundation of the application just as you did way back in Chapter 4.

2. Next, create a new database called railslist2_development, as you did for the original databases in Chapter 4.

3. Add the username and password for your MySQL server into the database.yml file in your new Rails app's config directory.

    The classifieds table needs to be created by default so that Rails' scaffolding generator won't throw an error, so let's create a migration for the new table.

4. Navigate into the railslist2 directory in the command prompt; then run the following command:

    ```
    ruby script/generate migration CreateClassifieds
    ```

    This command creates a migration file under db/migrate: 001_create_classifieds.rb.

5. Open the file and modify it to look like the following:

    ```
    class CreateClassifieds < ActiveRecord::Migration
      def self.up
        create_table :classifieds do |t|
          t.column  :title, :string
          t.column  :price, :float
          t.column  :location, :string
          t.column  :description, :text
          t.column  :email, :string
          t.column  :created_at, :datetime
          t.column  :updated_at, :datetime
        end
    end


      def self.down
        drop_table :classifieds
      end
    end
    ```

6. Save your changes.

    This is the same code you used a few chapters back to create the classifieds table, so all the code should look familiar to you.

7. Run the migration with the following command:

    ```
    rake migrate
    ```

    Next, you'll use scaffolding to create a new classified model and controller. The process is similar to creating a regular controller, but the wording is a bit different.

8. In your command prompt, type the following command:

    ```
    ruby script/generate scaffold Classified
    ```

    Your output should look similar to Figure 12-1.

12

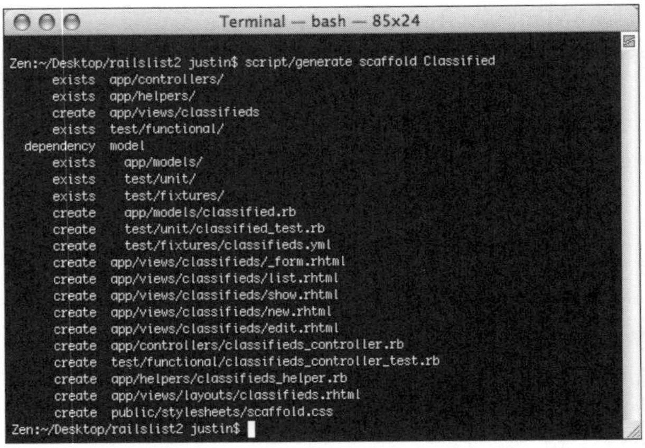

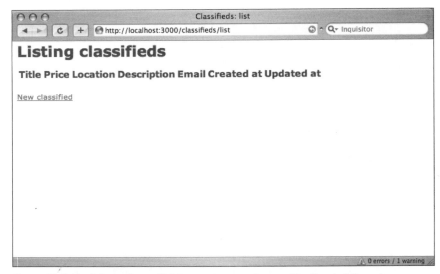

Figure 12-1. Running the scaffolding generator creates the models and controllers automatically.

When you created a controller before, it generated the controller file and some test files. By using scaffolding, you are getting not only those files but also a Rails model, the test files for it, a layout along with Cascading Style Sheets (CSS), plus all the default views. In other words, you are getting everything you need for a basic application automatically!

Testing the scaffolds

Before you even look at the basic code, let's launch the application and see how it works.

1. In your command prompt, start the server using the following command:

```
ruby script/server
```

2. Launch the browser and go to http://localhost:3000/classifieds/list. You should see a basic page with a headline, column headers, and a link to create a new classified, as shown in Figure 12-2.

Figure 12-2. By default, the scaffolding pages are not very attractive, but they give you a quick way to test your application.

3. Click the *New Classified* link to go to the New Classified form. It might not be the most attractive form ever created, but it enables you to hash out a data model.

4. Add a new classified to the database by filling out the form and submitting your information. When you are redirected to the list view again, there should now be a classified displayed (see Figure 12-3).

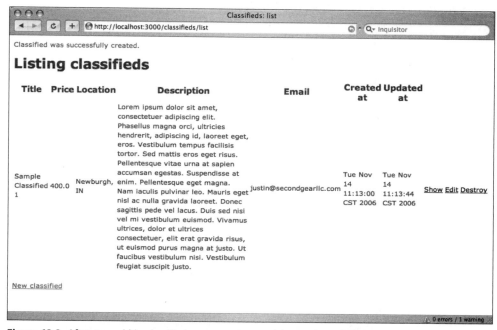

Figure 12-3. After you add in classifieds, you can see a quick overview of all the data in each row.

Again, the view isn't that attractive, but you won't keep it like this, so don't worry about it for now.

Analyzing the code

Since you know that scaffolding gives you a lot of basic functionality for free, let's look under the hood and see how it is done. First, let's analyze the scaffolding code created in the Classified controller.

1. Open up classifieds_controller.rb; it will look like so:

```
class ClassifiedsController < ApplicationController
  def index
    list
    render :action => 'list'
  end

  # GETs should be safe (see http://www.w3.org/2001/tag/doc/whenToUseGet.html)
  verify :method => :post, :only => [ :destroy, :create, :update ],
    :redirect_to => { :action => :list }
```

12

```
  def list
    @classified_pages, @classifieds = paginate :classifieds,➥
:per_page => 10
  end

  def show
    @classified = Classified.find(params[:id])
  end

  def new
    @classified = Classified.new
  end

  def create
    @classified = Classified.new(params[:classified])
    if @classified.save
      flash[:notice] = 'Classified was successfully created.'
      redirect_to :action => 'list'
    else
      render :action => 'new'
    end
  end

  def edit
    @classified = Classified.find(params[:id])
  end

  def update
    @classified = Classified.find(params[:id])
    if @classified.update_attributes(params[:classified])
      flash[:notice] = 'Classified was successfully updated.'
      redirect_to :action => 'show', :id => @classified
    else
      render :action => 'edit'
    end
  end

  def destroy
    Classified.find(params[:id]).destroy
    redirect_to :action => 'list'
  end
end
```

Although most of the preceding code is easy to follow, the verify command toward the top might not be familiar to you. This method runs a verification that certain prerequisites are true before allowing an action to be completed. If an action does not pass verification, the user is forwarded elsewhere. In this case, you are verifying that any data-manipulation method is sent using an HTTP POST call. If it isn't, the user is redirected to the list method. (This is a security precaution.)

If you look at the Railslist code you created, you implemented something similar to this in the actual method using a decision structure (if request.post?). Either method accomplishes the same goal; it's all a matter of personal preference.

The next bit of code that might not be familiar to you is in the list method:

```
def list
    @classified_pages, @classifieds = paginate :classifieds,➡
 :per_page => 10
end
```

Scaffolding uses Rails' built-in pagination methods to break up the classified listings into multiple pages. The preceding code gives each page access to an @classifieds instance variable that has all classifieds in the database. It also creates an @classified_pages variable that contains an instance of the Paginator object, which is what handles all the pagination and, by default, instructs Rails to split up each page to contain no more than 10 listings per page.

2. Now look at the list.rhtml view, and you will see how the Paginator is implemented:

```
<h1>Listing classifieds</h1>

<table>
  <tr>
  <% for column in Classified.content_columns %>
    <th><%= column.human_name %></th>
  <% end %>
  </tr>

<% for classified in @classifieds %>
  <tr>
  <% for column in Classified.content_columns %>
    <td><%=h classified.send(column.name) %></td>
  <% end %>
    <td><%= link_to 'Show', :action => 'show', ➡
 :id => classified %></td>
    <td><%= link_to 'Edit', :action => 'edit', ➡
 :id => classified %></td>
    <td><%= link_to 'Destroy', { :action => 'destroy', :id =>
classified }, :confirm => 'Are you sure?', :post => true %></td> ➡
  </tr>
<% end %>
</table>

<%= link_to 'Previous page', { ➡
 :page => @classified_pages.current.previous }
  if @classified_pages.current.previous %> ➡
<%= link_to 'Next page', { :page => @classified_pages.current.next } ➡
  if @classified_pages.current.next %>

<br />

<%= link_to 'New classified', :action => 'new' %>
```

12

The list view first creates a `<table>` to hold the classified listings. The table headers are implemented by iterating through the column names.

```
<% for column in Classified.content_columns %>
  <th><%= column.human_name %></th>
<% end %>
</tr>
```

content_columns is a method that gets the names of each column in the database. Rails then iterates through the database table and outputs the column name using the human_name method. Using human_name removes any underscores (_) or hyphens (-) and then capitalizes the first letter of each word. A column named first_name is output as *First Name*.

Next, Rails outputs the values of each column by iterating through the @classifieds array and puts the value of each column in its own table column. Of most interest is this line:

```
<td><%=h classified.send(column.name) %></td>
```

You are using Ruby's send method to extract the column value for the classified row you are iterating through at that moment. You are also wrapping the output using the h() method. This method strips any JavaScript code that might have been stored in the database to prevent XSS (Cross Site Scripting) attacks against your application. Another instance of Rails' scaffolding putting security first.

The final bit of code you should pay attention to are the lines that create the next and previous links:

```
<%= link_to 'Previous page', ➡
{ :page => @classified_pages.current.previous }
  if @classified_pages.current.previous %> ➡
<%= link_to 'Next page', { :page => @classified_pages.current.next } ➡
  if @classified_pages.current.next %>
```

You are using the @classified_pages Paginator object you created in the controller to create these links. Using that object, you can get the value of the current page and then create links using the next and previous values. All of it is pretty seamless because Rails takes care of most of the heavy lifting.

> *One of the points against pagination is that it slows performance of your application. There has been much discussion in the Rails community about the merits of pagination. It is a personal decision about whether you think pagination will benefit your application. If you have a lot of data and want to make it easier to navigate and stabilize page load times, do try pagination. Just be aware of the performance issues.*

Scaffolded model

The final piece of scaffolded code you should look at is the data model.

1. Open up the classified.rb model file. It's pretty bare, as you can see:

```
class Classified < ActiveRecord::Base
end
```

There's not much here since ActiveRecord takes care of the basic business logic. If you want to add in some validation methods you can do so—and the scaffolding picks them up immediately.

2. To illustrate this, add the following line to classified.rb and save your changes:

```
validates_presence_of :title
```

3. Now try to create a new classified but leave the title field blank—you will see the error_messages_for helper doing its job. Notice that scaffolding also styles the error messages by default, as shown in Figure 12-4.

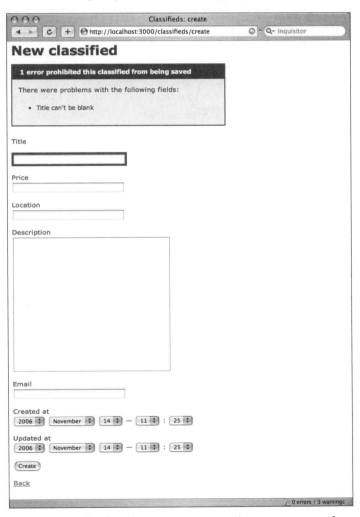

Figure 12-4. Notice that when an error appears, the error_messages_for helper is automatically styled by the scaffolded CSS file.

211

Just by adding that validation method to the model, you could put in a basic business rule and let Rails handle the rest. You can now add in all the other validation that you had in the original Railslist application, safe in the knowledge that it can be carried across more than comfortably.

Now that you have this basic classified creation implemented, let's investigate the Rails plug-in functionality and how you can leverage it to create categories in the application.

Adding functionality with plug-ins

Since this chapter is focused on getting *free* functionality, you should discuss the Rails plug-in architecture. A plug-in is an extension or modification to the Ruby on Rails core framework. Using plug-ins, you can add functionality to the application with little effort.

Plug-ins were created by the core Rails development team from a desire to add functionality to the Rails framework between releases. Developers wanted to add functionality to the framework, but the timeline for inclusion was either too long or their enhancement request was rejected. So the core team added a plug-in architecture to enable developers to release features separate of the Rails core.

A Rails plug-in is merely a collection of files comprised of models, views, and controllers just like a Rails application. The major difference is that a plug-in cannot be run independently of a host application.

Using plug-ins

Let's use plug-ins to add tagging capabilities to the new version of Railslist. In the first version, you created the own categories controller to help sort classifieds. This was similar to tagging in many ways, so it was certainly acceptable to use tagging in place of categories (in fact, it makes Railslist even more Web 2.0!).

The first thing you should do is search for a plug-in that will handle this functionality for you. The best way I have found to find plug-ins is through the Rails plug-in search engine at Agile Web Development (www.agilewebdevelopment.com/plugins).

If you search for a plug-in for *tagging*, you see there is a result that looks very promising: *acts_as_taggable* (www.agilewebdevelopment.com/plugins/acts_as_taggable), as seen in Figure 12-5. From the information page, you can discover more about the plug-in.

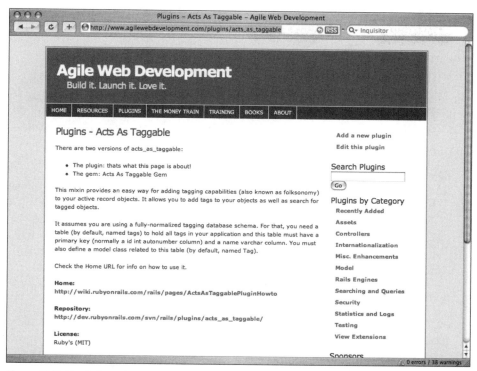

Figure 12-5. The Agile Web Development directory is a great resource for finding plug-ins to enhance your application easily.

This mixin provides an easy way for adding tagging capabilities (also known as folksonomy) to your active record objects. It enables you to add tags to your objects as well as search for tagged objects.

It assumes that you are using a fully normalized tagging database schema. For that, you need a table (named tags by default) to hold all tags in your application and this table must have a primary key (normally an id int autonumber column) and a name varchar column. You must also define a model class related to this table (named Tag by default).

It sounds like this is just what you need.

To install plug-ins, there is a script included in the `scripts` folder called `plugin`. You can take the repository URL from the Agile Web Development page and use that as the source.

1. At the command prompt, navigate to the `railslist2` folder, type the following, and press Return:

```
ruby script/plugin install ➡
http://dev.rubyonrails.com/svn/rails/plugins/acts_as_taggable/
```

12

This installs the acts_as_taggable plug-in in the vendor/plugins directory of the Rails application. The output should look like Figure 12-6.

Figure 12-6. Installing plug-ins pulls the code into your Rails application and stores it in the vendor/plugins directory.

2. You need to restart your Rails application after the installation. In fact, you need to do this before you can begin using *any* Rails plug-in. Do this as soon as it has finished.

Using acts_as_taggable

Now that you have installed the plug-in, the first thing to do is create the tags table.

1. At the command prompt, type the following:

```
ruby script/generate migration AddTagSupport
```

2. Open the migration file db/migrate/ 002_add_tag_support.rb and modify it to look like the following:

```
class AddTagSupport < ActiveRecord::Migration
  def self.up
    create_table :tags do |t|
      t.column :name, :string
    end

    create_table :taggings do |t|
      t.column :tag_id, :integer
      t.column :taggable_id, :integer
      t.column :taggable_type, :string
    end
  end

  def self.down
    drop_table :tags
    drop_table :taggings
  end
end
```

You are creating two tables, tags and taggings, to house the tag information. The tags table houses all the tags that are stored in the database, whereas the taggings table maps the relationships between a classified and its tags.

3. You now need to migrate the database so the new tables show up, so type the following command in your command prompt or Terminal window:

```
rake migrate
```

Now you need to let the classified model know that you have an association with the acts_as_taggable plug-in.

4. Open classified.rb in app/models and modify it to look like the following:

```
class Classified < ActiveRecord::Base
  validates_presence_of :title
  acts_as_taggable
end
```

Next, you need to implement the tagging functionality in the application.

5. Open the _form.rhtml file under app/views/classifieds/ and add the following bold lines to it:

```
<p><label for="classified_updated_at">Updated at</label><br/>
<%= datetime_select 'classified', 'updated_at'  %></p>

<p><label for="tags_list">Tags:</label>
<%= text_field_tag 'tag_list', @classified.tags.collect{|t| ➡
t.name}.join(" ") %></p>

<!--[eoform:classified]-->
```

6. Save your changes.

This creates a text_field called tag_list that enables users to add tags to describe their new classified item. Each tag should be separated by a space. If you want to have a multiword tag, put the full tag in parentheses.

Next, you need to tell the controller to save that information, so you can open the Classified controller and modify the create method.

7. Open up classifieds_controller.rb and add the code highlighted in bold (on line 3 following) to the create method. It should look like this:

```
def create
  @classified = Classified.new(params[:classified])
  @classified.tag_with(params[:tag_list])

  ...

end
```

The line of code you added uses a method created by acts_as_taggable called tag_with that will associate the user submitted tag(s) with the classified.

8. Now go back to your application and try creating a new classified with the New Classified form again. You will now be able to enter tags to describe your classified, as shown in Figure 12-7.

12

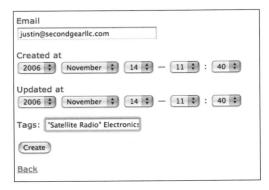

Figure 12-7. Adding tags is a process of putting descriptive words into a text field and separating them by a space.

Next, let's add functionality to show the tags when you view each specific classified.

9. Open up show.rhtml, add the following lines to it just before the two `link_to` tags, and save your changes:

```
<% unless @classified.tags.blank? %>
  <p><strong>Tags:</strong>
  <%= @classified.tags.collect{|tag| link_to tag.name,
    :action => 'tag', :id => tag}.join(", ") %></p>
<% end %>
```

10. Go to a classified and try it out. Your show view should now look as seen in Figure 12-8.

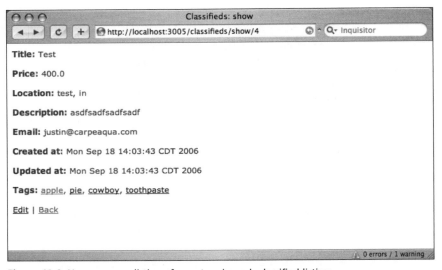

Figure 12-8. You can see a listing of your tags in each classified listing.

Finally, you want to be able to show other classifieds that share the same tag.

11. Create a new method called tag in the classifieds_controller.rb controller just before the last end keyword.

```
def tag
  @tag = Tag.find_by_id(params[:id]).tagged
end
```

Again, you are using a method given to you by the acts_as_taggable plug-in. You are using the plug-in's tag model to find the tag with the id passed.

You also need to create a view to give a listing of all classifieds that share that specific tag.

12. Create a file called tag.rhtml file under app/views/classifieds and add the following code to it:

```
<ul>
<% @tag.each do |t| %>
  <li><%= link_to t.title, :action => "show", :id => t -%></li>
<% end %>
</ul>
```

Now if you click on one of the tag links in the show.rhtml file, a new page appears with a basic listing of other classifieds sharing the same tag. Obviously, this needs some CSS to be production-worthy, but the main point of this exercise was to show you how easy it is to add functionality to your application using plug-ins with minimal effort.

Using engines in the application

Another method of adding almost-instant functionality to the application is the use of Rails engines. The Rails engines system is a plug-in that builds on the plug-in architecture to allow for more advanced use cases. Unlike a standard plug-in, an engine is capable of working with almost any type of file you would find in a regular Rails application: models, views, controllers, libraries, database schemas, and so on.

Like a regular plug-in, the engine is stored under the vendor/plugin directory of your application so that it is completely self-contained from the code that you have written yourself. Unlike a regular plug-in, you can also manipulate the behavior of the engine to suit your specific application needs easily.

For example, you can use Rails engines to implement a user account system in the application. Let's do that now.

The first thing you need to do is install the engine's plug-in itself, which gives you the foundation you need to use other engines built on top of that architecture.

1. At a Terminal or command prompt window, type the following commands:

```
ruby script/plugin source http://svn.rails-engines.org/plugins
ruby script/plugin install engines
```

These commands install the engines plug-in in your vendor/plugins directory.

12

2. Next, you need to install the login_engine, which provides the actual user account system functionality. Do this with the following command:

```
ruby script/plugin install login_engine
```

The login_engine is a bit more complex than the user system you created, but it covers the same basic functionality. It enables a user to create a new user account and log in to the system. Beyond that, it also allows you to enable account authorizations via e-mail if you wish.

> For a list of available engines, the best place to look is the Rails wiki at http://wiki.rubyonrails.org. Official documentation page for the login_engine can be found at http://api.rails-engines.org/login_engine/.

You have to tell the Rails application that you have added a new engine to the application and where to find it. You do this in the environment.rb file.

3. Open the file (it's in the config directory) and add the following to the bottom of the file, just below the comment that says # Include your application configuration below:

```
module LoginEngine
  config :salt, "rails-solutions"
  config :use_email_notification, false
end

Engines.start :login
```

You just set two parameters for the engine. The first is to use the phrase *rails-solutions* as the salt for the password encryption. Salting a password is a technique to enhance the security strength of a password. Before storing it as a hash (as you did in the previous login system), you append the *rails-solutions* string to the password to throw off hackers if the physical database is compromised—even if they get the information from the database tables, they still don't get the right values. (You don't necessarily have to use the phrase *rails-solutions*; it can be anything you want.)

The second configuration option is to disable e-mail notifications. By default, login_engine requires users to activate their account by sending out an e-mail and requiring the user to click on a link in the message to confirm their account. For the purposes of this exercise, it isn't necessary.

4. Save your changes and restart your Rails application so that your changes go into effect.

Migrating the database

Engines also provide us with a way to migrate the database easily to patch in the engine functionality. The login_engine includes the migration information for a users table, so let's run it to add the users table to the database.

1. In a Terminal or command prompt window, run the following command:

```
rake db:migrate:engines ENGINE=login_engine
```

The migration runs just like any other migration you have written yourself. The only difference is that you are telling Rake to get its migration information from an engine: the login_engine specifically. The output should look like Figure 12-9.

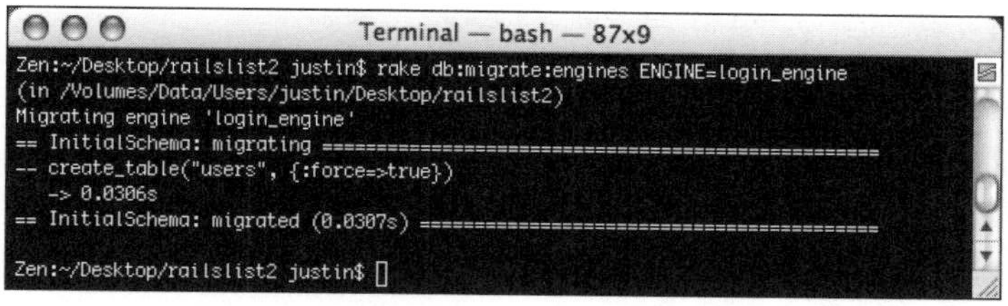

Figure 12-9. The command for migrating from an engine is a bit more complex than migrating from your own code, but it does the exact same thing.

Configuring login_engine

The first thing you should do to configure the engine is set up a default route so that the application is aware of the UserController that is packaged with the plug-in.

1. Open up routes.rb in the config directory and add the following line above the default routes:

```
map.connect '/user/:action', :controller => 'user'
```

2. Save your changes.

The next step in setting up the login_engine is telling it how to restrict access to certain functionality in the application.

3. Open up the application.rb file under app/controllers and modify it to look like the following:

```
require 'login_engine'

class ApplicationController < ActionController::Base
  include LoginEngine
  helper :user
  model :user
end
```

By adding the references to the login_engine in the main ApplicationController, you are ensuring that other controllers will be made aware of it without you having to declare it again.

4. Open the classifieds_controller.rb file and add the following filter just under the first line in the file (it restricts access to the data-manipulation methods in the file to users who are logged in):

```
before_filter :login_required, :only => ➥
[:edit, :update, :new, :create, :destroy]
```

12

219

5. Save your changes.

6. Now try to create a new classified, and you will be redirected to a login page like the one shown in Figure 12-10.

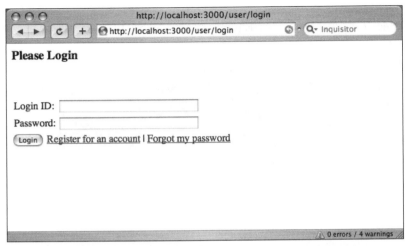

Figure 12-10. With just a bit of configuration, you have a fully functional login system in the application. You also are getting the forgot password functionality for free.

7. Since you don't have an account yet, go ahead and create one.

After you create your account and login, you should be able to create a new classified in the system.

Working with the login engine is pretty much the same as if you had created the code yourself. As you continue work on the application, you can set up relationships between the engine's user model and a classified to associate them with one another or restrict access to classifieds by a user (just as you did in the original Railslist application). The main difference is that you have built up the code base so much more quickly.

After you install and configure an engine, it's almost seamless to use it in your application as if it were your own code.

> For more information on the login_engine, visit http://api.rails-engines.org/login_engine/.

A note on components

There is another approach—components—which enable a developer to call actions from within another view or action. For example, if you were building an e-commerce site and had a shopping cart that would display the price and number of items in your cart on multiple pages in your application, you could create a component to do that.

The problem with components is that they are incredibly slow compared with other parts of the Rails framework and will most likely be removed from the Rails core framework and extracted as a plug-in by the time Rails reaches 2.0. So I decided not to cover them here. Besides, almost anything you can accomplish using components can be done using partials and/or plug-ins instead.

Summary

In this chapter, you built a basic skeleton application that had most of the functionality of the previous Railslist application using only Rails' scaffolding, plug-ins, and engines. The purpose of this exercise was to show you how easy it is to add functionality into your application using these powerful Rails technologies, ultimately saving you precious development time.

In the next chapter, you will learn how to deploy a Rails application to a remote Web server using Capistrano.

12

As you finish the development process of the Railslist application, you want to enable people to access it from the Web, just like any other website or web application. Therefore, you need to put it on a production server for all to come and find. The final step in the development process is configuring the application so that it can be deployed to and run on such a server.

This chapter discusses the following:

- What deployment is and why it is necessary
- What is needed for deployment
- Setting up the server for deployment
- Installing and configuring Capistrano

What is deployment?

Deployment is the process of transferring your web application onto a production web server so that it can be accessed by other users on the Web. In other languages you might have used, such as PHP, you go through the deployment process by removing comments, obfuscating code, and then uploading it to an FTP server. With Rails, after you finish developing your application on your local Mac or PC, you can finalize and transfer the code automatically to a remote web server that supports Ruby on Rails and your chosen database (in this case, MySQL). After configuring your remote database for storing your data and setting your Rails application to run in the production environment, your users can then access the application from their browsers over the Internet (the process is a lot more streamlined with Rails deployment than if you were to manually prepare your code and upload it). Figure 13-1 illustrates the setup between your development machine and the web server.

> In this Web 2.0 world, your first public access version will no doubt be dubbed beta.

Ruby on Rails makes deployment easy with its Capistrano utility, which was developed by Jamis Buck of 37Signals to enable developers to easily deploy new versions of their many applications to multiple servers with minimal effort. Prior to Capistrano, deploying a Rails application involved a complicated system of disabling a running application, moving the previous version and replacing it with the latest version, and trying to restart the application—hoping no issues would arise.

Imagine how this process might lead to problems as you build your application. The goal of deployment is to have as little downtime as possible so that your users don't notice. If you run into complications with deployment, you now have to trace your steps backward to get the application running again on the previous working version.

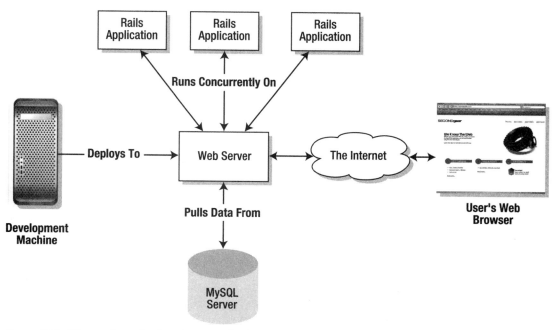

Figure 13-1. After you have developed your application locally, you can then deploy it to a remote web server where others can access it via a web browser.

Capistrano addresses this issue by providing a set of Rake scripts to automate the deployment by sending a set of tasks as a single command. Capistrano also makes it easy to handle problems during deployment because it can automatically roll back to a previous version of your application.

> *Capistrano, like Rails itself, is opinionated software. It assumes that you will be deploying to a Unix-based system such as Linux, Solaris, or Mac OS X. While it is possible to use Capistrano to deploy a Rails application to a Windows server, it's not easy to do. Maybe this is why no major Rails application has yet to be deployed onto a production Windows server?*

Second, Capistrano assumes that you have your code stored in a source code management repository. In this case, you use Subversion, which is a popular, open-source source code management system that is used by most Rails developers.

13

> *What about Concurrent Version System (CVS)? Subversion is a newer, more modern source code management system that addresses many of the weaknesses of CVS.*

Don't worry if this sounds intimidating right now. Capistrano makes it incredibly easy to get your application up and running on your production server(s).

Tool requirements

Deploying with Capistrano involves installing a few more utilities and applications on the local machines:

- Capistrano utility
- Subversion command-line utilities (http://subversion.tigris.org/)
- Geoffrey Grosenbach's Shovel scripts for Capistrano deployments (http://nubyonrails.com/pages/shovel)
- Web host that supports Ruby on Rails, Lighttpd, Subversion, and MySQL

For the purposes of the Rails deployment, I will walk you through the process using TextDrive (http://www.textdrive.com). While there are other web hosts on the Internet that support Rails, TextDrive is the official host for Ruby on Rails and has all the required tools you need for deployment. The Shovel scripts are built for easy Rails deployment on TextDrive.

> *If you are not keen on TextDrive, you can find a list of all the web hosts that support deploying Ruby on Rails web applications in the Rails wiki at* http://wiki.rubyonrails.org/rails/pages/RailsWebHosts. *Pricing ranges from a few dollars a month for a shared hosting account up to hundreds or thousands per month if you need a dedicated server.*

Installing Subversion for Mac OS X

If you are using Mac OS X, you need to install the Subversion binaries from Martin Ott (http://www.codingmonkeys.de/mbo/). Ott's binary package is a simple Mac OS X installer that will put the Subversion command-line tools on your system. svnX (a Mac Subversion client) requires them to communicate with the remote Subversion server.

1. Go to Ott's site and grab the latest version of the Subversion installer (I used *Subversion-1.4.2.pkg*) and download it to your Mac.
2. Launch the installer (see Figure 13-2) and click through the screens, selecting the default options.

After you finish the installer, the svn client is installed on your Mac.

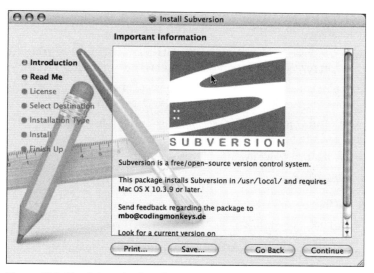

Figure 13-2. The Subversion installer walks you through the process of putting the Subversion command-line tools on your Mac.

Installing Subversion for Windows

The Windows installation is similar to the Mac installation. You need to download an installer that will install the Subverison binaries. You can grab them from http:// subversion.tigris.org/servlets/ProjectDocumentList?folderID=91.

1. Grab the latest svn-1.*x.x*-setup.exe (where *x.x* is a minor version number) from the preceding location.

2. Once downloaded, install it using the default options, as shown in Figure 13-3.

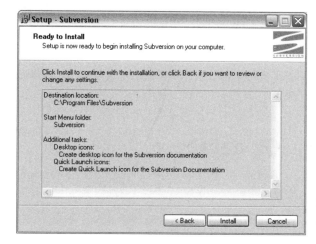

Figure 13-3. After installation completes, you can access remote Subversion servers from your Windows PC.

13

3. Open your command prompt and type svn help so Subversion will create its configuration settings.

Windows users need to download puTTY (http://www.chiark.greenend.org.uk/~sgtatham/putty/download.html) since Windows does not support SSH by default.

4. Download putty.exe and plink.exe. The download and install procedure is very simple. Move the files from your desktop into c:\putty.

5. Edit C:\Documents and Settings*yourname*\Application Data\Subversionconfig using your favorite text editor.

6. Change the line that looks like this:

```
#ssh = $SVN_SSH ssh
```

to look like this:

```
ssh = c:\plink.exe -ssh
```

7. Replace the path /to/putty with the actual path to the application.

8. Save your changes.

Before you begin

To host your Rails application to a production environment, you need a web host that supports Rails. Since you'll use TextDrive as the host, the first thing you need to do is sign up for an account. (Even the minimum plan—which as of this writing costs $15/month, plus a $25 initial setup fee—will suffice for what you'll be doing.) After you complete the signup process, you receive a welcome e-mail with all the relevant login and password credentials you need.

After you have your account set up, you need to submit a support request for a server port on which you can run the Rails application. A port is an access portal that enables you to access a web address from a URL such as http://www.railssolutions.com:8888 (*8888* is the port). You request a port by filing a support ticket in their web-based support system at http://help.textdrive.com/index.php?pg=request. All you need to do is tell them that you want to host Ruby on Rails applications and need a port for it.

The TextDrive folks will then assign a unique port number to you. Keep track of that number because you will need it later.

Creating the MySQL database

You need to create a database on the TextDrive server to hold all the data stored in the application. To do this, you first need to modify the database.yml file to let Railslist know about the new database.

1. Open up the database.yml file in the config directory and modify it to look like the following:

```
development:
  adapter: mysql
  database: railslist_development
  username: root
  password:
  host: localhost

test:
  adapter: mysql
  database: railslist_test
  username: root
  password:
  host: localhost

production:
  adapter: mysql
  database: yourtextdrivelogin_railslist
  username: yourtextdrivelogin
  password: yourtextdrivepassword
  host: localhost
```

You are modifying the values for the production environment's database to work with TextDrive. You have to replace *yourtextdrivelogin* with the relevant value in the database name. Also, replace *yourtextdrivelogin* and *yourtextdrivepasssword* with their respective values. If you aren't sure of them, check the welcome e-mail you received.

Next, you need to create the database. You can do this via the Web using a piece of software called phpMyAdmin, which is a tool written in PHP intended to handle the administration of MySQL through a web browser.

2. Open the web browser and go to http://mysql.*server*.textdrive.com/ (replacing *server* with the server you were assigned to by TextDrive).

3. When prompted, enter your TextDrive login and password.

The main phpMyAdmin window can be somewhat intimidating, as you can see in Figure 13-4.

13

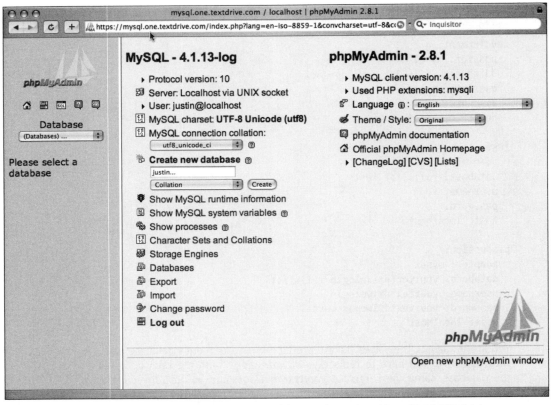

Figure 13-4. phpMyAdmin is a web-based management tool for creating and working with MySQL databases.

Luckily, you have to perform only a single task.

4. Find the text field below the *Create new database* text (where Justin... was entered in Figure 13-4) and enter the value for the production database you set when you modified the database.yml file. For example, if you set the database name to be *railslist_production*, enter it in the text field.

5. Click the Create button to create your new database.

This process creates your new database on the TextDrive server, so that you can begin adding new data to it after you get the application running on Capistrano.

Setting up the server

Subversion is a code-management repository that enables you to keep your source code stored on a remote server that can be accessed by multiple users. Subversion makes collaborating with multiple users a breeze because users can check out copies of the source code to their local machines, make edits, and then send the changes back to the Subversion server. At that point, team members can update their local copies with all the team's changes. Subversion manages the changes made to each file so that you aren't automatically overwriting your teammates' work: that's one of the biggest selling points of version control.

Even if you are a sole developer, storing your code in a Subversion repository is a great way to keep a remote backup of your code in case your development machine is compromised or if you fall victim to a situation resulting in data loss.

The first thing you need to do is set up a Subversion repository on TextDrive. You can manage it all by using Webmin, TextDrive's web-based control panel.

1. Log in to http://webmin.*server*.textdrive.com/, where *server* is the name of the server you were assigned to.

2. Once logged in, click Servers ➤ Subversion Repositories, as shown in Figure 13-5.

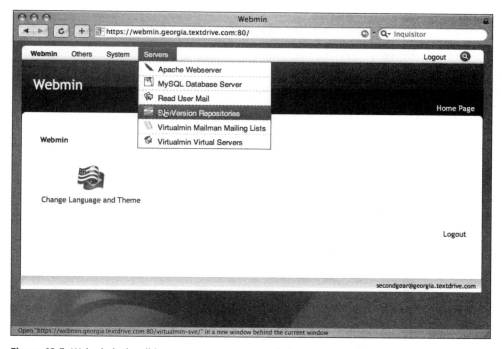

Figure 13-5. Webmin is the all-in-one management console for your TextDrive hosting account.

3. Enter railslist as the name for your repository, as shown in Figure 13-6. Leave all other fields at their defaults.

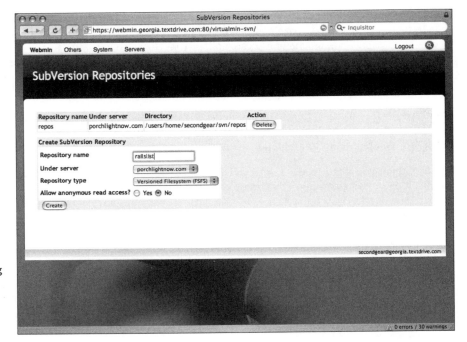

Figure 13-6. After naming the repository, Webmin takes care of creating everything you need to get started with Subverison.

4. Click the Create button to create your repository.

5. Click Return to return to the main page.

Next, you need to create a Subversion user to access the repository.

6. Under *Servers*, click *Virtualmin Virtual Servers*, as shown in Figure 13-7.

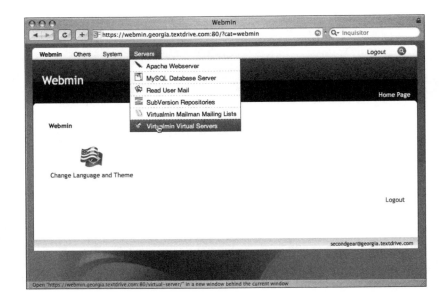

Figure 13-7. After creating the Subversion repository, you need to add a user to your account so you can access the repository.

7. From the list of domains, find the domain you added your repository to (if you are starting with a bare account, it should only be one account) and click the *List...* link under the Mailboxes column.

8. Click Add A User To This Domain to get to the screen shown in Figure 13-8.

9. Enter a username, real name, and password for the account.

10. Under Allow Access To Repositories, select your repository.

11. Change Primary Email Address Enabled? to No.

12. Set Home And Mail Quota to Unlimited.

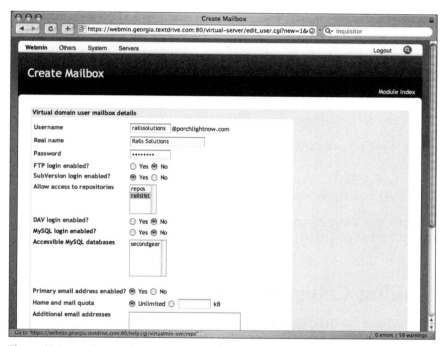

Figure 13-8. Creating a Subversion user involves creating a user Mailbox. Just make sure you disable the Mailbox and leave only the Subversion login enabled.

13. Click Create.

At this point you should now have the Subversion repository available at http://yourdomain.com/svn/railslist. You can log in to it using the username and password you created previously.

Committing the project to Subversion

Now that you have the repository set up, you need to commit the Railslist application. Committing is the process of sending code changes to the Subversion repository. The process is similar on both Windows and Mac OS X using the Subversion command-line utilities.

13

1. Open up the Terminal or command prompt window and go to the Railslist directory.

2. Run the following command to commit your project:

```
svn import --m 'Initial Import' . ➥
http://yourdomain.com/svn/repos/railslist/
```

3. You will be prompted for your Subversion username and password. Provide them.

    This process sends all the files that are a part of your project to the Subversion repository.

    Next, you need to check out a *working copy* of the application. Many first-time source code management users don't understand why they need to check out a copy of the code they just imported to Subversion, but it is necessary so that you are working with a copy of the code that has the hooks Subversion can use to determine changes in your code.

4a. In the Mac OS X Terminal, type the following:

```
cd ..
mv railslist railslist_bak
svn co http://yourdomain.tld/svn/repos/railslist
```

4b. If you are using Windows, type the following:

```
cd ..
ren railslist railslist_bak
svn co http://yourdomain.tld/svn/repos/railslist
```

Now you have a working copy of the code on the local development environment that you can set up for Capistrano.

Installing Capistrano

To install and use Capistrano, you use the Shovel script created by Geoffrey Grosenbach (http://nubyonrails.com/pages/shovel). Shovel automates the setup of Lighttpd and Capistrano on the TextDrive server using Rake tasks.

The first thing you need to do is install Capistrano.

1. In a Terminal or command prompt window go to your railslist directory and type the following commands, pressing Return at the end of each line (Mac OS X users should append the word sudo to the beginning of the first command to run it as root):

```
gem install capistrano --include-dependencies
cap --apply-to .
```

The first command installs the Capistrano gem onto your system.

2. You will probably be asked if you want to install a bunch of dependent software such as net-ssh along with Capistrano. Accept all of them because they are required for Capistrano to function correctly.

   The second command uses the actual cap application to put the Railslist application on Capistrano. It creates a deploy.rb file in your config directory. The deploy file contains all the tasks that you can perform via Capistrano. You will be overwriting this file with the Shovel file.

3. Open up your web browser and go to http://topfunky.net/svn/shovel/deploy.rb. The file should render as a text file in your browser.

4. Save it to your desktop.

5. Next, go to your Rails application's config directory and replace the deploy.rb file with the one you just downloaded.

   You just removed the default deploy.rb file that was created by Capistrano and replaced it with Shovel. If you examine the actual Shovel file you will see that it is filled with hundreds of lines of code. Luckily, you only have a few lines to manipulate.

6. Open up the deploy.rb file and modify the values in bold on following lines (which appear starting around line 40):

   ```
   set :application, 'railslist'
   set :user, "textdrivelogin"
   set :txd_primary_domain, 'yourdomain.com'
   set :lighty_port, 00000000
   ```

   :application is the name of the application. It needs to match the name of the folder you stored the application in on the Subversion server (*railslist* in this case). :user is the login name you set up when you signed up for TextDrive. If you don't remember this, consult the welcome e-mail you received from them. :lighty_port is the port that you asked TextDrive to assign to you earlier.

7. Save your changes.

Connecting to the server on a Mac

Next, you need to connect to the TextDrive server and check out a copy of the application so that the Subversion password is cached on the hosting account.

1. If you are on a Mac, type the following into your Terminal window, replacing *yourtextdrivelogin* and *yourdomain.com* with the relevant values.

   ```
   ssh --l yourtextdrivelogin yourdomain.com
   ```

2. You're prompted to enter your password; do so after confirming that you trust the identity of the remote server you're connecting to.

13

Connecting to the server on Windows

Windows users need to use puTTY since Windows does not support SSH by default.

1. Launch putty, as seen in Figure 13-9.

2. Under Host Name, enter yourdomain.com and then click Open at the bottom of the screen.

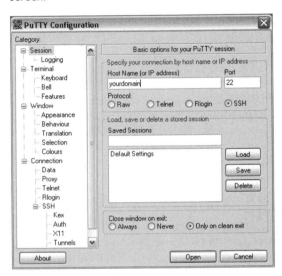

Figure 13-9. Windows doesn't support SSH by default, but the freely available puTTY client makes up for it.

3. You're prompted for your login; enter your TextDrive username.

4. When prompted for your password, provide it.

5. Once logged in, enter the following commands at the prompt:

```
mkdir tmp
cd tmp
svn co http://yourdomain.com/svn/railslist/railslist/
```

6. Enter your Subversion login and password when prompted.

7. After the checkout of your code is complete, you can enter the exit command to safely disconnect from the TextDrive server.

Now that you are back on the local machine, you are ready to start using Shovel.

Deploying the application

1. Now that you have everything set up, you should be able to run the following command from the Terminal or puTTY prompt to start the deployment process:

```
rake remote:exec ACTION=setup_lighty
```

2. You're prompted for your SSH password. Enter it.

This sets up the Lighttpd server on TextDrive and checks out a copy of the Railslist application to run against that Lighttpd instance.

3. Next, you need to migrate the database to the remote server. Type the following command in your Terminal or command prompt:

```
rake remote:migrate
```

4. Again you're prompted for your SSH password; enter it now.

5. Restart the application so that all the processes pick up the new database. Do this by entering the following command:

```
rake remote:restart
```

After the rake commands complete, you should be able to go to http://yourdomain.com:your_port and view Railslist running on a live server. If you don't see anything, you might need to SSH into your TextDrive server again and run the following command to manually start Lighttpd:

```
./lighttpd/lightttpdctrl restart
```

Now that the application is set up to use Capistrano, deploying changes is an easy process.

6. The first thing you need to do is commit the changes to the Subversion server. You can do this with a command similar to the following:

```
svn commit --m 'Commit Message' /path/to/railslist
```

7. After the commit is completed, you can deploy the changes using the following command:

```
rake deploy
```

This command checks out a new version of your code from the Subversion server and associates it with your Lighttpd instance.

Summary

This chapter covered a lot of topics. You only skimmed the surface of the power of Subversion, but it can be beneficial to learn more about how to work with it so that you are completely comfortable with your deployment environment. (If you want to learn more about Subversion, visit http://svnbook.red-bean.com/.)

You can also learn more about Capistrano by reading its online manual (http://manuals.rubyonrails.com/read/book/17). It is a powerful utility that can ease your deployment woes. It just has a bit of a learning curve.

Like most new things, deployment is by no means an exact science at this point. It has improved substantially over the past year thanks to Capistrano, but there is still room for improvement. To keep abreast of the changes in deployment, be sure to subscribe to the Ruby on Rails weblog (http://weblog.rubyonrails.org/).

13

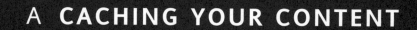

A CACHING YOUR CONTENT

As your database grows, and more users begin using your application, the web server will start to see some performance hits. Each time a user requests an action, the web server has to query your database and retrieve the information (among other behind-the-scene things). Each time this occurs independently is not much of a performance hit, but when hundreds and thousands of users are doing it at the same time, the performance loss becomes noticeable. Luckily, Ruby on Rails enables you to implement caching to keep the result of calculations, rendered views, and database calls around for subsequent requests. *Caching* is the process of saving a copy of the results of a web request on the server or a local machine for subsequent requests. Instead of having to query the database each time a user requests something, you can serve a cached copy of the result that one user retrieved to subsequent users in an attempt to save server resources and speed up the application.

With Rails, there are three types of caching. First, *page caching* is the fastest method of caching because the entire page is generated once and then stored on the server's hard drive, so the next time a user requests the page, it can just retrieve the cached page instead of invoking the Rails application. Page caching relies on the entire page being static. In other words, if you want to greet your user with a Welcome username message on your page, this wouldn't work for you since that username value changes per user. However, a page that doesn't change often—such as an about section—would be an ideal candidate for page caching.

Cache Type	When to Use
Page	You need to cache an *entire* static page
Action	You need to cache a page with dynamic content such as login information
Fragment	You only want to cache a portion of a page like a header or footer

The next type of caching is *action caching*, which is similar to page caching in that the entire response is cached, but differs because every request still goes through the Rails ActionPack. This makes action caching useful for any pages that need to be accessed by authenticated users. It also gives you the ability to keep dynamic content in the sidebar (Welcome username).

The final (and most flexible) type of caching is *fragment caching*, which is used to cache various blocks within templates without caching the entire action or page. It is useful when certain elements of an action change frequently, but others do not. Those parts that do not change can be wrapped in a caching statement in your templates.

Just as you did for storing your session data, you need to choose where to store your caches to use fragment caching by assigning a fragment store. There are four types to choose from, as follows:

- **MemoryStore**: This store keeps the fragments in your application's memory, which can potentially take up a lot of memory on your server. It is used by default, but it is hard to manage and scale if your application becomes popular.

- **FileStore**: This store keeps the fragments on the hard disk instead of in memory. It works well if you have a lot of file storage and have outgrown the MemoryStore.

- **DRbStore**: This store keeps the fragments in the memory on a separate shared Drb server (Drb stands for *Distributed Ruby*). It keeps only one cache around for all processes. This is a complex solution because it involves setting up a secondary server.

- **MemCacheStore**: Similar to DRbStore in that it stores your caches on a separate server, but uses the MemCache library. It also requires you to install the ruby-mem-cache library.

Setting up the caching strategy

For Railslist, I think the best solution is to use the default MemoryStore for caching. It has a no-frills setup and gives you the results you are looking for. If you notice that your application is starting to have more and more users, you can easily switch between the different types of stores used for caching.

By default, caching is enabled only in production environments. You can turn it on or off manually by setting the config.action_controller.perform_caching option in the config/environments/production.rb file.

If in the future you decide to use a cache store besides the MemoryStore, you can add one of the following lines of code to your config/environments/production.rb file:

```
ActionController::Base.fragment_cache_store = ➡
:memory_store
ActionController::Base.fragment_cache_store = ➡
:file_store, "/path/to/cache/directory"
ActionController::Base.fragment_cache_store = ➡
:drb_store, "druby://localhost:9192"
ActionController::Base.fragment_cache_store = ➡
:mem_cache_store, "localhost"
```

A

Implementing caching in the application

Let's implement page caching in the application. The most logical place is on a page like the signup form, since the form fields don't change too often.

1. Open up the user_controller.rb file in app/controllers and add the following line to it:

    caches_page :signup

That's all there is to it. Now when a user views the signup page for the first time, the page is on the server. Or is it?

2. Look at the signup form in a browser (see Figure A-1).

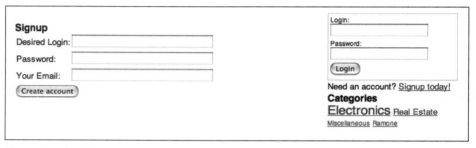

Figure A-1. The signup form for the railslist application with the login form in the sidebar

Notice the categories listing in the sidebar? It is dynamically generated in your application's layout template, so page caching is not a suitable strategy for this page; you can use action caching, however. Action caching is achieved in the same way as page caching except that you use caches_action instead of caches_page.

3. Modify the line in the user controller to use action caching and then save your changes.

Let's also implement action caching in the classified controller. You can cache the multiple listings, the single listing, and the new classified pages.

4. Add the following line to classified_controller.rb:

    caches_action :show, :list, :new

5. Save your changes.

Now when those three actions are accessed, the pages are cached. In the case of the show method, a new page cache is created for each classified listing because action caching uses fragment caching to store its data so that classified/show/1 will be a different cache from classified/show/2.

Using fragment caching explicitly

At the bottom of each classified listing is a form that enables you to contact the seller or e-mail the listing to a friend. These fields rarely change, so let's implement fragment caching to store those bits of data in memory.

1. Open up the show.rhtml template under app/views/classified and wrap that area of code with a cache do statement.

2. Modify the bottom of the file so that the interested and contact links are being cached. When you finish, it should look like the following:

```
<% cache do %>
  <p>Interested?
  <%= link_to_function('Contact the seller', ➥
"Element.show('contact_seller')") %></p>
  ...
  <p><%= link_to_function('E-mail to a friend', ➥
"Element.show('email')") %></p>
  ...
  <%= end_form_tag -%>
  </div>
<% end %>
```

Now that you have implemented this fragment cache, it will be bound to the name of the action that called it, which in this case is show.

> You can cache any block of code in your Rails app by enclosing the code block in a cache do statement.

Expiring caches

One issue with caching is that it can lead to out-of-date information being displayed to the user. For example, if you cache the listing of a classified, and the poster then goes to update the listing, you want to make sure that anyone who looks at the listing from that point forward sees the most up-to-date data. To do this, you need to set up expirations on the caches. You do this in the controller methods.

1. Open up the classified controller file classified_controller.rb, which is located in app/controllers.

2. Modify the update method to look as follows (you need to add only the line in bold):

```
def update
  ...
  if @classified.update_attributes(params[:classified])
    expire_action(:controller => "classifieds", :action => "show"),➥
:id => @classified
    redirect_to :action => 'show', :id => @classified
  else
    render :action => 'edit'
  end
end
```

A

The only change you made was to add the expire_action call after the update method. This tells Rails to wipe the cache you already created (if it existed) and recache the new data. If you want to expire the cache of a *page cache*, use expire_page instead of expire_action.

```
expire_page(:controller => "user", :action => "signup")
```

And if you want to expire a *fragment cache*, you have to pass the actual cache name.

```
expire_fragment("/classified/listing/1")
```

Obviously, expiring a fragment cache isn't ideal in certain instances, but the option is there if you need it.

Summary

This appendix covered the basics of caching, but there is much more to the topic that you can explore if you're interested.

- Rails documentation on caching: http://api.rubyonrails.com/classes/ActionController/Caching.html
- Scott Laird's presentation on caching: http://scottstuff.net/blog/articles/2005/09/28/rails-caching-presentation
- Ruby on Rails caching benchmarks: http://www.maxdunn.com/typo/articles/2006/09/12/ruby-on-rails-caching-benchmarks

B TESTING RAILS

As you develop applications with Ruby on Rails, you will undoubtedly be adding new features and functionality to existing code bases. If it's a large application with several users, the chances of creating a new bug in the application can be increased. If you deploy the new feature to your users with that bug, you might have to deal with hundreds of support requests from users who cannot get the application to work properly.

You shouldn't assume that you have the time or desire to manually run through every single method and function of the application. Luckily, Ruby on Rails comes with the capability to automatically test the functionality of the application using a little bit of Ruby code and few simple Rake commands. In short, Rails comes with test-driven development functionality built in.

This appendix covers the following:

- What test-driven development is
- Why testing is important
- The types of testing available
- How to implement those tests into applications

What is test-driven development?

Test-driven development is a programming technique that emphasizes writing *tests* that will check the functionality of the application's code before you actually write it into the production application. Test-driven development got its roots in the Extreme Programming methodology that many developers took to in the early 2000s. Now, testing has been extracted from Extreme Programming and is used in more general programming practice.

> For more information on Extreme Programming and the ideas behind test-driven development, visit www.extremeprogramming.org/.

Ruby on Rails includes the functionality needed to test the application by default when you first create the application using the rails command. The framework includes several different types of tests you can run. For testing models, Rails uses unit tests. Unit tests test the business logic and functionality of the data models. When you add a method to the model, you should write a unit test to test its functionality.

To test the functionality of the controllers, the framework uses functional tests. Functional tests help you to ensure that the methods perform as they should. If you were to test a login method, you'd check to see that it will display the login form, enable a user with the proper credentials to log in, and restrict unauthorized users from proceeding through the login process.

The last major type of testing, integration testing, tests the interaction between multiple controllers. In the case of the Railslist application, you can create an integration test that allows a user to sign up for an account, log in to that account, and then create a new classified ad. You are testing the interaction between both the user and classified controller.

Test directory

As outlined in Chapter 4, creating a new Rails application creates several directories. One of those directories is called test. Take a peek at the test directory; you'll see the following files and folders:

- fixtures: Sample data for unit tests
- functional: Functional test files
- integration: Integration test files
- mocks: Container for mock objects
- test_helper.rb: Ruby helper file used in testing
- unit: Unit test files

Fixtures folder

The fixtures folder houses YAML files containing sample data that you can run through the unit tests instead of having to worry about creating new data inside the actual test database itself each time you run the tests. You can define the data fields in an easy-to-read text file and have Rails import it automatically. Each time you create a new model by using the generator, it also creates a fixtures file that is associated with the model. Let's utilize the fixture files now.

1. Remove the existing code in the fixtures/classifieds.yml file; then add the following to it (this is a sample fixture for a classified from the Railslist application):

```
first:
  id: 1
  title: 60GB iPod For Sale
  price: 499.00
  location: Evansville, IN
  description: Black iPod video.  Like new condition
  created_at: <%= 5.days.ago.utc.to_s(:db) %>
  updated_at: <%= 2.days.ago.utc.to_s(:db) %>
  email: justin@secondgearllc.com
```

Pay special attention to the formatting of the following code. YAML is very sensitive in terms of spacing. Each item needs be spaced with a tab. If the YAML isn't valid, the testing will fail.

2. Replace the data in the categories.yml file with the following code (you will need this when you start testing the categories model):

```
first:
  id: 1
  name: Sample Category
another:
  id: 2
  name: Sample Category 2
```

B

Functional folder

The functional folder contains a functional test file for each controller you have created in the application. Since you have three controllers in the application, you have three functional test files: classified_controller_test.rb, category_controller_test.rb, and user_controller_test.rb. The code inside the classified_controller_test.rb file is not the same as the Classified controller; it instead calls the Classified controller's methods and tests functionality to ensure that things are working properly.

Integration folder

The integration folder is empty at first because you have to manually create each of the integration test files.

Mock folder

The most complex folder is mock, which contains a separate folder for each environment used by the application. Each folder contains mock object implementations. A mock object is a "double agent" used to test the behavior of other objects. If you are writing an application that checks the availability of a domain name through a third-party provider such as Enom (www.enom.com/), you can use mock objects to imitate the check so that you don't have to keep pinging Enom's servers while you develop the application. It also eliminates the dependency on an active network connection while you are developing the application. The mock objects are not covered in this book because they're a bit advanced and out of scope.

Test folder

The test_helper.rb file contains configuration options for the Rails' testing suite. (You won't be manipulating this file.)

Unit folder

The unit folder is the home of all the unit tests. Similar to functional tests, a file is created for each model you create in the application. You write the tests that will check the validity of the data models in the file associated with each model. In the case of the Classified model, you would write tests against it in the classified_test.rb file.

Creating a test database

As discussed before, a Rails application can run under several different environments, and each separate environment requires a database of its own. One of the environments created by default is *test*, so you need to create a new database for the test environment that you will be working with in this appendix.

Why can't you just use the same development database that you have already created for the test environment? Besides the environment issue, the test environment is designed so its database is completely erased each time you run the unit, functional, and integration tests. So each time you run the tests, you are running it against fresh data.

You should have created the railslist_test database in Chapter 4. In case you haven't, here are the instructions for creating it again.

On Windows

To create the database using SQLyog on Windows, launch the application and follow these steps:

1. Open the Connect To MySQL Host window.
2. Double-click the *Rails Development* session you created previously.
3. Under the menu bar, select Database ➤ New ➤ Database.
4. Name the database railslist_test. Leave everything else the same and click OK.

On Mac

To create the database using CocoaMySQL on Mac OS X, follow these steps.

1. In the dialog box that pops up, enter localhost as the host, root as the username, and the password as defined in Chapter 2. Leave everything else blank so it picks up the default values.
2. Click the Connect button.
3. Under *Databases* in the top-left corner, click the Add button.
4. Another sheet appears. Type in railslist_development and click Add.

Preparing the test database

After the database is created, you still need to populate it with the database schema by running migrations against it.

1. Open a command prompt or Terminal window and go to the `railslist` directory.
2. Type rake db:test:prepare, which populates the database with the same tables that are found in the development database because it is running the same migrations.

Now that you know the basics of Rails' testing implementation and have the test database ready to go, let's start by creating a few tests and running them.

Unit-testing the models

To recap: a unit test is a test that runs against a data model. When you created the Classified model in Chapter 4, it also created a unit test in the `test/unit` folder called `classified_test.rb`. Let's open that file and examine what is created by default:

```
require File.dirname(__FILE__) + '/../test_helper'

class ClassifiedTest < Test::Unit::TestCase
  fixtures :classifieds
```

```
      # Replace this with your real tests.
      def test_truth
        assert true
      end
  end
```

The first line is a require statement that imports the test_helper.rb file discussed earlier. Next, you have a class definition. Like almost everything else in Ruby on Rails, a unit test is just another Ruby class. In this instance, ClassifiedTest inherits the attributes and methods from Test::Unit::TestCase, which is a part of Ruby's unit testing implementation Test::Unit.

The second line imports the fixtures file classifieds.yml. Calling fixtures imports the data from the YAML file into the test database.

Below that is a single method that is created by default called test_truth. Starting the method name with test means that it will be run as a test by the Test::Unit framework. The test_truth method is merely a stub implementation method of a test that will always pass. It's like testing to see if 1 equals 1—the value will always be correct. It's basically just a placeholder for the real tests.

The assert method is another method that is part of Ruby's testing framework—it expects a logical expression as an argument. If the logical expression evaluates to true, the test is deemed to pass. There are many different types of assertions included with Ruby, such as assert_equal, assert_match, assert_not_equal, and so on. Notice that each one of these assertions has an easy-to-understand method name. For the most part, the functionality of the assertion is self-explanatory just by reading the name.

Running the first test

Let's see what its like to run a unit test inside of Rails before you start modifying the classified_test.rb file.

1. Type the following at the Rails command prompt:

```
ruby test/unit/classified_test.rb
```

The output should look similar to Figure B-1.

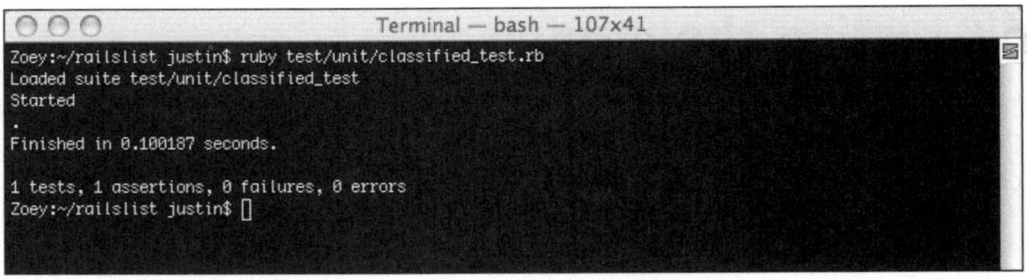

Figure B-1. After running a unit test, the results are shown like this.

What just happened? First, Ruby loaded the Test::Unit suite and then started executing the classified_test.rb file's methods sequentially. The period (.) is an indicator that a test method executed successfully. If the test did not pass, the period would be replaced with an F (for failure).

There isn't much going on here yet, so let's start adding some meat to this unit test file. The first thing you can do is make use of the fixture you created a few pages ago and test it against a newly created classified.

2. Add the following method to the classified_test.rb file, just before the last end keyword, and then save the file:

```
def test_create
    c = Classified.new
    c.title = "Test Title"
    c.price = 566.00
    c.location = "Chicago"
    c.description = "This is a sample description that➡
is not very interesting"
    c.email = "justin@secondgearllc.com"
    assert c.save

    # This will pass
    d = Classified.find(c.id)
    assert_equal c, d

    # This will fail
    e = Classified.find(1)
    assert_equal d, e
end
```

This method does a few basic things that should help introduce you to unit testing. First, you create a new Classified object, c, and populate it with some sample data. On line 8, you call assert c.save, which tests to make sure that the object will save. It should return true because you input valid data.

Below that you create a new variable, d, which is a clone of the c object. To test to make sure that they are exactly identical, call Ruby's assert_equal assertion against it. It should return true as well. assert_equal has a specific format that you should pass parameters to. The first parameter should be the expected value; the second value should be what the actual output is from the object. In this case, you expect the output to be the c object and the actual value to be the d object.

I added the last two lines to this method to give you a taste of what a failed test looks like. You create another Classified object that contains the fixture from before. When it was created, it had a database id of 1. The line below that tries to run assert_equal against the new e object and the preexisting d object.

What happens when you run a failing test?

B

3. Go back to the command prompt or Terminal window and run the test again. The output should look similar to Figure B-2.

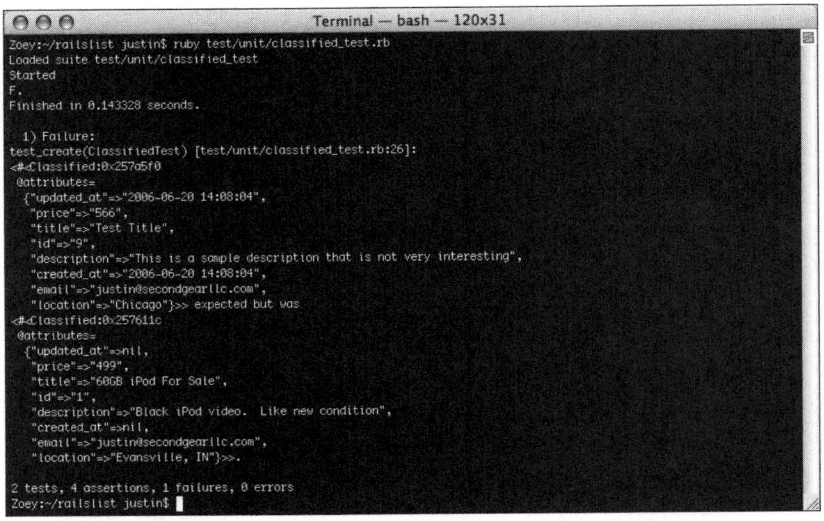

Figure B-2. After running the method, Rails tells you that it failed and how it failed.

The output for a failed test gives you a lot of useful information. It gives you the method name, the file in which it occurred, and the line number of the failure. In this case, that would be test_create, classified_test.rb, and line 26. Below that it gives an output of each of the objects you were using.

4. As you can plainly see, object 1 does not equal object 2. Let's fix this error by modifying the failing line to look like the following and saving your changes:

```
# This will fail
    e = Classified.find(1)
    assert_not_equal d, e
end
```

5. Run the test again and everything should pass.

You ran a different assertion method called assert_not_equal that checks to make sure that two objects are *not* the same. Obviously, they aren't, so everything will pass now.

Keep in mind that when you write the unit tests, you should write a test method for each method in the model class as well as for each validation method you have. For example, in the classifieds model, you have seven validations:

```
class Classified < ActiveRecord::Base
  validates_presence_of :title, ➡
:message => "cannot be blank. Make your title descriptive"
  validates_presence_of :price
  validates_presence_of :location
  validates_presence_of :description
```

```
      validates_presence_of :email
      validates_numericality_of :price
      validates_format_of :email, ➡
   :with => /^([^@\s]+)@((?:[-a-z0-9]+\.)+[a-z]{2,})$/i
   ...
   end
```

Each validation should have a corresponding test in the classified_test.rb file to ensure that they work properly in the application. Although you can write a single test method to test all the functionality of the classified model, the best way to accomplish it is with several small, to-the-point methods.

Other unit test assertions

You have been introduced to only two assertions thus far, but Rails offers quite a few more that you can use during the test-driven development. Here are just a few:

- *assert_block*: The base assertion upon which all others are based. Test whether the code you are executing returns true.

- *assert_nil*: Checks to see whether an object returns nil. If so, the test passes.

- *assert_delta*: A math assertion that checks to see whether an expected decimal value (float for the programmers in the house) matches the actual decimal value within a certain number of decimal points (the delta value).

- *assert_raise*: Checks to see whether an exception is called. Passes if it does.

- *assert_not_raise*: Checks to see whether an exception is not called. Passes if it doesn't.

- *assert_valid*: Checks whether an ActiveRecord object passes all its data validations.

1. Let's add a few unit tests to the Category controller as well. Open category_test.rb and add the following to it just before the last end keyword:

```
def test_valid
  c = Category.new(:name => "Furniture")
  assert_valid c
end

def test_unique_name
  c = Category.new(:name => "Sample Category")
  assert !c.valid?
end
```

The first test uses the assert_valid assertion to make sure that the Category instance passes all the data validations it finds in the model. The next test, test_unique_name, checks to see whether the assertion will fail. Unfortunately, there is no assert_invalid assertion built into Rails. Instead, the best way to do this is by using the standard assert keyword and Rails' valid? method.

B

2. Run the category_test.rb file and make sure that everything passes.

Functional testing of the controller

A functional test is a test against a single controller. When writing functional tests, the main goal is to make sure that each of the actions the user can perform results in a successful experience. If the user is creating a new classified ad, for example, you want to make sure that it goes off without a hitch. Functional testing makes it easy to test all the common problems that might arise from the development and squash them before the problem is pushed onto the users. Think of it as the computer imitating what users would do in their browsers when using the application for real.

Each controller you create also comes with a functional test file. You have only one controller in the application so far, ClassifiedController, so it shouldn't be too difficult to create a few tests to make sure that all the actions result in success for the user. Under the test/functional directory, there is a file called classified_controller_test.rb. Open it up and inspect it.

```ruby
require File.dirname(__FILE__) + '/../test_helper'
require 'classified_controller'

# Re-raise errors caught by the controller.
class ClassifiedController; def rescue_action(e) raise e end; end

class ClassifiedControllerTest < Test::Unit::TestCase
  def setup
    @controller = ClassifiedController.new
    @request    = ActionController::TestRequest.new
    @response   = ActionController::TestResponse.new
  end

  # Replace this with your real tests.
  def test_truth
    assert true
  end
end
```

The first line should look familiar to you because it's exactly the same as the first line of the Classified model test file. The test file imports the settings from the test_helper.rb file. Below that, the actual Classified controller is imported by calling another require statement.

The following line is used by the test controller to raise exceptions that are thrown. Exceptions are errors that arise from the application not behaving as it is expected to. The goal is to make sure that any time a user encounters one of these exceptions, you handle it appropriately. Functional testing is part of the cure that will help ensure it.

The actual class you are working with is called ClassifiedControllerTest and, like its unit test counterpart, it inherits from Test::Unit::TestCase. This sample contains two methods: setup and test_truth. The setup method, which is an integral part of functional testing, initializes three objects that will be used by all functional tests that you write:

- *@controller*: The actual instance of the controller you are working with. In this instance, it is ClassifiedController.

- *@request*: Contains the data from incoming requests sent by the user to the Rails application: POST and GET data, for example.

- *@response:* Contains the data you send back to the user's browser window. HTTP status codes and the actual data you are returning is encapsulated in an @response object.

> *Never remove the setup method from a functional test. It will cause much chaos.*

Similar to the Classified unit test, ClassifiedControllerTest also contains a stub test called test_truth that simply returns true.

Let's add a new functional to ensure that the user can get a listing of all the classified ads.

1. Copy the following code into the classified_controller_test.rb file, just before the last end keyword:

```
def test_list
  get :list
  assert_response :success
  assert_rendered_file "list"
end
```

This simple test_list method does three things. First, it calls the list action from the Classified controller using the get method provided by Rails. The get method simulates an actual request sent to a web server by a user's browser and then retrieves the response.

Second, it makes sure that the response you receive from that call is that of success (status code 200 for the HTTP geeks). assert_response has several different status code keywords it can accept.

- *:success*: The file was successfully retrieved with no problems.

- *:missing*: The file cannot be found (404).

- *:redirect*: The action redirected you to another page than the one you intended.

- *:error:* The request returned an error not covered by :missing or :redirect.

It can also take the actual HTTP status code instead of the keyword.

Finally, it ensures that the list template is rendered.

2. To run the new functional test, let's run the test. Type the following at the Rails command prompt:

```
ruby test/functional/classified_controller_test.rb
```

The output should be similar to what you received when you were working with unit tests because everything you are doing in functional testing is using the same testing classes as the unit testing side of things.

B

3. Let's create one more test that will test searching all the Classified objects. Add the following to the classified_controller_text.rb file, again just before the last end statement; then save the changes.

```
def test_search
  post :search, "search" => "iPod"
  assert_response :success
end
```

4. Run the classified_controller_test.rb file one more time to make sure that the method works.

The first line calls the post method to send a simulated HTTP POST message that calls the controller's search method. Along with the POST, you are passing the values of the new search as params[:search]. After sending the request, you use assert_response to make sure that it ran successfully.

Let's look at the actual controller code you wrote for the create method to see how it matches up with the functional test:

```
def search
  @classifieds = Classified.find(:all,
    :conditions => ["lower(title) like ?",
    "%" + params[:search].downcase + "%"])
  if params['search'].to_s.size < 1
    render :nothing => true
  else
    if @classifieds.size > 0
      render :partial => 'classified', :collection => @classifieds
    else
      render :text => "<li>No results found</li>", :layout => false
    end
  end
end
```

The bold lines are ones that are directly referenced in the functional test. Notice that the first line creates a new object using the params[:search] values. If results are rendered, you are given a successful response.

Running all the tests at once

It's not really convenient to run each test file manually, so Rails has a built-in way of running all the unit and functional tests at once. In the Terminal or command prompt window, type the following command and press Enter.

```
rake test
```

Running this command runs all tests that it finds in the test directory. It runs each file one by one and then outputs a final results tally on the tests at the end.

> *The ActionMailer tests fail because you changed how the scaffolded method worked in Chapter 8 by modifying the parameters it accepts. I left this in deliberately as a reader exercise—see if you can fix the test to match the modified contact method.*

Besides the rake test command, there are also more finely grained rake tasks you can run:

- rake test:functionals: Runs all tests that it finds in the test/functional directory and outputs the results.

- rake test:plugins: Runs all tests that are associated with any plugins that you installed during the course of the application development.

- rake test:units: Runs all tests that it finds in the test/unit directory and outputs the results.

Summary

This appendix gave you a basic introduction to test-driven development and its role in Ruby on Rails. You also learned how to write basic unit tests and functional tests. There is still a wealth of information related to test-driven development and Ruby on Rails that you might want to uncover. For more information, visit the following websites:

- A Guide To Testing With Rails: http://manuals.rubyonrails.com/read/book/5

- Why and How: Ruby (and Rails) Unit Testing: http://glu.ttono.us/articles/2005/10/30/why-and-how-ruby-and-rails-unit-testing

- Testing with Rails: www.linuxjournal.com/article/8625

B

INDEX

You Need the Companion eBook

Your purchase of this book entitles you to buy the companion PDF-version eBook for only $10. Take the weightless companion with you anywhere.

We believe this Apress title will prove so indispensable that you'll want to carry it with you everywhere, which is why we are offering the companion eBook (in PDF format) for $10 to customers who purchase this book now. Convenient and fully searchable, the PDF version of any content-rich, page-heavy Apress book makes a valuable addition to your programming library. You can easily find and copy code—or perform examples by quickly toggling between instructions and the application. Even simultaneously tackling a donut, diet soda, and complex code becomes simplified with hands-free eBooks!

Once you purchase your book, getting the $10 companion eBook is simple:

❶ Visit **www.apress.com/promo/tendollars/**.

❷ Complete a basic registration form to receive a randomly generated question about this title.

❸ Answer the question correctly in 60 seconds, and you will receive a promotional code to redeem for the $10.00 eBook.

2560 Ninth Street • Suite 219 • Berkeley, CA 94710

eBookshop

THE EXPERT'S VOICE™